GRAHAM TAYLOR

IN HIS OWN WORDS

PELOTON PUBLISHING

First published in Great Britain by Peloton Publishing, 2017

© Graham Taylor 2017

1 3 5 7 9 10 8 6 4 2

ISBN 978-0-9932899-2-7

Peloton Publishing Ltd
107 Jupiter Drive, Hemel Hempstead, HP2 5NU

Printed and bound in Great Britain by
CPI Group (UK) Ltd, Croydon, CR0 4YY

FSC is a non-profit international organisation established to
promote the responsible management of the world's forests.

It was Graham's wish that this book should be dedicated to
Rita, Joanne, Karen, Rhianna, Elsie and Jake

Contents

Foreword

by Sir Elton John

It is odd that two of the most important people in my life – Bernie Taupin and Graham – both hailed from Lincolnshire, but kismet put them together with me and I am forever grateful.

I have so many wonderful memories of Graham that I could write a whole book about our friendship, but I will try to be concise and human in my writing. He was without doubt like a brother – a man I befriended and loved from the day we first met at my house in Windsor. I was determined to sell him my dream – greatness and longevity for my beloved Watford Football Club.

There I sat nervously explaining why he had to come to this run-down club so we could go to the stars and back. We all know what happened. It was a partnership so binding and enjoyable; one that equalled my relationship with my brilliant lyricist.

We may have looked an unlikely twosome from the outside but if you had the time to spend in our company, you understood. We shared a fiercely ambitious, revolutionary approach to a football club and its community.

Passionate and committed we were, along with Bertie Mee, Eddie Plumley and the board of directors. An unstoppable force of nature. And how we all enjoyed it. How we laughed. It was for me like finding a new family. Then, of course, there were the players. I remember Graham saying to me when he took over that he couldn't get promotion from the Fourth Division in our first season because he had a bloody giraffe at centre-forward. We got promoted of course and our giraffe, Ross Jenkins, became a folk hero for the club, along with countless others.

What impressed me about Graham was his commitment to the community and the town. He wanted the club to be more accessible to families and children and he was adamant about change. What a dump the club was, we would say to each other at the beginning. Never could we have imagined the changes that would come.

The last time we spoke was just before Christmas 2016 and the conversation was all about how proud we both were of the club and how it is today. As chairman and manager, we were Batman and Robin. When Batman left to go to Aston Villa, Robin floundered without his mate. I missed him and I made some bad decisions but I'd had to let him go. It was time. He had done the work of a thousand men at Watford.

Our friendship remained close and connected. We spent time together and on the phone talking football, families and careers. Our friendship has been cast in stone and was as strong as ever. I am proud of that. I have cherished his advice and company during these latter years and he was so happy that I had become a father in recent years.

His honesty and kindness towards me will stay with me forever. His family and his daughters showed me something that I wanted in my life, but it was something I could not obtain because of my substance abuse. His lecture to me one day shook me to my core. He told me how foolish I was and how I was letting myself and, more importantly, the club down. As you can imagine, those words rang so true and I will never forget them. To love somebody, you must be prepared to be honest and open.

Graham was the most honest and open man I have ever met. He was successful but he cared about players, fans, family and friends. There were no airs and graces. He was just a genius from Lincolnshire.

Because of him, I have the name of Watford Football Club etched in my soul. I have memories that are sublime and a sense of achievement that no one can ever take away. He is a legend in football and in life. I love you, my friend. Thank you for everything.

Preface

I always planned to sit down and write a book about my life and my career in football but it never seemed to be the right time. Shortly after I'd finished as England manager I was approached to do something but the disappointment was still far too raw. I was still coming to terms with it and trying to work out why it had gone wrong. The last thing I wanted was for people to think I was making excuses for our failure to qualify for the World Cup (I still don't, by the way) and at that time it would have been easy to fall into the trap of blaming other people. Besides, I was only forty-nine years old and I wanted to get back into football management and prove to myself that I could still be successful. I didn't think writing about the biggest failure an English football manager can have would be particularly helpful when it came to persuading a chairman to give me a chance either.

There simply wasn't time to look backwards because I had to focus on what I was going to do next. I was in the middle of my career, and in the middle of my life, and it didn't appeal to me to tell the story *so far*. I have no problem with sports people who write a book while they are still playing or shortly after they have retired but I don't tend to read them. I prefer the ones written later on because I believe the passing of years adds perspective.

When I left Aston Villa for the second time in 2003 I had decided that I was no longer going to be a football manager. I was fifty-nine, which is relatively young when you consider

1

Arsène Wenger has continued managing well into his sixties and Sir Alex Ferguson retired at seventy-one. Some people told me I was going too soon but I wanted to retire as a manager when I chose and on my terms. I could see that things were changing, that it was becoming harder and harder to be the type of football manager I had been and wanted to be.

You might wonder why I didn't write something then but I went into radio and television and I still felt part of the game. I was busy, travelling up and down the country for the BBC, and abroad covering the England team. I was still too concerned with today and tomorrow to think about yesterday.

But eventually, we all reach a point where there is much less life to live than has been lived. If I am honest with myself, I recognise now that it took me time to accept that my management days were over because football had been such a huge part of my life for more than half a century. It had been a privilege to wake up every day and go to work with players, to spend time on the training pitch and in the dressing room, trying to improve myself and improve a football team. Life had unfolded season by season, match by match, and then one day it was over and from that moment on I did feel a bit like an outsider, even if I was still earning a living from watching football. For a while, the idea of writing a book felt a bit like drawing a line under my career before I was ready, even though I knew I would not give another team talk or take my place on the bench again.

Every now and then I would look at the league tables in the newspaper, see Lincoln City languishing outside the Football League, and joke to Rita that I could go back to Sincil Bank and do it all over again. She would roll her eyes in the way I suspect the wives of many men my age do when their husbands say something ridiculous.

As for the book, there were times when I began working with one journalist or another on my book but I think there was always something holding me back, perhaps it was because I had imagined sitting down at a computer and writing it myself. My father had been a sports journalist and so from a young age I had been around newspapers. I would sit with him in the press box at Scunthorpe United's Old Showground and after he'd finished work we'd head back to the office in time to see the papers being printed. I can still remember the smell of the ink and newsprint as they came flying off the press. I had always considered journalism as a possible back-up if football didn't work out for me. When I was a player at Grimsby Town, I took night classes to learn shorthand and typing skills and I swear my motivation was absolutely nothing to do with the fact I was the only man in a class of thirty women. I wanted to sit the shorthand and typing exams so that I had a formal qualification, but because I was not employed as a journalist or in local or central government, they wouldn't let me. It was something to do with the National Union of Journalists' rules, which annoyed me. My dad was the head of the local NUJ chapel, or whatever it was called, and I gave him some right stick about it.

Over the years, I have written columns for *The Times*, the *Telegraph* and the *Express* and I've always enjoyed the process of sitting down and constructing an argument, looking at an issue from several different angles and trying to draw some conclusion. Whenever I did sit down to try to start work on the book, which wasn't often, I found that there was a big difference between writing an 800-word column for a newspaper and trying to sort through the memories of a lifetime. I knew that if this book were ever to see the light of day, I'd need some help. The problem was, I had a very particular idea of how I wanted this book to turn out, and journalists – quite rightly when writing for a newspaper – want to start with the most eye-catching stories first. Many people reading this will want to know why I substituted Gary Lineker, or what it felt like when the *Sun* turned me into a turnip, or what I thought when we failed to qualify for the World Cup, and that is perfectly understandable because being the England manager was the most high-profile job in my career. Those stories, and many more, will be in this book but I didn't want to start there because my life didn't start there. I wanted to tell the story of my life, not just of what happened when I was England manager but how I got there and what I learned on the way. Many people may think they know me but this is my chance to tell my story my way. I certainly don't want to settle scores, but I also don't want to gloss over the bad bits because they are all part of my life.

So, what changed? What finally persuaded me to get on with it?

One night, while we were visiting my sister Christine in Scunthorpe, I got up in the middle of the night to visit the loo. It was dark and I was still half-asleep and in my daze, I'd forgotten I was not at home. Instinctively, I turned left, presumably thinking I was heading to our bathroom at home, only to tumble down the stairs, landing very heavily at the bottom. Rita jumped out of bed, turned on the lights and when she saw me twisted and unconscious at the bottom of the stairs she thought the worst. That accident meant I needed an operation on my shoulder and it began a long, slow rehabilitation process that often put me in a reflective mood. While I was recovering from the operation, I turned seventy and I thought to myself: 'Graham, you've lived more years than you have left, so if you are going to do this book, you'd better get started.' I finally felt I could talk about a life because I had lived it.

I know that many people reading this will be football supporters, perhaps supporters of one of the clubs I played for or managed, or perhaps people keen to know what happened when I was England manager, but if I am writing this for anyone it is for my three grandchildren, Rhianna, Elsie and Jake. At the moment they are not very interested in granddad's boring old stories because they are young people looking forward to their own lives, but they might be interested in the future and I'd like to think that when they are older they will pull the book from the shelves and have a read. My playing days happened in black and white and almost all of my management career happened before they were born so it's not surprising they think of it as ancient history. I was the same at their age but, as we grow older, we naturally become more interested in what our parents and grandparents did and I know there are things I wish I had asked my own parents before they passed away. So this book is for my grandchildren.

There was another more practical reason for getting on with it. At our house in Little Aston there was a summerhouse in the garden which became a dumping ground for all my old junk. I have collected a lot of things over the years, much to Rita's annoyance, I suspect. There were scrapbooks of newspaper cuttings from my playing days at Grimsby and my years in management at Lincoln, Watford and Aston Villa. There were suitcases full of old photographs, piles of football programmes, a complete set of *Rothmans Football Yearbooks* going back to the early 1970s, ring-binders of letters I'd received and notes I'd made, diaries and notebooks documenting certain times in my career, even an envelope full of embroidered badges I'd cut off shirts and blazers, including the three lions from the official jacket I wore at my first match as England manager. If you asked me, I think I'd say that I am not a sentimental person and that I don't look back with misty eyes at the things I've done, but perhaps the contents of my summerhouse say otherwise. As we planned to move south, back to Kings Langley in Hertfordshire, where we had lived for a time when I was Watford manager, I knew I had to sort through it all. Rita was in favour of throwing it all in a skip – not because she's unsentimental, but because she can't stand clutter. I couldn't bring myself to do that because I thought some of it might spark some memories for this book, which it did.

In autumn 2014, I began working on this book with a journalist I have known for a few years called Lionel Birnie. After our first few meetings, he suggested we visit some of the places that mattered most to me, and so one morning before Christmas we met in the car park outside Glanford Park, Scunthorpe United's ground. It wasn't the Old Showground, where I spent many happy Saturday afternoons watching my heroes Jack Haigh and Jack Brownsword in claret and blue because that was knocked down years ago. As I stood outside Glanford Park I remembered the England under-21s beating Germany there in September 1991, the day before my first defeat as manager of the senior side. It was a relatively new ground then but I can't help noticing it's showing signs of wear now.

Together Lionel and I visited places in Scunthorpe, Grimsby, Lincoln, Watford and the Midlands and so the memories in this book are partly inspired by that journey. Even though some of the places have changed significantly in the years that have passed, it brought back many memories. It may well be that the journey meanders a bit at times, but anyone who knows me will tell you I do often go the long way round in conversations.

In football, you win, you lose and sometimes you draw. Hopefully you win more than you lose but whatever happens you are learning all of the time because no matter how good you are, you cannot crack the game. I think the same can be said about life. Of course, we are all selective in our memories – we tend to remember the good times much better than the bad, or we remember the bad times in a way that shows us in the most positive light. But this is the story of my life as I saw it.

1

'Leave your mark, son'

At the end of Axholme Road in Scunthorpe there's a little patch of grass. It's not quite square and it slopes a little bit, but to us – the small boys who lived in the nearby streets – it was a special place. It was Wembley in the winter and Lord's in the summer. It's also where everyone gathered to celebrate the Coronation in 1953 and where the dads and sons' cricket matches would take place involving all the boys in the neighbourhood. We spent hours – whole days – playing there and wouldn't go in until the light faded, making it impossible to see the jumpers for goalposts or the stumps. We'd head home for tea, bathtime or bed, knowing there'd be a game going on when we returned the next day.

The house I grew up in was only supposed to last twenty-five years but 74 Axholme Road is still standing. It was one of the prefabricated steelhouses built quickly after the War to meet the housing shortage. The ground floor is brick and upstairs is made of sheets of corrugated steel bolted together. Some of the houses have been covered in pebbledash or cladding but the house I lived in with my mum and dad and two sisters, Christine and Margaret, in the 1950s is much the same now as it was then. I can see the window I climbed out of on the few occasions I ran away from home and, looking at it now, it doesn't seem like it can be as far to jump down to the ground as it is in my mind's eye.

It's only a short walk from Axholme Road to my old primary school at Henderson Avenue. I can remember the route off by heart – up through the housing estate to the Doncaster Road, then up the hill past what was Scunthorpe Grammar, where I later went to school. A bit further on, near to the big crossroads, there's a Sainsbury's supermarket and Scunthorpe United supporters will know that's where the Old Showground used to stand before it was knocked down and the club moved to Glanford Park on the outskirts of town. The offices of the *Scunthorpe Evening Telegraph*, where my dad worked as a sports reporter, were just the other side of the old football ground but the newspaper has moved now too.

Not many people will know this but just behind the supermarket there's a development of new houses built in 2011 and one of the little roads there is called Taylor Court. Although I was born in Worksop, not a million miles away in Nottingham-shire, my family moved to Scunthorpe when I was three and so I consider it my home town. You might not think it particularly unusual that they named a road Taylor Court – after all, I managed the England football team, you know – but the street isn't named after me, it's named after my dad.

In fact, both my mum and dad were well known in the town and they enjoyed being a part of the community. My dad was a sports journalist, covering not only the town's Football League team but all the local sports – cricket, athletics and bowls in the summer, rugby, football and even darts in the winter. Mum was a postwoman. She would get up early in the morning to sort the mail and then complete her round before starting her day as a mum to Christine, Margaret and me. As a result of their work, everyone knew Mum and Dad and would wave and say hello if they saw them out and about.

The idea of being part of a place and contributing to the town was something I learned from them, something that stuck with me, and I don't think it's a coincidence that they both did jobs that took them out into the community and made them feel that they were participating in life. They encouraged me to always give my best and to know that if you asked the most of yourself, no one could criticise you for a lack of effort.

The proudest moment of my career was when I watched as my parents arrived at Wembley on 12 September 1990, the night I managed England for the first time, against Hungary. They knew where I had come from and how hard I had pushed myself to get the opportunity to manage my country. It was so important that they were there to share the occasion with me, even though I didn't have all that much time to say anything other than 'hello' before the match.

Dad always said to me: 'Leave your mark, son. Whatever you do, leave your mark.' Years later, when Scunthorpe's town council decided to honour my dad by naming the little cul-de-sac Taylor Court after him, I was every bit as proud of him as he had been of me. In their own ways, Tom and Dorothy Taylor had left their mark on Scunthorpe.

We were not a wealthy family but I don't remember ever feeling we were going without. I don't think my parents would have considered themselves middle class because the house we lived in was very modest, but compared to many they were doing well. Scunthorpe was a steel town and the big employers were the steelworks at Lysaght's and Redbourn. The work there could be hard, dirty and dangerous, so my dad going to an office to write about sport for the paper was a pretty middle-class job.

My dad, Tom, was born in Westerham in Kent. His father was a baker and so as a boy my dad would cycle off to deliver the freshly baked loaves in the morning. One of the addresses on his rounds was Winston Churchill's home at Chartwell. When he was nineteen, he met a seventeen-year-old girl called Dorothy, who was working as a parlour maid. They started going out, got married in Worksop, my mum's home town, in 1940 and had their first child, Christine, a year later. I arrived in September 1944, just a few months before he was sent to Burma with the Royal Electrical and Mechanical Engineers. I don't know much about his military service other than that he came home with malaria. It's funny, really, because the two World Wars are eras of history that really interest me and I'll read books and watch television programmes about them but I don't know too much about my dad's experiences because he didn't talk about them.

The only story my dad told me about the War was when I was about six. We were in the garden on a warm, sunny day and Dad was wearing shorts so I noticed the scar on his knee.

'How did you get that, Dad?' I asked.

'That's from the War,' he said. 'I saw this bullet coming and I knew it was going to hit my general, so I stuck my leg out and deflected it away. I'm a hero, son!'

Mum was listening, shaking her head, saying: 'Tom… Don't! Tell him what really happened.'

'OK,' said Dad, smiling. 'It was a bee sting. A very vicious bee, mind.'

Mum and Dad both enjoyed a joke and our house was always full of laughter. I'm sure there was the occasional argument, although I don't remember too many. I was a pretty well-behaved boy but I wasn't a saint. I know Christine and I ganged up on Margaret a bit because she was the youngest. When I was seven or eight, I was sent to my room by my mum. I can't remember what I'd done wrong but I can remember I tried to fib my way out of it and, angrier at the lie than at what I'd done wrong in the first place, Mum hurled a bar of soap she'd been holding towards my head. With the reflexes of a champion boxer, I dodged my head to the side to avoid the missile.

'Graham, you can help a thief but not a liar,' she said, which was one of her phrases. 'Get up to your room.'

I decided I'd had enough and that I was going to leave home, so I packed a little suitcase and climbed out of my window onto the porch, jumped down and announced that I was leaving and never coming back.

'Oh good,' said Mum, which was not the reaction I'd been expecting.

I headed into the field that backed onto our house, keeping our back garden in sight the whole time, and sat on the banking as it began to sink in what leaving home would mean. Where would I sleep? What would I eat? What would I do if it rained? It didn't take long before I realised that perhaps living at home wasn't so bad after all. Eventually I picked up my case and walked back.

'I've decided to come home,' I said to Mum, who was gardening and had, she admitted later, been watching me the whole time, shaking her head gently and smiling to herself as she watched me come to my senses.

'Oh dear,' she said. 'Oh, I'm not too keen on that idea. I thought we'd got rid of you. Well, if you insist but I hope we're not going to have any more lies.'

I can't say that the occasional 'porkie' has never passed my lips in all the years since, but I can say that I've never told a white lie without my head flinching to dodge an imaginary flying bar of soap.

I inherited a few interests from my dad – he was a keen reader and loved poetry and Shakespeare – but it was sport that captured my imagination as a child. It's a cliché, no doubt, but for children brought up after the War, it seemed we spent our entire lives playing outdoors. All we needed for amusement was a tennis ball. The streets were quiet – there were no parked cars like there are now – so we had the roads to ourselves. We knew the bus timetables off by heart so we'd know when to pause the game to let the bus go past. We'd make up games of football and cricket that only we knew the rules to – for example, if the ball hit a certain part of the wall it counted as a goal, or six runs. We learned to use the kerb so the ball would bounce to our advantage and fool the opposition but we were careful not to get too cocky in case the ball hit the kerb at the wrong angle and flew straight back past us for an own goal.

Perhaps once or twice each summer, all the dads would come down to our little version of Lord's and we'd have a 'dads versus sons' cricket match. These games didn't happen all that often but they stick in my mind so vividly because they were special afternoons – everyone outside, playing cricket and treating it as seriously as if it were the Ashes.

One day, I was trying – unsuccessfully – to get the ball to spin. I was wrapping my fingers round the ball like the diagrams in my *Boy's Own* book or wherever it was I'd seen it. My dad was at the crease, tapping his bat on the ground, looking a bit too pleased with himself for my liking because he knew I was getting frustrated.

Each time I tried to spin the ball, it would fly out of my hand badly, pitch and bounce straight on without turning. After a few attempts, my dad was shaking his head at me, which just riled me up more. As I walked back I thought to myself: 'Right. I'll show you.'

This time, I got everything right – the grip, my timing and the release of the ball were perfect. The ball flew towards Dad. He watched it as it bounced just in front of him and, expecting it to bounce straight on again like all the rest, he decided not to play a shot. But this time the ball pitched, spun and clattered into his stumps.

'Howzat!' I shouted in celebration.

Dad turned and looked at the stumps in disbelief, tucked the bat under his arm in an exaggerated, defiant fashion and walked, as if he were Don Bradman marching back to the pavilion, with a look of fatherly pride on his face.

'Do you know,' he said to the other dads, 'I've been trying to teach him that for ages and he's finally got it.'

I thought: 'No, you haven't. I learned that all on my own.'

I enjoyed cricket and, although I'm right-handed, I batted left-handed. Don't ask me why, it just felt natural to pick up the bat that way. Typical Graham, doing things differently to everyone else. I would go in at number three and I can remember scoring a half-century for Scunthorpe Grammar School once, although athletics was more for me in the summer because I could run. I was quick and I had endurance but I never quite managed to break the two-minute mark for 880 yards, which really set you apart as a decent runner.

In any case, it was football that really excited me, probably because it was the sport I was best at. I played inside-forward for my primary school team, Henderson Avenue, and I scored most of the goals. One of my team-mates was Tony Jacklin, who went on to be a pretty decent golfer – a sport I never really got to grips with, perhaps because it didn't feel natural whether I tried to play left-handed or right-handed.

Later on, I passed the eleven-plus and moved to Scunthorpe Grammar School, where I was captain of the football team and leading goalscorer. Mum would come and watch our matches on a Saturday morning after she'd finished her post round, as would Dad if Scunthorpe were playing at home. If we won, which we often did, it was my job as captain to lead the three cheers for the opposition. 'Hip-hip, hooray!' It was always easier when we won, but if we lost – even if I was feeling annoyed – I tried to sound as loud and enthusiastic as I could. We beat John Leggott Grammar School, which was the other grammar school in Scunthorpe and our big rivals, 16-0 once. I think I scored eleven of them and at the end of the game we celebrated a bit too much considering it had been a total mismatch. I was still feeling pleased with myself when I got home but Mum brought me down to earth over lunch, saying: 'No one likes a bad loser, but an ungracious winner is just as bad.'

Having said that, neither Mum nor Dad objected to the idea of winning 16-0 because they always encouraged me to give my best on the basis that there was no point wishing later on that you'd tried harder.

They are happy memories that have stayed with me my whole life: playing football, running home and finding the greengrocer, Tom Goy, still in our street with his van full of fruit and veg. He'd ask if we'd won and sometimes he'd chuck me an apple. I'd head upstairs and lie in the hot bath, eating my apple, having just played football and knowing Scunthorpe United were at home that afternoon. Life really was fantastic.

I played for the school team, I played when the best players from all the schools in Scunthorpe were selected to play against other towns, I played for the county and I was called up to play for England Grammar and Public Schools after a trial at Oxford University. We played against Scotland and Andy Roxburgh played for them. No one would have known then that the future England and Scotland managers were playing against one another.

I also had a trial for England Schoolboys at Barnsley but when the squad for the next trial was named I wasn't in it, which was very disappointing. It was the first time I'd not been picked for something. When I got back to school, Mr Hill, our geography master, who had been at the trial, had told the games master Mr Warburton that I'd played well and was unfortunate not to be selected. Mr Warburton called me into his study and sat me down. He had a list of the players who had been picked.

'Let's have a look at who's been selected, shall we, Taylor?' he said. 'This boy is from Sheffield, and what do we know about Sheffield?'

I didn't really understand what he was asking me, so I probably looked confused.

'Sheffield is a city, isn't it, Taylor?' Mr Warburton continued. 'And what about this lad here? He's from Manchester. Another city. And these boys are from London. In fact, if you look at the list you can see that there are no boys from towns like Scunthorpe. If you look at the names of the people on the selection committee, they all come from cities too. Now, you may not understand what I am saying to you at the moment, but you may do in later life. The point is not to let the decisions of others deter you from trying your best to prove them wrong.'

At the time, I probably thought Mr Warburton was just trying to be kind, cushioning the blow of not being selected for the England Schoolboys squad but perhaps he was planting a seed for later life because I have always tried not to be put off by people who don't believe in me. Maybe it also helped me to identify with the underdog or, more to the point, it has taught me not to judge people by where they come from but by their abilities and their character. I can't say that at the time Mr

Warburton's words meant a great deal to me but I think it's telling that I remember the conversation more than fifty years later.

Scunthorpe Grammar School played a hugely significant part in my life, not just because it's where I spent a big chunk of my childhood, but because it's where I met the girl who would become my wife.

I met Rita Cowling in March 1958. It was just before the dress rehearsal for the school play, a production of *The Tale of Tom Thumb*, in which I was to play the part of Lord Grizzle. I don't remember very much about the play at all but it was one of the most important events in my life.

We had to have some make-up put on for the play and so I entered the little room where there were a couple of chairs for us to sit in while the make-up girls did their job. I was sitting waiting to get made up when I heard a very attractive laugh behind me. I turned round and saw a girl in a yellow cardigan who was making up the boy in the other chair and I thought, as thirteen-year-old boys do: 'I fancy her.'

The next night – the night of the play – I had butterflies in my stomach but it was nothing to do with the fear of performing in front of an audience or worry that I might forget my lines; it was because I had a plan to catch the eye of the girl in the yellow cardigan. I got there early and deliberately sat in the other seat, gambling that she would apply my make-up. I was right and we had a laugh and joke about it and it went from there. She had cycled in from her home in Winteringham and I had cycled in too, so after the play we cycled off together. Our first kiss was across the handlebars of my bike, although I should point out it was just a peck on the cheek.

From that moment on I was convinced that Rita would be the girl I would marry and so six years later, when I was still a teenager, I found myself round at her house seeking her father's permission to ask her to marry me. Rita's dad was in the bathroom at the time, shaving. He had foam all over his face and his back to me, although he could see me in the mirror. I asked him if I could marry Rita. He didn't stop shaving, but he did look at me in the reflection of the mirror and said: 'As long as you know what you're doing.'

We had two beautiful daughters, Joanne and Karen, who now have children of their own. As important as football has been, I am a very family-orientated person and I have been so lucky to have had Rita by my side through all the ups and downs. I have to be honest, I've never asked Rita if she enjoys football but she has watched hundreds of matches over the years and always has an opinion, so she must do.

Rita allowed me to immerse myself totally in the job so that I could always do it the way I wanted to, but she has also managed to remind me at crucial times that there is more to life than team selection and tactics. She accepted that it wasn't just a job for me, that it was a passion, and that I wanted to live it fully. If you're not careful, football management can completely take over. There is always something to do, whether it's travelling to watch a match because you want to see an opposition side or a particular player, or just staying late at the training ground or the office to make sure everything is under control. She also knew it wasn't something I could leave behind when I came home, that I would sit at home mulling over decisions or making plans and, for the most part, she allowed me to do that. But she also had a knack of snapping me out of it. Rita knew when to give me space to work or perhaps to sulk over a bad performance or result. She knew better than to tell me it didn't matter, or that it was just a game, because she knew it *did* matter. But she was able to remind me that I was a husband and a father as well as a football manager. It was usually very simple and to the point – she'd say: 'OK, football is over now, Joanne needs help with her homework,' or: 'You'd better cheer up because we're going out tonight.'

I was a family man and I wanted the supporters of the clubs I managed to know that. Over the years, Rita has had an opinion on players and I've always listened because she watched the games and often had a different perspective. I joke that she's picked my teams for me over the years, although it's funny because she never takes responsibility for the England side. Before I go on, I'd better make sure you realise that's a joke, otherwise there'll be headlines saying: 'England manager's wife picked team.'

When I was a teenager, as far as I was concerned, I was going to become a professional footballer. Although I was pretty good at school lessons, I worked hard and behaved well most of the time, football was my preoccupation and every time I was stuck in a classroom and saw the Scunthorpe United players jog past on their regular runs from the Old Showground I knew I wanted to be one of them.

Some of the teachers at the school had other ideas though. I passed my O Levels and when I moved up to the lower sixth form I was made a prefect by the headmaster Mr McIvor, which was quite unusual because it was usually only students in the upper sixth who were given that responsibility. No one said this to me but it probably meant I was one of the pupils being considered by the staff to be the school's head boy when I reached the upper sixth. I suppose I had shown some leadership qualities, in that I was captain of the football team, and I was pretty well-liked by the pupils and caused the teachers very little trouble.

One of the jobs for the prefects was to make sure everyone was wearing the correct school uniform, but there was one rule I never enforced: I hated wearing the school cap because I thought they were daft and so I let that one go. If one of the teachers pointed out to me that someone wasn't wearing the cap, I'd say: 'Yes, I'll make sure I have a word with him about that,' but I never did. You have to take these small victories where you can.

During the school holidays, Scunthorpe United had invited me and my best friend Alan Morgan (who would be my best man when I married Rita) to train with them, so I knew the club were interested in me, and by the time I was reaching the end of my year in the lower sixth I had made up my mind that I needed to leave school if I was going to join a professional club. I had seen Derek Hemstead and Barry Lindsey leave school early to join Scunthorpe United and I wanted to do the same because I knew that if I waited another year while I did my A Levels some other young striker might come along and take my place.

When I made my decision to leave school a year early – to join Grimsby Town rather than Scunthorpe United, as it turned out – I was summoned to see the headmaster, Mr McIvor. He was Scottish and very stern and we nicknamed him Jock, although we were careful never to call him that when he was in earshot. I can still remember the look of anger on his face when I stepped into his office. He didn't invite me to sit down, so I knew it was something serious, and I was trying to think what it was I had done wrong.

I was on the receiving end of the biggest telling-off I'd had before, or since for that matter. It was the quiet anger and disappointment that rose and swelled as he spoke that sticks with me to this day. As far as he was concerned, I was a disgrace to myself and the school for choosing to throw away an education unfinished. His closing words were: 'You do not come to grammar school in order to become a professional footballer.' The way he spat out the word 'footballer' left me in no doubt he had very little respect for the game as a career.

Of course, there was nothing like the money in professional football that there is today. This was before the abolition of the maximum wage, which kept players more or less in line with what ordinary people earned. Football was also a short career, although it was better paid than a life spent in the steelworks. I don't think in any way Mr McIvor was a nasty man and so I will give him the benefit of the doubt and say that he probably had my best interests at heart; it's just that, as the headmaster of a grammar school, he expected his pupils – particularly one he had selected as a prefect – to aspire to more than kicking a ball about for a living.

But even a dressing-down that had my knees buckling and my heart racing was not enough to make me change my mind.

2

The Poacher's Boy

I thought my dad had the second-best job in the world. He was paid to watch and write about sport, got into Scunthorpe United home games for free and travelled on the team coach to away games. Other than actually being a professional footballer, I thought it couldn't get any better than that.

As soon as I was old enough to sit still for ninety minutes, Dad used to let me join him in the press box at the Old Showground. After lunch I'd head up to the newspaper office and then we'd walk across to the ground where they'd let us in through the door marked 'Players & Officials'.

Everyone knew Dad because he covered the team home and away. He wrote a column in the paper under the pseudonym 'The Poacher' – a reference to the local cheese, Lincolnshire Poacher, I suppose – but it was an open secret that it was him. People knew me as Tom's Lad or The Poacher's Boy before they knew me as Graham. It felt very special to be acknowledged by everyone as we made our way up to the little wooden press box at the back of the main stand.

I loved the buzz of the press box at the Old Showground in those days. The little wooden benches were divided by a sliding wooden panel, a bit like a serving hatch, that split the press box in two. The reporter from the town's other newspaper, the *Scunthorpe Star*, would sit on the other side from my dad. Scunthorpe United was a club on the up in the 1950s. They had joined the Football League in Division Three North at the beginning of the decade and won promotion to Division Two in 1958. During those years there were some big FA Cup ties at the Old Showground – against Tottenham Hotspur, Sunderland, Portsmouth and Liverpool – and the ground would be full to bursting, as would the press box. I noticed early on that having a successful team made the whole town walk with a spring in its step and people looked to their local newspapers to find out what was going on behind the scenes at the club.

My job was to be in charge of the stopwatch for my dad. As soon as the game kicked off, I pressed the button on the stopwatch and then I made a note of the times of any goals scored. Sometimes the little hatch door would slide open and the man from the *Star* would say: 'What time did you make that, Tom?' Dad would look at the note I'd made and say: 'Twenty-five minutes,' and the hatch would slam shut again.

Every quarter of an hour or so, Dad would pick up the phone and dictate his match reports in chunks to a copytaker at the other end of the line. It used to amaze me that he could reel off his report off the top of his head, although I think he wrote the odd sentence down as the game went along. He'd spell out the names of the players letter by letter and while he was dictating he'd have one eye on the game to make sure he didn't miss anything important for his next update. The reason for phoning through his report in bits like this was because the paper went to press within minutes of the final whistle so that copies could be printed ready for people to read that evening.

It was always exciting when a late goal was scored because Dad and the other reporters would quickly reach for the phone and start reeling off new copy. In fact, when I was a manager it used to tickle me when one of my teams scored a late equaliser – or even better, a late winner – because I knew the reporters would be having kittens. I would joke with them: 'That's pressure, isn't it, boys? You had your report all finished in good time and all of a sudden you have to redo it.'

After the match, Dad would speak to the manager and a few of the players for his follow-up articles for Monday's paper and we'd arrive back at the *Evening Telegraph*'s office in time to see the papers coming off the press. I'd turn to the football page and scan the results for the times of the goal. There it would be, '25 minutes', printed in the paper for all to see. I always had a thrill thinking that was my little contribution to the whole operation.

I am probably biased because he was my dad, but I think he was respected not just by the readers but also by the people he was writing about because it was a job he did for more than thirty-five years, until he retired in 1983. I'm sure he upset managers or players every once in a while with something he wrote, but he was always accountable and would stand by his words if he was challenged. Dad travelled to Scunthorpe United's away matches on the team coach and he would have formed relationships, perhaps even friendships, with the players. When Kevin Keegan first broke into the team in the late Sixties, he would sit on Dad's lap and pretend to be a ventriloquist's dummy while Dad did the voice and cracked the jokes. But Dad was always aware that he had to be objective, otherwise he was short-changing the supporters, and that meant sometimes having to be critical of the players while remaining fair to them.

It was probably a much more innocent age, and it's fair to say that the stakes were not quite as high at Scunthorpe United as I was to experience when I was England manager, but I admired the way my dad did his job.

People might assume – because of the treatment I received from some of the newspapers, particularly the *Sun*, when I was England manager – that I must dislike journalists and news-papers, but I don't. Not all of them anyway. I like to think that I got on well with the majority of journalists I worked with and I came to count some of them as friends, but it was impossible for me to win over everyone. I am not being boastful but I perhaps had a better insight into their world than they did into mine because I did understand some of the pressures they were under.

I always recognised that they had an important role to play in communicating with supporters because often a newspaper's coverage was the biggest insight they had into what was going on behind the scenes. I did sometimes feel that reporters thought they knew more than they did, or believed that they were entitled to know everything that was going on, but I always thought it was better that a journalist be reasonably well informed because it might help them when they watched the matches. Often they wouldn't be aware of everything that had happened on the training pitch or in the dressing room. They wouldn't know of any issues that might have been affecting the players, or be party to all of the factors that influenced my decisions, and yet they would be expected to offer informed and opinionated comments in their reports. Because of that, I tried to shed light on things when I could without breaking confidences or causing embarrassment to players or other people at the club, but it was a difficult balance to strike because no matter how much information you give a journalist they always want more.

Possibly I was too open for my own good at times, particularly when I was the England manager. I tried to treat everyone fairly but there were too many newspapers and too many journalists and they were all competing for stories. If I held a lunch for journalists from the daily papers, the writers for the Sunday papers would be upset. If I then held a lunch for the Sunday newspaper writers the journalists from the dailies would wonder what I'd said that I hadn't told them. I couldn't win.

In the main, the journalists who covered the matches and came to the press conferences were fine. I realised that the extreme headlines and the harshest commentaries were usually not written by those reporters but by editors and sub-editors, people sitting in the safety of their offices knowing they would never come face to face with those they were writing about so critically.

I could cope with criticism, as long as it avoided becoming vitriolic. I knew they had a job to do and I understood long before I wrote newspaper columns of my own that it was not the journalist's job to butter up the people they were writing about. I understood that an opinion, particularly a critical one, could upset people but I also accepted that if the writer could look the subject of their criticism in the eye and say it was their honestly held view then that was fair enough. Once or twice over the years I did challenge journalists on what they wrote and sometimes they stood by it and on other occasions they avoided eye-contact and looked a bit sheepish. Both responses told me what I needed to know about the sorts of people I was dealing with.

I also knew that journalists, particularly those covering the England team, could be emotional from time to time. After the game against Holland in Rotterdam – the one where a couple of very bad decisions by the officials contributed to costing us a place in the 1994 World Cup – I saw a reporter from one of the tabloids with his head round the door of the referee's dressing room, giving the officials both barrels. I can tell you he wouldn't have been able to print his comments in his family newspaper without a handful of asterisks. The following morning, I read his report in the newspaper and later that day I bumped into him in the hotel lobby. I was still hurting from the previous night's result but I managed half a smile. 'I heard what you said to the referee last night,' I said, 'and yet when I opened your paper this morning I found it was all my fault.'

So I understood a little bit about how the newspaper game worked. I have always read a newspaper and I do enjoy reading something that challenges my opinions as long as there's some substance to it, but I wonder if everyone who works in the industry – particularly those who enjoyed the power and reach of the tabloids in the 1990s – understands the consequences of their printed words once millions have read them.

It was largely my respect for dad's job that meant I knew I could not sign for Scunthorpe United when I was a teenager, even though they almost tricked me into doing so. Perhaps 'tricked' is too strong a word but they certainly tried to pull a fast one.

Alan Morgan and I had trained with Scunthorpe United during the school holidays and, although I'd have liked nothing more than to pull on the claret and blue shirt worn by my childhood heroes, I knew it would be difficult to do so. As it turned out, Scunthorpe helped make the decision for me. At the end of our last session of the summer holidays, Dick Duckworth, who was Scunthorpe's manager, said that he wanted all the young players who had been training with them to be able to watch the first-team games free of charge. He gave Alan and me a piece of paper to sign, saying that if we showed it at the turnstile on matchdays we'd be let in for free. We signed quite happily, without reading the large print, let alone the small print.

When I got home and showed my dad what I had signed, he was furious. In those days, professional clubs could retain amateur players – in effect reserving first refusal on them and preventing other clubs from moving in – just by getting them to sign amateur forms. I'd not realised that the pieces of paper I'd signed not only gave me free entry to Scunthorpe's games but also gave Scunthorpe my consent to be retained as an amateur player. Dad went up to the club and got the paperwork ripped up.

And that is where Grimsby Town came in, which spared both Dad and me the awkwardness of him having to report on his son's career. It sounds presumptuous of me to assume that I'd have made it into the first team anywhere, but at the time that's where I thought I was headed. I knew it would be awkward for both of us – he'd be in a position where he might be accused of showing favouritism to his son, or perhaps feeling he had to be extra critical of me to avoid being seen as biased, and I would be on the inside at the club, hearing bits of gossip that I couldn't pass on to him. And if Dad did get wind of a story at the club, there would always be the suspicion that I'd given it to him, even if I hadn't.

So Dick Duckworth's tactics made it easy for me to follow up on Grimsby's interest, and I left school and signed a one-year contract with them. Grimsby was only thirty miles down the road but it felt like I was taking a risk. When you are seventeen years old, twelve months feels like all the time in the world, but as soon as I arrived in Grimsby I realised that the world of professional football was a lot more cut-throat than the

Scunthorpe players jogging past my school had made it look. Playing football for a living meant it was no longer just a game and I realised very quickly that I was going to have to toughen up if I was to survive.

3

Baptism of fire

I am tempted to say I have always felt happy and comfortable in a football club's dressing room, and almost consider them to be like a second home, a place of laughter and togetherness, passion and determination and, yes, the odd flying teacup on a bad day. The dressing room is for the players and the staff to work and prepare in, somewhere to celebrate and commiserate. Before a match, there's an energy in there that you cannot feel anywhere else in life. There's a smell too – of embrocation ointment and nerves – and whenever I get a whiff of it, I'm transported back to the sound of a thousand team talks I've given, or listened to, the clack of studs on the floor and the shouts and backslaps of encouragement. 'Come on, lads, this is ours today.'

And it was 'our' place. What gets said in the dressing room stays in the dressing room – at least it should. I'm not saying that Heneage Dove, Elton John and Doug Ellis didn't pop into the dressing rooms at Sincil Bank, Vicarage Road and Villa Park from time to time, but when they did they knew that although they may have been in charge of the club, the dressing room was not their space. They were welcome until we told them it was time to go. They had no authority here.

So although I was tempted to say I've always felt happy and comfortable in this environment, as I step into the cramped away-team dressing room at Grimsby Town's Blundell Park now, I note that not only has it barely changed in half a century but I remember a time when I was anxious, insecure and painfully quiet.

In May 1962, Grimsby had just been promoted from the Third Division to the Second Division and there was a sense of excitement around the club. I was not foolish enough to think I had made it, but I couldn't have been happier. I thought of my heroes at Scunthorpe United jogging past the school while I'd been stuck in the classroom, and I felt like I was one of 'them'.

What I hadn't really appreciated from afar was that the life of a professional footballer was not just about enjoying the cheers of the crowd on a Saturday afternoon and getting out of lessons during the week. There was uncertainty right from the start because pretty much the day after I had signed my contract, the manager who had offered it to me, Tim Ward, left to join Derby County. Mr Ward had told me that he had recommended me to the board of directors and assured me that the club wanted me, but it was very disconcerting to know that the manager who had been prepared to offer me a job was no longer going to be around.

My first meeting with Mr Ward's successor, Tom Johnston, an intimidating Scotsman, didn't go too well. I had a holiday booked at Butlins and, not fully appreciating that pre-season training was not optional, had planned to go.

'Do you want to be a professional footballer or not?' he said to me with a look that suggested I might as well get on the bus back to Scunthorpe.

'Yes,' I said, quietly.

'Well, you'll be in with the others then, not taking part in the knobbly knees competition.'

At Grimsby, the first team changed in the home-team dressing room and the reserves and young players, like me, changed in the away-team dressing room, which was smaller and much more cramped. My peg was on the end of the row, which was reserved for the newest of the new boys. As we got changed we'd hear the laughter and jokes from down the corridor and I always noticed that it was louder, more raucous and bawdier than in our dressing room.

I learned a few things very quickly, some of which shocked me. I had assumed that because we were all Grimsby Town players that we'd all be in it together, but I realised we were not all on the same side all of the time. The group was split into two – those who were in the first team and those who wanted to take their places – and that meant there was always a sense of competition and rivalry between the two groups. And the fact we changed in different dressing rooms only emphasised that divide. Because I was a new lad, I had naïvely expected to get a bit of a welcome but I was more or less left to my own devices at first. I suppose I had to prove myself before I would be accepted because I was just another youngster who might or might not make it.

The atmosphere in the dressing room took me by surprise too. I am not saying I was a wallflower but the language was new to me. Of course I had used swear words before, and I'd heard my dad curse every now and then, but I had been at a grammar school where swearing was not part of our everyday language – certainly not to this extent. There were some sentences that seemed to have almost as many swear words as normal words and there was also an edge to the language. I am not saying it was offensive, it was just that swearing was normal and accepted and that was new to me, as was the sight of twenty naked blokes all climbing into the communal bath. I remember early on when I was sitting in the bath, one of the senior players standing on the edge of the bath, stark naked, waving his willy round and round at eye level, saying to me and one of the other young players: 'Hey, lads, when you've got one as big as this you'll be ready for the first team.' I am not saying it was right, but it was what it was like and it was accepted.

In those days, a football club was an entirely male environment – certainly on the playing side of things – and most of the players came from working-class backgrounds. Had they not been footballers, I expect many of the players would have been in the mines or at the steelworks. That is not to be in any way dismissive or disrespectful of those professions, by the way –

they were honest and tough ways to make a living – but at that time football was an escape for the working class rather than an aspirational career for the middle class. I began to see what Mr McIvor had meant – a grammar school education had not prepared me for the dressing room. However, I certainly wasn't going to complain about the language; in fact, I realised that I would need to adapt in order to fit in.

There were other things to adjust to, such as living away from home for the first time. I was only thirty miles from Scunthorpe but I may as well have been at the other end of the country because the opportunities to go back home were few and far between, simply because I didn't drive to start with. Grimsby put their young players into digs, which in my case meant living with an elderly lady in Cleethorpes who, I think, offered to put up a young footballer just so she would have some company. She didn't like me going out in the evenings and she always asked me where I'd been if I was more than half an hour late back home after training. I could understand the club wanting their landladies to keep an eye on the players and make sure they weren't out until the early hours or getting up to mischief, but I think in her case she just wanted someone to talk to. The final straw was when I snuck in one afternoon and crept upstairs without her hearing me, simply because I didn't want to get into a long conversation about anything, and she found me lying on my bed eating a packet of biscuits.

'Right,' she said, 'that's it. There's no eating biscuits in bed – you'll get crumbs all over the sheets.'

I think she complained to the club because I was offered a move to another house, and that suited me just fine. It turned out to be with two other players a little bit older than me – Jimmy Thompson and Brian Hill – at a good-sized house on Carr Lane, Cleethorpes, with a smashing couple called Mr and Mrs Wakeham. They had a son, John, who was a bit younger than us and a massive Grimsby Town supporter, so he was happy to have three players living in the house with him like adopted older brothers, not least because it meant he got in at Blundell

Park for free and heard some of the gossip from the training ground over the dinner table.

The early months flew by and I played a mix of youth-team and reserve fixtures and gradually got to grips with the routine of being a professional footballer. I'd walk to training in the morning, we'd generally be done by lunchtime and then some of the players would meet for a coffee in the café round the corner from the ground before heading home. It wasn't as glamorous as I'd expected, although that wasn't my main concern. It sank in pretty quickly that I had a contract for just one year, and that the club had an option to extend that if they thought I was good enough or to let me go if they didn't. It dawned on me that a year was not a long time to make my mark and that at the end of the season my fate was out of my hands. And then what? Go back to Scunthorpe and tell my dad I'd not made it? Prove Mr McIvor right – that grammar-school boys were wasting their time trying to become professional footballers?

I'd been used to scoring plenty of goals at whatever level I'd played but this was different. The standard of opposition was higher and it was harder to make an impression in training because I was a seventeen-year-old boy coming up against experienced defenders – strong men who knew every trick in the book and had no interest in letting the new lad catch the manager's eye by making them look foolish.

As the weeks went by, I was getting more and more concerned. There was little in the way of feedback from Tom Johnston, the manager, and I wouldn't have dreamed of going to see him to ask how he thought I was getting on. I wasn't expecting to be in the first team but I had hoped to get some idea of whether I was progressing OK.

Then, in November, we had an FA Youth Cup tie against Doncaster Rovers and the manager spoke to me to tell me he wanted me to play out of position, at left-back. I was right-footed so I wasn't keen but I didn't dare object because I believed that if the manager asked me to do something, I would do it to the best of my ability. Jack Catley, who played outside-right, was also pushed back to right-back. This was no great tactical masterstroke, by the way; we simply didn't have anyone else.

We won the match comfortably – 5-1 according to a newspaper cutting I pasted into my scrapbook all those years ago. Apparently we scored three goals in six minutes, although I must admit I don't remember that, but I do remember very well that Mr Johnston came into the dressing room afterwards, pointed to me and said: 'Taylor, that's your position now.'

I was disappointed. I didn't want to be a defender because what appealed to me about the game was attacking and scoring goals but I also wasn't daft. I knew that if the manager thought I was better suited to playing as a left-back rather than as an inside-forward then I should listen to that and try to turn myself into a Football League left-back.

Without our trainer, George Higgins, I don't think I'd have made the grade. In many ways I owe that man my career in football because he spent hours and hours teaching me first the basics and then the finer points of full-back play. George had been a full-back with Bolton Wanderers in the First Division and he was an excellent teacher.

After training with the squad in the morning, I'd go back to Blundell Park in the afternoons and George and I would head out onto the pitch with a ball and we'd go through all different aspects of defending. He taught me so much not just by telling me what to do but by describing a scenario and asking me what I thought the best approach would be in the circumstances, then suggesting alternatives. He taught me how to think about the game, how to tell what an opposing winger liked to do and what he didn't like. George taught me how to identify which was an opponent's stronger foot, whether he liked to try to attack around the outside or cut inside. Bear in mind in those days there was no video footage to watch, so each opponent was a new one to try to work out. George encouraged me to keep notes about each match and each opponent so that if I came up against them again I could refer back and remind myself of what he was good at and what he was less comfortable

31

doing. In short, George taught me how to be a professional footballer and treat it as a job.

One thing I did find, following my conversion from forward player to full-back, was that I was happier playing with the game in front of me. A forward spends a lot of time with his back facing the goal he's attacking and, although I was comfortable with that, I found that playing in the defence, knowing that most of the time only the goalkeeper was behind me, I could begin to read the game and watch things as they unfolded. I spotted danger early and could not only reset my position but help to organise the rest of the defence, or shout to a midfield player or the winger on my side to drop back ten yards, or watch out for an opposition player's run. As a forward I had always tried to anticipate where the ball was going to end up. If the cross was headed away, where would it fall? If there was a deflection, where should I be to give myself the best chance of having a shot on goal? So I understood what forwards were trying to do, because I had been one, and that undoubtedly helped me as a defender. Playing at the back gave me a completely different impression of the game and, although I didn't realise it at the time, I was learning all the time not just about my own job in the team but also about what everyone else should be doing.

I relished the challenge because of all that learning and then, on a matchday, I could put what I'd learned into practice. I was becoming a right-footed left-back and slowly growing into the position, although I was no more confident about the club keeping me on at the end of the season. As we reached the spring, I really was beginning to panic because no one had said anything to me or given me any reason to think I'd be OK. One day I was called into the manager's office and Mr Johnston told me that the club would be taking up the option of giving me another year. I can't tell you the relief I felt. My bottom lip was starting to go so I got out of his office as quickly as I could. I was pacing round outside in the car park, breathing deeply as the news sank in, when Clarrie Williams saw me. Clarrie was a lovely man who had been Grimsby's goalkeeper for many years and was now part of the backroom staff.

'What's the matter with you?' he said.

'They've just told me they're keeping me on,' I said, as the tears started to roll down my cheeks.

'I could have told you that, son. I knew they'd keep you on,' he said, with a big smile.

I still wasn't all that comfortable swearing, especially not to one of the members of staff, but I couldn't help it. 'Fucking hell, Clarrie, why didn't you tell me? I've been worried sick the last few weeks.'

'Well, they don't want you feeling too comfortable, do they?'

Not everyone was given such good news. For some, their meeting with Mr Johnston meant the end of their time at Grimsby and the beginning of a period of uncertainty and insecurity. As the season wound down, we had a practice match, eleven versus eleven, on the pitch at Blundell Park. I was at left-back, up against a winger called Johnny Scott who had just been told he was not being kept on and was free to look for another club. Johnny was a good player, a Belfast lad who had started at Manchester United and had been at Grimsby for seven years, but he was coming towards the end of his career and although he knew it he perhaps wasn't ready to accept it. I could see in his eyes that he was hurt and angry about being rejected and frightened about what the future might hold. I wonder if he could see the confidence in my eyes and the spring in my step and resented it. Perhaps he thought he'd teach the young lad who thought he'd made it a lesson.

Early on in the match, I took the ball off him cleanly and cleared it up the line. Just as I had played the ball he came in on me late and strong, catching me on the shin hard. I went down to the ground and the fact he didn't offer to help me up, or say sorry, told me it was deliberate. The rest of the match was physical too. Johnny tried to push me off the ball, using his weight and strength to get the better of me. It taught me another valuable lesson – that football was a man's game and that I had to be stronger if I was going to make it.

That summer, I got a job at Lysaght's, the steelworks, partly because our wages went down during the close-season and partly because I wanted to get fitter and stronger. Cleaning the steel mills was hard, dirty and dangerous but it was exactly what I needed. It was a full-time job but I also volunteered to work on the company's sports ground, mowing the bowls court and the cricket pitch, pushing the heavy lawnmower and pulling the even heavier rollers. I also ran every day because I felt that I had got lucky, to some extent, to be kept on and I didn't want to take any chances. Yes, I'd been given another year but that came with no guarantees either and I was determined not to spend another season worrying about whether I'd be able to keep my job. I was also convinced that the best way to prove I was good enough was to treat every training session and every reserve fixture as if it were an FA Cup tie. When we played an eleven-versus-eleven game I knew that if I could stop the first-team winger, he might say something to the manager like, 'he's quick,' or 'he's hard to play against.' I knew the first-team left-back wouldn't be in a hurry to put in a good word for me, whereas the winger would. So I worked all summer and returned for the 1963-64 season feeling like I belonged in the squad.

At the start of my second season with Grimsby, I sensed I was getting closer to the first team, although I'd still not made the move across the corridor to the home-team dressing room. I came on as a substitute in a pre-season friendly against Leicester City, who had played in the FA Cup final at the end of the previous season. They had Gordon Banks in goal and in my scrapbook there's a photograph from the newspaper of him diving to make a save. I can't help noticing he's wearing a flat cap, as goalkeepers sometimes did in those days, which dates it. The last paragraph of the report reads: 'Young Graham Taylor took over from Donovan for the last ten minutes and he, too, kicked a goal-bound effort from Keyworth off the line.' The match ended 1-1 and I got a mention in the *Grimsby Telegraph* so I imagine I was pretty pleased about that.

A few weeks later, the *Grimsby Telegraph* had an exclusive story headlined: 'Taylor (18) makes debut for Mariners'. It read: 'Grimsby Town bring in eighteen-year-old reserve full-back Graham Taylor for his Football League debut against Newcastle United at Blundell Park tomorrow (3pm). He replaces Don Donovan, who is rested, at left-back and with Jimmy Thompson (20) makes up a young full-back combination.'

Reading that now, I am quite surprised that the local paper had such specific team news to print the day before the game and I wonder if Don Donovan found out he was being rested by reading it in the press or whether the manager told him first. I can't remember the specifics of it but I assume Tom Johnston told me I was playing before mentioning it to the local reporter. Either way, I was named in the team to make my Football League debut on 14 September 1963 – the day before my nineteenth birthday. It's a good quiz question, this, because on the same day another of the game's greats made his first-team debut. Can you guess who it was? You give up? It was George Best, playing for Manchester United against West Bromwich Albion. OK, I will concede that he was a bit more talented than me, but I do like to tell people that George Best and I had something in common.

We won the match against Newcastle 2-1 that afternoon and I don't need to look at the yellowed cuttings in my scrapbook to know that for an eighteen-year-old boy it was a special occasion. I must have bought all of the Sunday papers because there are match reports from at least half a dozen papers stuck into the scrapbook. It's quite amusing to see the different accounts of the game. There are three headlines that make us sound ever more heroic – 'Ten-man Grimsby hold out,' 'Gallant nine hold out,' and 'Eight survivors rock Newcastle' – and reading through the reports it seems that Newcastle's physical play meant we sustained injuries and finished with ten, nine or eight fit men, depending on whose report you want to believe. I don't know, you can't rely on journalists to get everything right all of the time, can you, eh? There were no substitutes in those days (we still had to wait a couple of years before the Football League allowed one substitute to be used) so it seems that we were hanging on a bit having gone 2-0 up against promotion-chasing Newcastle before losing Dick Young to injury and having two other players no more than walking wounded.

Now, more than half a century later, my eyes scan the reports for a mention of my name and I can't help but smile as I read the words: 'Alan Suddick found himself up against a most promising eighteen-year-old full-back in Graham Taylor,' says one. 'Graham Taylor and Cliff Portwood were playing it cool in the face of this amazing Newcastle attitude,' says another, and a third says: 'It was a game eighteen-year-old Grimsby left-back Graham Taylor will always remember. It was his baptism of fire in league football and he played as well as anyone in his side.' One of the reports also has player ratings, which I never liked when I was a manager because players paid far too much attention to them and, frankly, it was irrelevant if a reporter sitting in the stand thought a player's performance merited a nine if I thought he was worth a seven. Anyway, this particular reporter gave me an eight for my debut, so I will most certainly take that.

For a few weeks after that, I felt on top of the world. I'd made my debut in Grimsby's first victory of the season and I was living in digs with my two pals Jimmy Thompson, who had broken into the first team at right-back a little while before me, and Brian Hill, who tended to play on the left wing, directly ahead of me. Every day revolved around football. We'd talk about it over breakfast, then go to training, then talk some more in the afternoon and evening.

Not long after that, though, I felt what it was like to be left out of the team and all the insecurities came back. We had two away games in the space of a few days, against Cardiff City and then Plymouth Argyle, that meant a couple of nights on the road, which was another new experience for me. On the Wednesday night we drew 0-0 with Cardiff and then stayed in a bed and breakfast somewhere on our way towards Devon and then trained for a couple of days before facing Plymouth. The night before the second match, I was told I was not in the team – Brian Keeble was taking my place – and I was so disappointed. I wondered what I'd done wrong. I don't remember Tom Johnston explaining his decision to me. Maybe he did and I'm doing him a disservice here but I'd be surprised if I was given any detailed reasons, so my mind raced away with itself, imagining that he'd had a look at me for a few games and decided I wasn't up to it. I'd played half a dozen times in the first team and done well on my debut but there was no way I could consider myself established. There was also no certainty that I'd get back into the side and so I was worried. You might wonder why I didn't ask the manager to explain his decision but that wouldn't have crossed my mind for a moment. Back then, players simply didn't challenge the authority of the manager in that way. The manager picked the team and that was that, end of discussion. Later on, when I was a manager, there would be conversations between me and my players about team selection. My decision was still final but I did listen to players and try to explain and encourage if I could. But a nineteen-year-old in 1963? Forget it. At most I might have had a word with one of the senior players to see if they could give me any indication as to whether I might get back into the team in the near future.

It was a new experience for me and not just because I had been looking forward to playing in the match. On wages of £14 a week (which went down to £12 in the summer), the bonuses of £4 for a win and £2 for a draw were important. The club deducted money to pay Mr and Mrs Wakeham for putting me up and there wasn't an awful lot left after that.

On the day of the match itself, there was another shock because although I was not in the team, my lunch was still the small, light pre-match meal that the other players were having. So while the directors sat at another table tucking into steak and chips or lamb chops, I was eating scrambled egg or a small piece of chicken or whatever it was knowing that I'd be sitting in the stand at Home Park that evening with an empty feeling in my stomach. In more ways than one.

I wrestled with the emotions that afternoon because I had not expected to feel the way I did. I didn't like being dropped, of course, but there was more to it than that. I considered myself a team player and before I had broken into the first team, I had always wanted Grimsby Town to do well and win matches, but that night I hoped Plymouth would win and I particularly hoped Brian Keeble would have a stinker. People might be surprised to hear that but it was how I felt and, I suspect, how all players feel when they have been dropped by their manager. Supporters, in particular, may not want to hear that their players are not as interested in the team's result as they are in their own success but on occasions that is certainly the case. Speaking as a manager, I never wanted a player to be happy about being out of the side. I wanted him to be agitated about it, angry even, as long as he channelled that anger in the right way and fought to get his name back onto the teamsheet rather than creating waves in the dressing room. You can do without those ones.

So, I sat in the stand with another young player called Dougie Collins, who had also played at Cardiff but had been dropped for the Plymouth match, secretly happy that my team were slipping to a 3-2 defeat because I already knew that there were a few certain ways to get back in the side. You could either play well for the reserves and hope the reserve-team trainer said something to the manager or you could do particularly well in training, but by far the easiest route back into the team was if they lost a game and the manager decided to respond by making changes.

I felt guilty about that for a little while but soon learned that it was perfectly normal. I didn't expect the second-choice left-back to be over the moon if he heard I'd played well, which made it all the more remarkable that Brian Keeble and his wife, Diane, were so kind and generous to me, inviting me round to their house for dinner once a week and offering me advice and encouragement.

I got back into the side for the next game and made the number-three shirt more or less my own until I picked up an injury in the spring and missed the last seven games of the season. We were relegated from the Second Division and I won't try to pretend that my absence had anything to do with that because we had been in trouble for most of the year. We were neck-and-neck with Plymouth but went down on goal average – calculated by dividing the number of goals scored over the season by the number of goals conceded – which is how they separated teams that were level on points before they switched to using goal difference. It was sobering to think that if we'd managed to turn one draw into a win, or a defeat into a draw, we'd have stayed up and I can remember realising then that every match in a season was of equal importance. That sounds blindingly obvious, doesn't it? Of course every match counts but it's funny how games towards the end of the season take on greater significance if you are pushing for promotion or battling relegation and yet there's still the same number of points on offer (two for a win, in those days).

Early the following season, Tom Johnston left to take over as Huddersfield Town manager just as we were beginning to put together a push for promotion, and another Scot called Jim McGuigan came in. In all, I had six managers during my time at Grimsby Town (if you count Tim Ward, who left as soon as I arrived, and George Higgins, who was caretaker-manager so often he has to go on the list) and another couple at Lincoln City later on, but I have to say that Jim McGuigan was by far the best I played for.

Although we were only treading water during McGuigan's three seasons in charge – finishing mid-table in the Third Division a couple of years and towards the bottom in the final year – I learned so much from him about coaching, much of which I had never experienced before. McGuigan was the first man I'd encountered who had coached the whole team as a unit.

He encouraged the two full-backs to get forwards but insisted that midfield players would sit tight and cover, just in case we got hit on the counter-attack. He wanted us to be much more aware of what was going on round about us, not just to be concerned with doing our own jobs but also to make sure we were well positioned to fill in gaps.

It was the first time I had ever been coached in 'shadow-play', which is a training technique where you line up in your positions and kick off against nobody – it's eleven versus none – and you run through the ideal moves up the pitch. For example, if the right-back hits a diagonal pass up to the centre-forward, where should the two midfield players be? Should one of them run forwards to support while the other sits back? If the left-back goes forward, should the centre-half move across a bit to cover the space? We ran through all manner of scenarios, thinking about the best place for each player to be wherever the ball was on the pitch. It sounds crackers, the idea of eleven players kicking off with no opposition but it made us think as a collective rather than a collection of individuals, and a number of top managers have used it including Arrigo Sacchi at AC Milan in the 1980s and, I've read recently, Antonio Conte at Chelsea.

McGuigan also liked to play a style we called 'third man running'. The defender would play the ball up to the centre-forward, who would bring it under control and lay it back to a midfield player who would then quickly play a pass splitting the defence, or over the top, to the other forward, who was the 'third man' running into space. It was quick, direct and could be effective, even when the opposition knew it was likely to happen.

I am not saying McGuigan invented either of these things, because he didn't, but I learned about them from him and I took them into my own coaching later on. Now, you might ask me how I can say Jim McGuigan was the best manager I played for if his team was not particularly successful and that's a fair question. I'd answer it by saying he was the first person to make me think about the game in a broader way. He encouraged me to study how a game was being played rather than to simply react to what was happening at each given moment. Without any television coverage of matches, we couldn't film a game and watch it back, freezing the picture to see who was where and what was happening so we had to remember what had happened in matches and train ourselves to anticipate the play. McGuigan was a very intelligent man who made his coaching sessions relevant to the sort of situations we faced on matchdays. He also had an excellent temperament and I can't remember him losing his rag with us very often. I am sure he got frustrated with us but he never let it boil over and he always had the patience to go back and make sure his point was being understood. If any of my old players are reading this I can imagine them thinking: 'You lost your patience with us plenty of times, gaffer.' Well, none of us is perfect and I'm certainly not, but as I used to say: 'If you'd got it right the first time it would have saved us all a lot of bother.'

Perhaps my memory of Jim McGuigan is biased because I knew he liked me. After all, I had not been in the team all that long when he made me captain of Grimsby Town, and I was still only twenty. When an old teacher of mine, Owen Roberts, suggested I take a preliminary coaching qualification McGuigan encouraged me to do it. I'd bumped into Owen, who was very keen to hear how I was getting on at Grimsby and, after listening to me talk about it for a while, he pulled me up short by saying: 'Have you thought about what you'll do when it's all over?'

I was surprised because here I was, twenty years old, captain of the team and imagining I had a good decade or more ahead of me as a player. He wasn't quite as blunt as this but he asked what I'd do if my career ended tomorrow and it started me thinking, so I enrolled on an FA coaching course and worked towards getting a coaching qualification. I became an FA staff coach when I was still only twenty-one. At the time, I was the youngest person to qualify as an FA coach.

As the months went by, McGuigan took me into his confidence. He used to invite me to his house for a drink and a chat – not all that often, but often enough for me to be concerned what the other players might think if they found out. He'd talk to me about management, about some of the dilemmas he faced, although he was careful never to put me in a position where I might have a problem with the other players. Looking back, I have a lot of respect for the skill that style of man-management took. He wanted to know a bit about the atmosphere in the dressing room and what the players thought but he never compromised my relationship with my team-mates by asking me to rat on them. And he never, to my knowledge, said to another player: 'Graham Taylor has said something about you.' My confidence rose because the manager was choosing to let me in on some of his thoughts and decisions and I was learning too. At one point he told me that he thought I could be a manager one day which, when you consider I was in my early twenties, was quite unusual.

Unfortunately, we were not able to regain promotion to the Second Division and, as the seasons went on, players left Grimsby Town and were not replaced adequately. I don't know the full ins and outs but I think the board were selling players without telling McGuigan and eventually he'd had enough and it came to a head. He left in the summer of 1967 and was replaced by a man called Don McEvoy, who was the complete opposite of McGuigan.

I was still only twenty-two but I was the club captain and I also had a few responsibilities in life. Rita and I had got married in 1965 and our first daughter, Joanne, was born – with perfect timing – on FA Cup final day in May 1966, the day Everton beat Sheffield Wednesday 3-2. When we first got married, Rita and I lived in a rented house on Hainton Avenue that Don Donovan had been living in before he was released by Grimsby. We had one room at the back which had a settee in it that folded out into a bed. We weren't there long before we got our first house together in Cleethorpes, and as I drive around the streets now – remembering my walk from home to Grimsby's Blundell Park ground, through Sydney Park, where we used to take Joanne to play on the swings when she was old enough – I am taken back to those days when we had just started a family. Being a professional footballer was a privilege, and it was one I took seriously, but it was not making us rich in those days. Short-term contracts meant that it was very difficult persuading a bank manager to lend us money to buy a house. Our wages may have been a little bit above the average but there was very little security. The clubs held all of the power. Even though the maximum wage had been abolished by that point, it did not mean much for the players in the lower divisions because the clubs still set the wages and there was very little negotiation. The chairmen could plead poverty, which in many cases was probably true because in those days they balanced the books with the money that came in through the turnstiles or a bit of sponsorship from local companies and the shortfall was covered from the pockets of the owner and other directors. It was not a wealthy game, certainly not at Grimsby Town's level where attendances could easily slip to the 3,000 mark if we were on a bad run.

I can remember buying my first car – a secondhand Mini – and moving into a rented house of our own that had a garden, and feeling like I'd taken a big step up in the world. But the uncertainty about my future, and the responsibility of supporting a family, did weigh on me at times, although that was mainly because I badly wanted to stay working in the game for the rest of my career and I knew that not every ex-player could do that. Having a young daughter with another one on the way meant I felt under pressure to not only make the most of my playing career but continue to lay the foundations for my future when my playing days inevitably came to an end.

The 1967-68 season was to be my last at Grimsby and it was not a particularly happy one. The new manager, Don McEvoy, was not my cup of tea. He wasn't a bad person but I didn't enjoy his style of play or his style of management. He didn't want his full-backs crossing the halfway line, which restricted what I could do on the pitch. Compared to McGuigan, his training techniques felt like a step backwards, and as a team we were deteriorating.

In early December, we went to Watford and lost 7-1. We were terrible that day and I had a very difficult time against their winger, Stewart Scullion, who I later found out was quite a favourite at Vicarage Road. When I took over at Watford, one or two people asked me if I remembered that game and I always furrowed my brow and pretended to search my memory banks before telling a fib – 'No, it doesn't ring a bell…' – but I remembered it very well because I'd had a particularly bad afternoon. I don't think Scullion actually scored but in my mind he turned me inside-out and it wouldn't surprise me if he set up all seven.

When we got back into the dressing room, we could tell Don McEvoy wasn't happy but the bollocking we were expecting didn't happen. We washed and dressed in near-silence, exchanging a few glances and all wondering when the manager was going to lay into us. We trooped out onto the team bus, thinking he might let rip once we pulled away from Vicarage Road, but McEvoy sat at the front of the coach in silence, staring straight ahead. The coach made its way out of Watford to a hotel on the main road where we had been booked in for an evening meal before completing the journey back to Grimsby. All the players got off the coach but McEvoy stayed in his seat. Over dinner we wondered what he was up to and were convinced he would say something at some point. As we got back on the coach he didn't acknowledge us and he stayed quiet all the way home, which meant the rest of us stayed quiet too.

As we pulled up outside Blundell Park he stood up and turned to face us.

'Right, here we go. This is it,' I thought.

Standing in the aisle of the coach, leaning on the two seats either side, he said calmly: 'I'll see you all back here at ten o'clock tomorrow morning.'

Training on a Sunday wasn't unusual if a performance had been very poor, and it was often a punishment, but I was not expecting what happened the following morning. I arrived at the ground and one of the trainers was standing outside waiting for us.

'You'd better get in the dressing room and get kitted up,' he said. 'The gaffer's waiting for you on the pitch.'

McEvoy was standing on the centre spot. He had his whistle round his neck and there was a cardboard box of orange segments on the ground next to his feet.

Finally, he broke his silence.

'When I blow this whistle, I want you to start running round the pitch,' he said. 'And when I blow it again for half-time, you can have a bit of orange.'

He blew his whistle and we started running, not quite sure what was going on.

As we got going he shouted: 'If you bastards won't run for me for ninety minutes on a Saturday, you'll fucking well do it on a Sunday instead.'

And that is what we did. We ran for forty-five minutes, stopped when he blew his whistle, started again when he said so and ran for another forty-five minutes. By the end of the session, he had a group of demoralised, pissed-off players.

As I said, he wasn't an unpleasant man, and I can well understand that he was fed up with our level of performance, but I didn't think the way he chose to react to it was in any way constructive. I've never shied away from running, or from making my players run, but I never used running as a punishment for poor performances. Some players might dispute that but I always tried to make them understand that running and physical work was to attain high levels of fitness that were for their benefit. I didn't want players who saw hard physical work as a punishment for playing poorly. I couldn't understand why McEvoy wanted us to associate physical work with failure when fitness and strength were so important to players.

For the first time in my life I was not enjoying playing football. I remember lying in bed one morning, not wanting to get up (which was very unusual for me) and thinking: 'If I'm ever a manager, I don't want my players feeling the way I am feeling now.'

McEvoy didn't last long after that 7-1 defeat at Watford and he was replaced by Bill Harvey, who was a physiotherapist by trade. He had been on the books at Grimsby as a player and had been a manager briefly at Luton Town, before coaching at a couple of clubs, but it was a surprise appointment. McEvoy and I hadn't been close but we hadn't clashed, whereas it was clear that Harvey and I didn't get on. I can be pretty certain that he didn't like the fact that I had a coaching qualification and I think that was the root of his dislike of me.

Right from the start he took the mickey out of me in front of the other players. He'd run through what we'd be doing in our training session then turn to me and say sarcastically: 'If that's OK with the head coach?' Or he'd see me and say: 'Here he comes, England's best coach.'

I hope I didn't wander around with a big head on my shoulders because I certainly didn't feel like I knew it all, and I didn't see it as my place to contradict the manager, even if I didn't like what he was telling us, so I can only assume he felt threatened. It made me unhappy because I felt I was being picked on for wanting to better myself and showing a desire to learn. I knew I was doing the right thing by taking my coaching badges but it wasn't doing me any favours day to day. I'd go home and say to Rita that I had to get away from Grimsby.

My other problem was that I didn't feel I was being fairly paid. I'd been captain for almost three years and my wages had barely risen in that time. I saw new players come in on more money, getting signing-on fees that I'd never had because I'd joined the club from school. I went and asked for more money but was turned down.

The season ended unhappily, with relegation to the Fourth Division. Again we finished level on points with the club that had just survived – this time Mansfield Town – and went down on goal average. We missed out by less than a tenth of a goal so if we'd won our final game of the season against Swindon Town either 4-2, or 3-1, instead of 3-2, we'd have stayed up. Having said that, Peterborough United were only below us because they'd been deducted a load of points for some kind of financial irregularity, so we can't in all honesty say we deserved to stay up.

In the summer, Grimsby refused to budge over my wages. Having been captain of a side that had been relegated to the Fourth Division, I knew I was not in a strong bargaining position and my options were limited. I spoke to a few clubs but it came down to a choice between Mansfield Town, who had stayed in the Third Division by the skin of their teeth and at our expense, and Lincoln City, who were in the Fourth Division and had been forced to apply for re-election to the Football League after finishing in the bottom places four times in the previous six years. I thought to myself: 'Well, Graham, they're not exactly queuing up for you here, are they?' and realised I had to make the best decision for my family.

Both Mansfield and Lincoln agreed to pay me the wages that Grimsby were refusing to meet and it came down to the fact that Lincoln were prepared to pay me a £300 signing-on fee.

So that was it, one of the biggest decisions of my entire life decided by a few hundred pounds – admittedly it went a lot further then than it does now. I was not driven by money but I can't pretend it wasn't a factor. Our second daughter, Karen, was born not long before we left Cleethorpes for Lincoln and I had to think about my family. The transfer fee was £4,000 and I can still remember shaking my head when I realised that, in pure monetary terms, I – a Fourth Division left-back – was worth £800 more than the semi-detached house we bought on the outskirts of Lincoln. I might not have been rich but it seemed to me the money in the game was ridiculous.

4

Learning to coach

I had been a professional footballer for six seasons and in that time I had gone from playing in the Second Division to playing in the Fourth Division and I was acutely aware that if things didn't go well at Lincoln City I could very easily slip out of the game if I wasn't careful. In those days, non-league football was part-time and, as there was no automatic promotion between the top divisions of non-league and the Football League, many players who were let go by league clubs knew they were making a one-way journey if they joined a non-league outfit.

Although I was working my way through my coaching qualifications, I knew I needed to remain a professional player and so I was encouraged and relieved when the manager, Ron Gray, made me his captain as soon as I arrived. It wasn't easy because the captain before me had been a local lad called Jimmy Grummett, a centre-half, who was popular in the team and with the supporters. He could have been difficult about it because I wouldn't have liked to be in his position, watching a new player come in and take the captaincy from him, but he was absolutely fine with me.

My first game for Lincoln was at Sincil Bank in August 1968, against Notts County. We won 5-0 and I scored what turned out to be my only league goal for the club, although I did get another one in a League Cup tie at some point. I hit the ball from outside the penalty area and apparently it went in like a rocket. I didn't get to see it fly into the net because as soon as I struck the ball, a challenge came in that knocked me over and

48

before I could get up I had half a dozen team-mates on top of me celebrating.

Looking at the results now, I see we won our first four league games and were top of the Fourth Division table and remained in and around the promotion places all season, but I don't recall feeling like we were in the thick of a genuine challenge to get out of the division. When we finished our season, we were fourth in the table (the last of the promotion places) but several teams below us including Darlington, Bradford City, Halifax and Southend United had several games in hand – I assume because of bad weather over the winter – and they all overtook us, pushing us down to eighth. That wouldn't happen these days because the Football League wouldn't allow so many postponed games to be played after the official end of the season but that's how it was then.

I missed a chunk of that season with injury and so I was very fortunate that I had my coaching work to keep me occupied. I already had my full Football Association coaching badge and in my spare time I coached the National Association of Local Government Officials (NALGO) team. I always found it very valuable to coach players who were playing the game for enjoyment and didn't have the time to work on their technique or their tactics very often. A year or so earlier, while I was still at Grimsby, I went to Zambia with a group of Football Association coaches during the close season. We'd been invited to tour the country, coach a variety of clubs and play matches against the Zambian national team and a couple of their sides. It was a really eye-opening trip because parts of Zambia in the late 1960s were very, very poor but their passion and interest in football could not be doubted. I don't mean to be in any way disrespectful but what was amazing to me was how little the Zambians knew about the game of football. When I think about it now it's obvious that they couldn't have a deep understanding of the game because they had almost no opportunity to watch matches. Maybe in the larger towns and cities they could have watched World Cup games on television, I don't know, but their exposure to top-level football would have been extremely limited.

What I noticed was that they played with enthusiasm and an instinct to attack. That's perfectly natural because if you put a group of people on a football pitch, give them a ball and tell them what the object of the game is, they will try to score a goal as quickly as possible. It's what makes the game appeal to children and it's what makes millions of people around the world want to watch football. Coaching the Zambian players was such a good experience because I could see them learning very quickly when we explained to them some of the finer points of the game.

Back at home, coaching amateur players – whether it was the NALGO team or, later on, a side in the Lincolnshire League – helped me enormously. Because I had limited time with the players, it taught me to find ways to simplify things so that we could work quickly on a particular aspect of the game that they would then be able to take into their matches to give them a better chance of winning. These were not professional players and so I had to work with their limitations rather than get exasperated by what they were unable to do. I have always been the sort of person to look for the positives, so it wasn't particularly hard for me to focus on what people could do rather than worry about what they couldn't do. That doesn't mean players shouldn't try to improve their weaknesses but I always felt that a happy, confident player performed better than a worried one and so there was very little to be gained from telling someone they were slow or they couldn't trap a bag of cement. It was very likely they'd be well aware of their own shortcomings anyway so I saw my role as a coach to encourage people. I knew enough to know that a word of praise could make someone stand up a little straighter, pull their shoulders back and lift their head up, altering their entire demeanour for the better.

These were people who were playing football for fun, after work or at the weekend, as a diversion from the stresses of everyday life and so I had to find ways to make their training enjoyable as well as informative. No matter what level of football you're operating at, being organised and ensuring that every player in the team knows their job can improve results, and helping amateur players to understand how they could make small improvements was a challenge I enjoyed.

Meanwhile, at Lincoln City we were treading water. Ron Gray was sacked at the end of the 1969-70 season, after we'd finished eighth, and Bert Loxley, who had been the team's coach, trainer and physio, took over. Bert was a lovely man and he became one of my dearest friends. On my first day at Lincoln he and his wife Sylvia invited me to lunch at their house, and Rita and I ended up buying a house a hundred yards down the road from the Loxleys in North Hykeham. Bert would probably admit he was a bit too nice to be a manager. He was great towards the players and he always had a word of encouragement when we needed it, but perhaps he lacked the ruthless edge required to be the boss. Bert stepped back when the next manager came in.

David Herd had been a top-quality player for both Arsenal and Manchester United and he had won two league titles at Old Trafford, so it was a real coup for a club like Lincoln City to get him as our new manager in March 1971. I was more than interested to see what someone of his calibre could pass on to a group of Fourth Division players, but it didn't take me long to realise that playing at the top level is not necessarily an advantage when it comes to trying to manage and coach a team of people who do not know what it is like to be that good.

To be fair to David, he did turn a struggling side around and in 1971-72 we finished fifth, just one place out of the promotion places. But I wasn't all that keen on his management style. It was nothing personal but I found him difficult to get on with because I didn't get the feeling he was managing us for our benefit. For a start, he still lived over near Manchester and he'd drive over to Lincoln every day, which was a difficult drive in those days. He was very rarely on time but because he was the manager there was no one to pull him up on it. We'd turn up at 9.45 ready to start training at 10 a.m. and the manager sometimes wouldn't arrive until half past. Of course, once the players knew that, they started drifting in whenever they fancied, knowing that more often than not if they were late they'd still be in before the manager. I've always placed an importance on punctuality and it used to drive me mad that the manager wasn't in on time. Sometimes he'd travel to away games direct from home and we'd go on the coach and then after the match he'd head off in his car and leave us to go back to Lincoln, so a lot of the time we were a rudderless ship without anyone in charge.

Training was rarely structured. We would play eight-a-side matches across the width of the pitch and David would join in. He was in his late thirties and had not long retired from playing himself so he was fit and sharp and we knew that whichever side he was on in these training games would win because he was better than all of us. He was a goalscorer and he was clever and he scored most of the goals, which was all very well, but what was he teaching us?

He very rarely coached us, although I do remember one session clearly. We'd been having a problem with keeping possession of the ball at throw-ins. I think we'd had a throw-in, lost possession and conceded a goal on the break a couple of games in succession. One day he stopped training to demonstrate something to us.

'At Manchester United, what we did was, Paddy would get the ball,' he said, referring to Paddy Crerand, 'and throw it to Bobby Charlton. All Bobby would do was shape his body as if he was going to run one way but then drop his shoulder at the last minute, just as Paddy was throwing the ball to him and go the other way, into the space he'd just opened up, and look for a pass to Denis Law.'

'Boss,' I said, 'I don't mean to be disrespectful but we haven't got anyone who's as good as Paddy Crerand or Bobby Charlton.'

I shouldn't have said it really, because I was the captain and I wasn't helping the situation by embarrassing the manager, but I knew that as a group of players we needed better coaching than this. Everything was all a bit loose. We rarely had team talks – the starting eleven just went up on the board and we went out to do our best. Now, David Herd might say that for a season and a bit his approach worked because we weren't all that far away from getting promoted, but it wasn't going to work for long.

At that time I had no thoughts about management; I was concerned with continuing my career as a Football League player because if there's one thing about being a professional sportsperson it's that you can never be sure what the future holds. Sometimes it is the most innocuous thing that can change the course of your life so dramatically. In February 1972, I sustained a freak injury that would bring my playing career to an end at the age of twenty-eight. We were playing an away game at Northampton Town's County Ground and had just got a free-kick on the halfway line around the left-back position. I placed the ball and took a few steps backwards to prepare my run-up. I was going to just send a simple lofted pass up towards Percy Freeman, our centre-forward. Just before I struck the ball, my right foot clipped the ground and my whole leg collapsed under me and the ball could have gone no more than five yards. I can still remember hearing the Northampton supporters laughing and I can't blame them because it must have looked funny, but I was immediately in a lot of pain. My knee had gone and I'd also dislocated my hip joint. I went to hospital and, after looking at my x-rays, the doctor said I'd do well to recover sufficiently to play professional football again. I did manage to come back in time to play the final game of the season but that was the beginning of a persistent hip problem that wasn't going to get any better. I had a build-up of calcium in the hip joint and it caused me quite a lot of pain, particularly when the pitches were hard or muddy, which in the 1970s was pretty much all the time. I knew that my career as a player would probably end before I reached the age of thirty and suddenly my decision to take my coaching qualifications looked like a very sensible one.

5

A game for the people

In 1968, a journalist called Arthur Hopcroft wrote a book called *The Football Man*. I read it for the first time shortly after it came out and I returned to it a number of times over my career, often when I needed to give myself a boost or a reminder of why I was putting so much time and energy into my work. It remains my favourite football book because not only is it beautifully written but it puts into words so eloquently many of my own thoughts about the game of football and the role it plays in our society.

Hopcroft writes: 'The way we play the game, organise it and reward it reflects the kind of community we are. ... What happens on the football field matters, not in the way that food matters but as poetry does to some people and alcohol does to others: it engages the personality. It has conflict and beauty, and when those two qualities are present together in something offered for public appraisal they represent much of what I understand to be art.'

Reading Hopcroft's book forced me to ask myself a question and examine the worth of my chosen career: 'What is the point of professional football?' My answer has always been that it should be a form of entertainment, something that brings people together and gives a town or city a sense of pride in their team. That entertainment at a game can take many forms. Sometimes there can be no greater sense of enjoyment than winning a match against the odds. Seeing your team score a late winning goal in a game that – on the balance of play – they probably didn't deserve to win can be more satisfying than watching a controlled and technically proficient performance and a relatively stress-free victory. I've always believed that supporters remember most strongly the feeling they had at the end of the game as they walk out of the ground, and so in a funny way a late scrap and battle to hold onto the points can leave someone with a greater sense of having enjoyed the experience than an easy 2-0 win with both goals scored in the first twenty minutes. This is not a scientific survey, by the way; it's just a sense of how I understand the game's appeal to people.

You may have noticed that I never refer to the supporters as fans. That's because I have always preferred to think of them as supporters, people who support their team through thick and thin and try to remain positive even when things are going badly. Of course, I know that there are people who love to moan and complain about anything and everything, those for whom even a comfortable victory is never enough because of the missed chances or mistakes, but I like to think that even they are won over when their team plays well.

The game in this country has changed in many ways in the past twenty-five years, largely as a result of the creation of the Premier League. Top footballers are now fantastically well paid, earning sums of money in a week that a great many people will not earn in a year and that money has put distance between the players and the supporters in some respects. Although a lot of very wealthy business people are now owners of our clubs, it is worth bearing in mind that a great deal of the money in the game comes – directly or indirectly – from the pockets of supporters, either from ticket revenue or television subscription fees or from people who buy the goods and services of the companies that sponsor the game. Without the supporters, the game could not possibly generate the money that it does and I sometimes wonder if we forget that.

The game has always been for the people. Back in the late 1950s, Scunthorpe United's Saturday home games kicked off at 3.15 p.m. – as many other clubs did – to allow the workers to finish their morning shift at work and have a pint or two in the pub before the game. The pubs closed at 3 p.m. in those days, re-opening in the evening, and the clubs realised that if they kicked off at 3 p.m. many supporters would still be in the pub. That has all changed now, of course, and kick-off times often do not suit the supporters' best interests but are arranged for the benefit of the television companies, but I can understand that because those companies are handing over hundreds of millions of pounds to the clubs every year.

All the money in the game has changed things and I wonder if some of the cautious, defensive play we see in the Premier League is a result of the fear of dropping out of the league and losing access to those riches. I am not saying that there was no such thing as a dull game in my day because of course there was, but I do look back at the start of my managerial career with Lincoln and recall that I was determined to do two things to ensure that we connected with people. One was to create a team that would excite supporters; the other was to take the players out into the community so that people could see that the club was representing them.

Most supporters would love to be footballers if they were talented enough, and they would certainly give their all for their team if they were ever given the chance to pull on the shirt, and so I knew I wanted a team of players who understood that they were representing not only themselves but their team-mates, me as their manager, the club, the supporters and their town or city.

If we could be successful, we could create a two-way relationship between the club and the supporters, attract more people to the matches and generate a buzz, and the way to do that was by creating a football team that played attacking football, tried to score goals and win matches with a bit of style. I can already hear plenty of you saying: 'But Graham, surely every football manager and football team is trying to do that. They're all trying to score goals and win matches,' and of course you are right to a degree. We all know that there are no guarantees in the game. On plenty of occasions a team can dominate a match, create the most clear-cut chances and yet

Christmas in the Taylor house in Axholme Road, Scunthorpe. Graham with his sisters Christine (left) and Margaret. From the Taylor family collection

Graham sitting front and centre as captain of the Scunthorpe Grammar School football team for the 1957–58 season. From the Taylor family collection

Graham's playing career started in the black and white stripes of Grimsby Town. He made his first-team debut against Newcastle United in September 1963, the day before his nineteenth birthday. From the Taylor family collection

Graham was thirteen when he met Rita Cowling at school. They got married in Scunthorpe in 1965. From the Taylor family collection

As manager of Lincoln City with his physio and coach Bert Loxley (left) and assistant George Kerr. From the Taylor family collection

Having narrowly missed out on promotion the previous season, Lincoln City stormed to the Fourth Division title in 1975–76, scoring 111 league goals in the process. From the Taylor family collection

In 1977 the Taylor family moved to Watford, and Rita, Karen, Joanne and Graham made their home in Mandeville Close. From the Taylor family collection

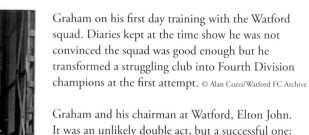

Graham on his first day training with the Watford squad. Diaries kept at the time show he was not convinced the squad was good enough but he transformed a struggling club into Fourth Division champions at the first attempt. © Alan Cozzi/Watford FC Archive

Graham and his chairman at Watford, Elton John. It was an unlikely double act, but a successful one: the no-nonsense football manager and the flamboyant millionaire pop star. From the Taylor family collection

On the bench at one of Watford's first home games, a League Cup tie against Reading in August 1977. Elton's enthusiasm for Watford could not be doubted but his habit of sitting on the bench and getting a little too involved was not to Graham's liking. Boundaries had to be set. From the Taylor family collection

Graham back in the press box at Scunthorpe United's Old Showground with his dad, Tom, a journalist for the *Scunthorpe Evening Telegraph* after Watford had clinched the Fourth Division title in April 1978. From the Taylor family collection

Graham's job at Watford was to build a club, not just a team, and the management and board were integral to that. Here Graham sits next to his assistant manager, Bertie Mee, who had led Arsenal to the Double in 1971. © Alan Cozzi/Watford FC Archive

Graham uncorks the bubbly as the Watford players and Elton John celebrate promotion to the Second Division in 1979. © Alan Cozzi/Watford FC Archive

In 1982 Graham criticised Watford's supporters for being quiet at home games and questioned whether they had the desire to reach the First Division. After the inevitable backlash, Graham admitted he was wrong, taking to the field before a game with a written apology. © Alan Cozzi/Watford FC Archive

Luther Blissett was one of the players who made the journey from the Fourth Division to the First. He scored twice against West Bromwich Albion on 11 September 1982 to send Watford top of the First Division for the first (and so far only) time. © Peter Robinson/ EMPICS Sport

Graham's hero in football management was Bob Paisley, who led Liverpool to six league titles. Paisley's last game in charge of Liverpool before retiring was at Vicarage Road in May 1983. Liverpool had already been crowned champions but Watford won the match 2-1 to clinch the runners-up spot.
From the Taylor family collection

Watford faced Everton in the 1984 FA Cup final and a coach brought Graham and Rita's family from Scunthorpe to Wembley. Graham's parents, Dorothy and Tom, are in the middle, four from the right.
From the Taylor family collection

The result at Wembley did not go Watford's way but the town turned out in force to thank Graham, Elton and the team the following day. Graham stayed at Watford for three more years but by 1987 it was time to move on. © PA/PA Archive/PA Images

After joining Aston Villa, newly relegated to the Second Division, Graham had to confront some hard truths about the state of the club. He addressed shareholders and supporters at a meeting shortly after arriving and what he said made uncomfortable listening for his chairman Doug Ellis. From the Taylor family collection

lose the game because of a moment of brilliance from the opposition or a mistake or a slice of bad luck. I was not going to guarantee the supporters success but what I could do was commit fully, and without wavering, to building a team that worked very hard, tried to attack the opposition as much as possible and tried to create goalscoring opportunities, knowing that if we got more right than we got wrong we would be rewarded over the course of a season.

Go to a game at any level where spectators have paid to watch and you will notice that the crowd responds positively when their team is on the attack, moving the ball forwards quickly and with purpose, trying to breach the opposition's defence. They will pay more attention, they will crane their necks for a better view or stand up from their seats in antici-pation, and they will roar encouragement. That, to me, is what the game is all about, and reading *The Football Man* reinforced my beliefs about what sort of football team I wanted to manage.

All I needed was my opportunity, and that came less than three months after my twenty-eighth birthday. I had been appointed player-coach by the directors, which I don't think pleased David Herd, who was still the manager, all that much. My leadership skills, my coaching qualifications and my eagerness to work on improving my coaching away from the club in my spare time had been noticed by Heneage Dove, one of Lincoln City's directors. We had a first-class board of directors – including Dennis Bocock, who owned the building company that had built a great many homes in and around Lincoln, and Charles Warner, who owned the local Vauxhall car dealership – but it was Heneage Dove who impressed me the most. He was a pig farmer, a man from the countryside, but he was also sharp and shrewd and he put a lot of faith in me right from the start.

I don't know the full circumstances that led to them sacking Herd and giving me his job but I have a feeling they ran out of patience with him commuting from Manchester. I don't think it was because we were under-performing on the pitch because we started the 1972-73 season quite well. A look at the records shows we were third in the table in mid-October, although we slipped away and were in ninth position when Herd was sacked in early December.

Dove, Bocock and Warner invited me to a board meeting and asked me if I felt I was ready to become the manager. And so one day I was a player, one of the lads, and the next I was the youngest manager in the Football League. The directors left it to me to break it to the players and so I gathered them round and said: 'I like to think I've got on with most of you and if any of you really dislike me you've hidden it well, but I've got some news for you. For some of you it'll be good news and for some of you it might be not so good news, but I am your new manager.'

Goodness me, I was confident, wasn't I? I was younger than some of the players I now had to manage, I had no experience of running a team and yet I felt totally ready to take it on. I wasn't a fool, I knew I had a lot to learn, and I knew I wanted to make some changes but I accepted that I had to go steady to start with. I wasn't sure the players would accept me so I had to earn their respect and I knew I couldn't make dramatic changes overnight. One thing was going to change immediately though: training would start on time every day.

My first match as a football manager was a Lincolnshire Senior Cup tie against non-league Boston United on 11 December 1972. We lost 2-0. I am stretching my memory here but I have a feeling I picked a strong side for the game, so it wasn't the greatest of starts.

A look at the results now tells me that when I took over, we were on a run of seven league matches without a win, stretching back to 21 October. My first couple of months did not show any sign of improvement and I failed to win any of my first eleven games as a manager. The first match was at Newport County, where we drew 2-2, but after that we lost at home to Barnsley and then drew away at Doncaster Rovers and Aldershot and at home to Exeter City and Crewe Alexandra. Not a very good start.

The first few weeks were difficult. Many of the players were my friends. We had socialised together and we had been equals but now I was their boss and they were looking to me to lead them and wondering, no doubt, if I was up to the task.

I can remember at half-time during one of my early games – it might well have been that first home defeat against Barnsley – walking from the dugout to the dressing room and wondering what I was going to say to them. We were not playing well but I didn't feel I could have a go at them, even though they needed to know a few home truths. I decided I had to try to encourage them, so I said: 'I think we're better than this, but you need to show it on the pitch.'

In a funny way, I felt tentative about taking charge. It wasn't that I was reluctant to do so and yet there was something holding me back and I couldn't quite put my finger on it until one night, sitting at home, mulling it over, I realised what it was.

The next morning, I said: 'OK lads, I know I said I've been perfectly happy with you calling me Graham but that has to stop now. From now on, it has to be gaffer or boss. You can call me what you like behind my back, as long as I don't hear you, but to my face it's gaffer or boss, OK?'

It was such a simple thing but it established that there was a hierarchy, that I was no longer one of the lads but that I was running the show. Now, some of them might not have liked it, and I am sure the older ones might not have been too happy that they were being managed by someone who was younger than they were, but I had to put a distance between me and them. I couldn't pretend they were my team-mates and friends, and I had to stop going out for meals with them and their wives, which was a shame, but if I was going to make a success of being the manager, I had to manage. I knew that, in time, I'd have to let some of them go, I knew I'd have to lay down the law every now and then, and so I couldn't be friends with them one minute and the boss the next because it just wouldn't work. I wasn't worried about what they said about me because I knew that players always talked about the manager, and sometimes not terribly favourably. I didn't necessarily need my players to like me though, but I did need them to respect me, listen to what I said and do what I asked.

I'd love to be able to say that I brought about an immediate improvement to performances and results but the facts are there in black and white. It was a tricky time and I wouldn't have thought many people were making a note of my name as a future England manager at that point, even though we were very unlucky not to beat Bury.

As I walk into Sincil Bank now I can see in my mind's eye where there was a little group of Lincoln supporters in the corner of the terrace behind the goal chanting: 'Taylor out! Taylor out!' after one of our home defeats. I think there was a letter printed in the local newspaper too, saying I was too young and too inexperienced for the job. Having the backing of Heneage Dove was so important because, inevitably, there were whispered conversations in the corridors at Sincil Bank from people wondering where our next win was going to come from and whether appointing me had been a terrible mistake.

I was still registered as a player and, although I had no intention of carrying on playing long-term, I did put myself in the team for three games – a defeat at Hereford United, a draw at Northampton Town and a draw at home to Bury. I knew more or less straight away that I couldn't do both jobs. We were terrible at Hereford and I'd been as bad as anyone so I could hardly get stuck into them afterwards. It was a relief when I packed in playing at the end of February 1973. My last game as a player was a 2-0 home defeat to Newport County and my eleventh winless game as a manager. It is perhaps no coincidence that the next game, against Darlington at Sincil Bank, brought my first victory. It wasn't pretty – we needed a late goal from centre-half Terry Branston to clinch it – but it was a huge relief.

Maybe that was what I needed to do – to give up all intention of being a player and commit fully to management. Or maybe the first signs of some of the work I had done were beginning to pay off, and when we turned the corner we finished the season quite well, winning nine of the last fourteen, starting with that game against Darlington, and hauling ourselves up to tenth place in the table.

Boy, did I work hard. I am not making out that I was in any way unusual in this regard because football managers do put in the hours, but I worked six days a week, at least, and committed everything I had to the job. Rita knew, and accepted, that I had to do this and I am so grateful that she allowed me to spend so much time at work. Not that it felt like work because I was loving it and relishing the challenge. The sense that we were making small improvements felt so satisfying, especially when we began to win a few games.

I'd been careful not to change too much too soon but I did introduce some structure to the training. I'd been on a coaching course where the Sunderland manager Alan Brown, the founder of the shadowplay training method that Jim McGuigan had first shown to me at Grimsby Town, reintroduced me to the technique and I began to work on our organisation, explaining to the players where they should be when we were both in and out of possession, and on creating goalscoring chances.

I made a few changes to the squad, shipping out three or four who did not live in the Lincoln area. I had made it clear to the players that I wanted them to live within twenty minutes or so of the city, because it reduced the chances of them being late for training and also because I wanted them to be a part of the community. Very early on, I explained to the players that I wanted them to be active in Lincoln and I began to organise trips to work places, schools and pubs and social clubs so the supporters – or potential supporters – could meet them. We also held evenings where supporters could come in and ask me and a couple of the players questions. I took the players into local offices and factories too, which made it easy for me when they moaned that our training sessions were too hard. 'Hard?' I'd say. 'You could always be doing nine to five in a factory – you've got the afternoon off today.' On a bad day, we struggled to drag 2,500 people through the turnstiles and, although I knew we could never be a big club, I also knew that in a town the size of Lincoln there were a lot of people we might be able to convert into supporters if we began to be successful. We had an even better chance if people identified with the players too and, although there was the odd grumble about giving up their evenings every now and then, the players bought into the idea and committed to it. Slowly we reaped the rewards.

Despite the poor run of results at the start, the board backed me and gave me a little bit of scope to bring in some new players, although I knew money would be tight and so I could not afford any extravagant mistakes. I spent the first three months watching game after game, all over the country. There were some weeks when I watched five or six matches and I would go anywhere – from the First Division to non-league and, particularly, to watch reserve-team games at Second and Third Division clubs because that was where I felt I might pick up a few out-of-favour gems.

I realised that Lincoln did not have any scouting system to speak of and so I began to put one in place, although my scouts were really only a second pair of eyes. At the time, I was still honing my own judgement and the only way I could be sure of a player was to go and watch him myself. My first signings, in February and March 1973, included two players who would go on to play a big part in our success – Dennis Leigh, a full-back who came from Rotherham, and Alan Harding, a tricky right-footed left-winger I'd been impressed with when I saw him play against us for Darlington.

When I was trying to strengthen my team, I called two of the most successful, most famous and, to me, most intimidating managers in the country to see if they would let me have one of their players on loan. One afternoon, I asked my secretary to tell people I would be busy for the next hour. I locked my office door so I couldn't be disturbed and I picked up the phone, my hand trembling slightly as I began to dial the number for Arsenal Football Club. I asked to be put through to Mr Bertie

Mee, their double-winning manager and one of the most respected figures in the game.

'Mee here,' said the voice on the other end of the phone, rather abruptly.

My voice was shaking a bit as I explained who I was and asked politely whether he would consider lending me one of his reserve-team defenders (I can't remember who it was now) for a month or two.

'Young man,' said the voice, sounding slightly irritated, 'I have twenty-six players at the club and at the moment seven are injured and three are suspended. So, answer me this, why should I help you?'

I really didn't know what to say to that, so I thanked him for his time and hung up.

Refusing to be put off, I called Bill Shankly at Liverpool and asked him the same question.

'Listen, son, do you like your centre-halves to be tall, quick, strong and brave?'

'Yes, Mr Shankly,' I said.

'Call me Bill. That's good. But let me tell you this: Liverpool defenders have to be tall, quick, strong and brave, even the ones in the reserve team. And that is why ye cannae have any of them. But good luck.'

One man had turned me down in an obnoxious manner and the other had done so in a wonderful manner, and it taught me something about how to deal with people a little lower down the ladder. I resolved that if I ever reached the top of the game, I would not speak to a lower-division manager the way Bertie had spoken to me. (Bertie always denied he'd spoken to me like that when I reminded him of our phone call years later, though. Besides, as I was to find out, that was just Bertie's way. I don't think he was being deliberately rude.)

Another thing I learned early on was about the players' contracts and the bonus clauses they contained. I was quite surprised to see how many of them were on more money than me – because I had not been given a pay rise when I became manager, or if I had been it was a very small one. I said to Heneage I felt that as manager I should be secure in knowing I was earning more than the players because the buck stopped with me and I would get the blame for bad results.

Heneage invited me up to his farm and asked me to join him out in the barn where all his pigs were kept. He told me he was going to show me how to milk the pigs. Goodness knows why he was milking the pigs by hand, presumably to get some milk to feed to the piglets, but that's what he was doing. He got these two pigs and handed one to me and began to show me how to squeeze their teats so the milk squirted into a jug.

'So, Graham,' he said, 'you wanted to talk to me about a new contract?'

This was a ludicrous situation. I was lying down underneath the rear end of a pig, trying to aim the milk into the jug, thinking that if this pig needed a shit I was going to get it all over my face. It was clever of Heneage, really, because it took all the tension out of what could have been a tricky conversation. I made my case as best I could. I got a pay rise and, although it wasn't quite as much as I'd asked for, it was more than my best-paid player so I was happy. I also learned how to milk a pig, although that's not a skill I've had to call on since.

In summer 1973, I bought two more players who were building blocks in the team I was putting together. From Doncaster Rovers I signed Ian Branfoot, a very good full-back who went on to have a successful managerial career with Reading and Southampton, and Sam Ellis, a centre-half who, as a nineteen-year-old, had played for Sheffield Wednesday in the 1966 FA Cup final defeat to Everton. Ellis cost us £7,000 from Mansfield. A bit later, I got Peter Graham from Darlington for £12,500 and then, in February 1974, I picked up Dennis Booth, who I'd seen playing for Southend reserves and couldn't believe he wasn't in their first team. He came on loan first and then we signed him.

We finished twelfth in my first full season, 1973-74, and although that was two places lower than the previous year, I felt we were moving in the right direction. I was learning on the job and there was nothing quite as exhilarating as that. I'd studied coaching and had run sessions for players of all abilities but spending a year and a half working with a squad of players and putting into practice the things I had learned was exciting. I'd written coaching plans that built up day by day, week by week and I enjoyed the job of trying to get my ideas over to the players in a way that they could understand.

I am sure the players will say that at times it was repetitive and it was boring but they recognised that it did work and it did help them win matches. They may well have grumbled about it when I was out of earshot, but players will embrace anything that helps them get a result.

One afternoon I wanted to work on a particular free-kick routine that I had devised. We sat in the dressing room and I had my Subbuteo pitch laid out on a board balanced on a couple of stools. I had tiddlywink counters to use as the players – red for Lincoln, blue for the opposition – and I was moving the counters around to show them what I wanted them to do, going through the runs and where I wanted the ball played.

'OK, lads? Have you got it?' I asked before we went outside to the training pitch opposite the ground to start running through the moves. I can't remember exactly what was supposed to happen but I know Dennis Booth had to do a little decoy run in front of the ball and into a wide position to draw a defender away just before the free-kick was taken.

They just couldn't get it right. Time after time, they made a mistake and got the sequence of runs wrong or the delivery of the ball wrong, and I was getting very, very frustrated. Over the years Dennis reminded me: 'Do you remember the time you made us do that free-kick routine thirty-six times?' I can't be sure how many times we did it but I wouldn't be surprised if it was about that many. Poor Dennis didn't even have to touch the ball, he was just running backwards and forwards, which he liked to remind me about.

It was getting dark when eventually I snapped. 'Right, you lot, back in the dressing room.'

I went through the moves with the tiddlywink counters again and asked if they had it this time. One of the players, I can't remember who, started to ask a question and I lost it. I thumped my fist on the Subbuteo pitch, sending all the little tiddlywink counters flying. 'Forget it, we'll do it again tomorrow morning. Get out of my sight, you're worse than useless at the moment.'

The following morning, they were sitting in the dressing room, looking a bit sheepish. I looked at the Subbuteo table and the tiddlywinks were back in the right positions for the free-kick routine but two or three of the red ones had little bits of sticking plaster on them.

'Why have these got plasters on?' I asked.

Dennis Booth said: 'Well, gaffer, when you sent them flying yesterday one or two of them have picked up knocks, but they should be alright for Saturday.'

I had to laugh. I did enjoy that sort of reaction from my players and, although I'd been really annoyed with them the previous day, I liked it when they had a little bit of fun at my expense. I have to give them credit too because when we went out onto the training pitch to go through the free-kick routine they got it right first time.

I was adding to and developing my coaching repertoire all the time. I was determined to play fast, attacking football and the style of play that we developed at Lincoln was similar to how my teams later played at Watford. There were some accusations that we were a 'long-ball team', and I have some strong views on that, but if you ask Lincoln City supporters now whether we smashed the ball forwards and ran onto it, they would tell you there was more to it than that. I won't deny that my aim was always to get the ball forwards quickly. I'd read an article somewhere, possibly in a coaching manual or at one of the courses I attended, about where goals are scored from. If you draw an imaginary semi-circle from the goal line, taking in the two corners of the six-yard box and the penalty spot, you will find that a very high percentage of goals – perhaps seventy-five per cent – are scored in that area. Whoever had done the research had found that the percentage was roughly the same no matter what level of football you were talking about, from international matches down to non-league games. It made perfect sense to me and so I started making a note of where our goals were scored from and found it to be true.

I found that if we could concentrate on getting the ball into that goalscoring area at a pace that the opposition defence found hard to handle, we could create chances and score goals. And if we closed down opposition defenders in the final third of the pitch and won the ball back close to the penalty area, we could cause them real problems and force mistakes. Next time you watch a game, see how many goalscoring chances come from a mistake in the final third. A lot is made now of the pressing game but it's not a new thing. We were doing it at Lincoln in the 1970s, and it wasn't new then but it was as effective then as now. By closing down the opposition and restricting the passing options for the man with the ball, a team can either force a bad pass that can be intercepted or force the opposition to play a long pass, which also gives you a chance to win possession.

We should have got promoted in 1974-75. I was continuing to improve the team and – although we lost Dixie McNeil, a very good goalscorer, because we got an offer from Hereford United that we couldn't turn down – I had created a striking partnership I still think of very fondly. I brought back Percy Freeman, a tall centre-forward who had been a favourite with the City supporters before I sold him to Reading, to partner a smaller, quicker centre-forward called John Ward. Together they were excellent, and in a way they were the blueprint for many of the forward pairings I had later on.

Early that season, I signed Peter Grotier, a goalkeeper who had been a first-teamer at West Ham United but was now in their reserves. He came on loan to begin with. He was powerful and commanding and had the ability to pluck the ball out of the air with one hand. He also organised the defence and told them that they had to expect him to drop the ball or miss the cross, even though he rarely did. It was his way of making sure the defenders did their job properly rather than rely on him. When we were facing a corner, he'd say to the defence: 'You'd better be ready because I am not coming for this.' Then, when the cross came in, he'd power off his line and catch the ball. I really wanted to buy him but he was way out of our price range. West Ham wanted £20,000 for him and there was no way we could stretch to that. £10,000 was about our limit at that time.

But my work trying to strengthen the club's relationship with the supporters over the season and a half I'd been in charge soon paid off because I had the confidence to go to the local newspaper and make it clear how much I wanted to sign Peter Grotier. I explained that we couldn't afford to pay what West Ham wanted. I made no bones about it, I asked the supporters to raise some money if they wanted us to be able to sign him and they responded magnificently and found about £6,000 – which was a very decent sum then – that helped us buy him. I pleaded poverty to West Ham, Peter made it clear he wanted to join us, and somehow we managed to get him for £16,666.

I can tell you this, though: it's one thing spending your club's money or the chairman's money, but spending your supporters' money brings a whole different level of pressure. I backed my judgement and knew I was signing a very good goalkeeper for a Fourth Division side but knowing that the supporters had raised so much meant I was thinking: 'Come on, Peter, don't let us down here,' and he didn't. He was magnificent for us, and arguably the final piece of the jigsaw for me.

We did well in 1974-75 but the season ended with such disappointment that I worried over the summer if we would recover from it. We won our penultimate match, at Workington, 2-0 to end the day in the fourth and final promotion place. Everybody in the Fourth Division had finished their season bar us and Southport and we were due to meet on the Monday night. We were tied with Chester City on fifty-seven points and just ahead of them on the dreaded goal average – a system that had not been my friend when I'd been at Grimsby, remember.

All we had to do was go to Southport and avoid defeat. A win or a draw would be enough. Southport were in mid-table and had nothing to play for, so we travelled across feeling very confident. The directors had agreed to fund an overnight stay even though it was not a long journey, and everyone was thinking we'd be enjoying a late night in the hotel bar, celebrating promotion. I think we even took some bottles of champagne on the coach with us. I can promise we were not taking the match lightly, but we were confident. Talk about tempting fate.

We lost 3-2 and our goal average slipped below Chester's and we missed out. I can think of several disappointments later in my career but I have never known a group of players so low as the Lincoln City squad that night. We were absolutely devastated and there were tears over our beers. We felt very hard done by because not only had we missed out by 0.03 of a goal but we had scored seventy-nine to Chester's sixty-four (although admittedly we'd conceded forty-eight to their thirty-eight). Had goal difference been the tie-breaker that year we'd have gone up. It's all very well saying it was a daft system to decide teams that were level on points, but we all knew the rules before the season started and we hadn't done enough to make sure.

The next day we travelled back to Lincoln and that evening had to play the Lincolnshire Senior Cup final against Grimsby. A big crowd was at Sincil Bank and in different circumstances it would have been a big promotion party. The atmosphere was very flat but I remember the warm reception and encouragement of the supporters. None of my players felt like playing football but I gave them a calm team talk saying that they had a duty to the supporters who had turned up. I also said that the recovery process started here and, although it was just a county cup final, I was so proud of my players that they went out and did a very professional job, winning 2-0 when they could have been forgiven for feeling sorry for themselves. That night, I felt we'd laid the groundwork for promotion the following season.

6

We. Will. Win.

When we returned after the summer break I kept my message to the players simple. We were not going to make the same mistake again. The goal-average system was still in place (although the Football League changed it to goal difference the following season, partly because of how it had affected us at Lincoln), and I told the players that we had to be ruthless and show our opponents no mercy. If we were 2-0 up, we would push for the third and if we were 3-0 up we'd still keep going at them.

Before the season, Heneage Dove set me a challenge. He bet me that we could not score more than a hundred league goals. The deal was that if we achieved the target he would pay for a garage to be built at our house in Matlock Drive, North Hykeham, and if we fell short I'd pay him £100, which is almost £1,000 now and so not the sort of money I wanted to lose.

When we returned for pre-season training, I very quickly sensed that the players were still hurt after missing out at the end of the previous season but that the hurt they were feeling had lit a fire in their bellies. I was confident enough in them as individuals and as a team to know that I did not need to make major changes. I brought in John Fleming, a terrific little midfield player, on a free transfer from Oxford United and that was it.

I look back at that season as arguably my finest achievement in football because it was my first promotion and certainly the Lincoln City side that won the Fourth Division championship was the best I ever managed in terms of their ability relative to the division we were playing in. We walked away with the title and set records that still stand today. I never tire of looking at the league table and seeing our record. We won thirty-two out of forty-six matches, lost only four and were unbeaten at home. We scored 111 goals, which delighted Heneage Dove and particularly Rita because it meant work started on the garage at our house. On a recent trip to Lincoln I stopped in Matlock Way and I had to chuckle to myself about how innocent it all sounds now – in this world of multi-million-pound transfer fees and wages – that my reward for winning the championship was a garage. I was pleased to see the current owners of the house have kept the garage door nicely painted too. Our points tally of seventy-four is a record for the era when only two points were awarded for a win and if you translate our total into three points for a win it would have been 106, which has only ever been matched by Reading in a forty-six-game season.

I feel so fondly about that team and I know that people in Lincoln who remember them think the same. We had five players in the Fourth Division PFA team of the year but what is remarkable to me is that, for a team that scored 111 league goals, one of those players was the goalkeeper, Peter Grotier, and three of the others were defenders – Ian Branfoot, Sam Ellis and Terry Cooper. John Ward was the only attacking player who made it, and he had scored twenty-nine goals. But I think half a dozen other Lincoln players can feel unfortunate not to have been recognised by their fellow professionals that year and it wouldn't have been an injustice if all eleven had been Imps.

Branfoot and Dennis Leigh were the ideal full-backs and yet so different in playing style. Branfoot was a good player – too good for the Fourth Division, really – and he was so reliable. He liked to play it out from the back and then get forwards and overlap the attacking players. Leigh was the opposite – he kept it tight, didn't push forward, and was very difficult to beat. He was one of my favourites in the sense that I knew he would produce for me on a Saturday. And he was tough. I won't say dirty – because he played fair – but if you were tackled by him you knew about it. Midway through the season he got appendicitis and Phil Neale came in. Like me, Phil was from Scunthorpe and I knew his father, which is how we came to sign him. He was not a typical footballer because he signed for us after leaving university, where he got a degree in Russian. He was also a first-class cricketer and as soon as the football season ended he'd go off to spend the summer playing for Worcestershire. He was an intelligent and quite sensitive man and I remember we had to educate him a little bit so he could survive in the dressing room. I am not saying he was picked on but he could be the butt of the jokes sometimes and he would just take it. I called him into my office once and told him he needed to give a bit back every now and again so that the other players knew he was not a push-over, and he got pretty good at delivering a decent put-down.

Our two centre-halves were Terry Cooper and Sam Ellis, and Lincoln supporters who remember just what a magnificent partnership they had may be surprised to know that they didn't get on at all. Terry was a fiery Welshman who could give as good as he got. I remember early on being so frustrated with him during one match that I stormed onto the pitch and had a fistful of his shirt as I went face to face with him because he kept trying to play the offside trap, which I didn't want him doing. That would make headlines now and I'd probably be sent off and banned from the touchline for half a dozen matches, but the referee just asked me what the hell I thought I was doing and I came to my senses, realised I was on the pitch and ran back to the dugout feeling rather embarrassed. Sam was one of the finest people I've worked with but he was not the best in training. He saved everything for matchdays and I had to come to terms with that. If I'd picked my team based on what I'd seen in training on a Friday, Sam would rarely have got a game, but he was my captain because of what he delivered on a matchday. He'd played for Alan Brown at Sheffield Wednesday, so he was familiar with the type of coaching I was doing, and he was a leader. Terry and Sam barely spoke from Monday to Friday – they were just very different people and didn't get on – but when they crossed the white line on a Saturday they had each other's backs, they communicated well and they were tremendous together.

Everyone in the team knew what was expected of them. When we had the ball, we were an all-out attacking 4-2-4 side, with two of Dave Smith, Alan Harding and John Fleming getting wide and looking to get crosses into the box. Dennis Booth was possibly not appreciated enough until he was missing from the side. He was so funny in the dressing room that he made himself the heartbeat of the team. On the pitch, he was a holding midfield player years before anyone knew the phrase. I thought of him as our 'continuity' player because he would win the ball and move it on to someone else, while helping to keep the team's shape in case the opposition broke on us. He would pick the ball up and pass it on, and make himself available to team-mates if they were in trouble. Other players loved that reassuring presence but I don't think supporters necessarily noticed what he was giving to the team because none of his work was that spectacular. In fact, he rarely passed the ball over ten yards. He was the sort of player who made others look better and – even though he never won Man of the Match himself – we were always a poorer side without him.

Up front we had Peter Graham, who was a skilful, clever player and one of the first to complain that my fitness training was excessive. I did make them run because I wanted them to be fit enough to close down defenders in the last ten minutes of games, because that was when the opposition would be tiring and prone to mistakes. I said to him: 'The supporters will see you giving everything at the end of the game. You might not always win the ball but they will like you for it and it will help them appreciate the other things you do.' Peter understood that there were simple ways to get the supporters on side by showing effort and desire, particularly when things weren't going well for us.

Our regular front pair, though, was the classic little-and-large combination that I liked throughout my managerial career.

Percy Freeman was tall and strong and John Ward was smaller and more mobile and another intelligent man who thought about the game. I hope he won't take this the wrong way because I thought of him as a manufactured footballer in that he made a lot of effort to learn the game and particularly improve aspects of his forward play that would help him score goals. Of his twenty-nine goals that season, I think only one was from outside the eighteen-yard box, and that was because he thought about his movement and tried to second-guess where the ball would land if it was cleared or headed away by the defenders. Between them Percy and Wardy scored fifty-four goals in league and cup – not far off half our total tally – and at times they were unstoppable. They would do these cross-over runs which would confuse the defenders they were playing against because they weren't sure whether to follow their man or hold their position on the pitch, and that used to open up space for the midfielders to attack into.

As the winter schedule and heavy pitches took their toll on the squad, I took two strikers on loan from Nottingham Forest to cover for injuries. One of them was Tony Woodcock, who Brian Clough had been playing at right-back in Forest's reserves and who came with the less-than-ringing endorsement: 'See if you can get anything out of him.' The other was a powerful lad called Bert Bowery.

I asked Woodcock where he preferred to play and he told me he was a striker. We had a practice match in training and he absolutely tore Terry Cooper and Sam Ellis to pieces, so I stuck both him and Bowery in the side for a midweek league game against Southport. Cloughie came up from Nottingham to watch. We won 6-0 and both Bowery and Woodcock scored. Afterwards, Brian came to see me in my office and we had a quick drink. I was keen to see if he'd be interested in selling Woodcock but Brian was in no mood to discuss a transfer. He downed his drink and said: 'I can't believe you lot are top of the league – all you do is kick it forwards and score goals. You've got nothing else about you at all.' He was half-joking but there was a compliment in there, I think, although you could never be quite sure with Brian. It was nice that Tony Woodcock – who went on to win the league championship and European Cup with Nottingham Forest as well as play in Germany and for England – always remembered the positive impact of his month at Lincoln City.

We worked hard on the training pitch to build up these understandings and I broke the team down into little two- or three-man partnerships and worked on them so that when we hit our stride we were like a machine. We won so many matches by convincing margins and scored so many goals – I look at the results now and see we beat Southport 6-0, Watford 5-1 (sorry, Watford supporters), Bradford City 5-1, Workington 4-0, Exeter 4-1, Torquay United 4-2. Because there were only two points for a win we had to wait a long time to confirm promotion and it wasn't until 17 April – our fourth-from-last league game and our final home match of the season, against Doncaster Rovers – that we had the chance to clinch the championship. It was one of the few occasions that I didn't need to give a team talk because just as I was about to address the players, Percy Freeman stood up and went round the room, addressing each of his team-mates in turn with a short but well-chosen line: 'Right, we do it today, OK?' I loved Percy for that. After the game, he got me in such a bear hug it felt like he had cracked my ribs, and I didn't even mind that either.

We won 5-0 and at the final whistle the supporters ran onto the pitch to celebrate with the players. There were more than 14,000 at Sincil Bank that day and it felt like we had built something that would last long in the memories, even if I wondered whether we could continue progressing as we were.

I kept the side together and we did well in the Third Division, finishing ninth, which was Lincoln City's highest position since 1961, but I could sense that I was beginning to outgrow them. Heneage Dove was not unambitious but he was realistic. He knew that a city the size of Lincoln might be able to sustain

Second Division football, but he always gave me the impression he thought I could make it to the top.

Bobby Robson came to watch us once when he was manager of Ipswich Town and I remember walking across from our training pitch to the office, through the car park at Sincil Bank, and I saw his car. It was a beautiful silver car – either a Jaguar or a Bentley – and it was about twice the length of anything else in the car park. I went up to the office to see Heneage and I stood at the window and said: 'Have you seen Bobby Robson's car?'

'One day, Graham, you'll have a car like that,' he said. 'Not at this club, you won't, but you're too good a manager to stay at this club for too much longer.'

Reading this, you might have got the impression that managing Lincoln was a walk in the park, that the precocious twenty-eight-year-old got everything right first time (apart from the sticky first couple of months), but that wasn't the case. Although the general trend was one of improvement, and I managed to build a side that could win the Fourth Division and survive comfortably in the Third, I made plenty of mistakes. But I developed as a manager at Sincil Bank because I was backed by a wonderful chairman who believed in me and, most importantly, told me he that he believed in me. I had the support of Rita at home, who knew and accepted that there would be times when I would be preoccupied by football matters. I remember Heneage telling me that he didn't like workaholics or people who complained that there weren't enough hours in the day, but I worked hard because I enjoyed it and because I was learning. Lincoln City was the place that gave a young manager with bags of energy the space to learn, the freedom to make mistakes and the encouragement to do things his own way and I didn't take that opportunity for granted.

I learned so much at Lincoln, especially about managing people and recognising that not everyone responded in the same way. The dressing rooms at Sincil Bank have changed since my day but when I was back at the ground I remembered a team talk I gave before a match against Cambridge United, who were managed by Ron Atkinson. We'd lost an FA Cup tie to West Bromwich Albion the previous weekend and training had been flat, perhaps because they were not used to losing or perhaps because they had realised the gap between the First Division and the Fourth. I didn't really know what to say to them and, if truth be told, I felt things were getting a bit repetitive so I decided to mix things up.

I asked them all to stand up, still not quite sure what I was going to say. I was making it up as I went along. I found myself asking them to jog on the spot. Once they were jogging on the spot, I still wasn't sure what I was going to ask them to do next. I don't know where this came from but I asked them to turn round to face the wall so they could step up onto the bench. I demonstrated what I wanted. I wanted them to step up onto the bench, clap once and then slap the wall with their open palms. One-step, two-step, clap, slap, slap. One-step, two-step, clap, slap, slap.

Once they got into the rhythm of it I told them to start chanting: 'We. Will. Win,' as they clapped and slapped the wall.

They weren't keen to start with but soon got into it: one-step, two-step, 'We. Will. Win.' One-step, two-step, 'We. Will. Win.'

I knew the Cambridge players in the other dressing room would hear this and wonder what the lunatics next door were doing, although I wasn't prepared for what came next.

One-step, two-step, 'We. Will. Win,' we chanted again.

Then we started to hear some noise from the Cambridge players next door. They were clapping and stamping their feet to the same rhythm. It took a while before we could work out what they were saying but gradually they got louder.

We carried on: one-step, two-step, 'We. Will. Win.'

And then came their reply…

One-step, two-step, 'No. You. Won't.'

That had us falling about laughing.

We won the match 3-0, so it just shows that sometimes players don't need a complicated team talk and a set of detailed instructions at all.

7

The million-pound challenge

Having fought my way out of the Fourth Division with Lincoln City, how did I end up back at the bottom of the ladder with Watford? I must admit, it's a question I've pondered many times over the years and each time I think of it my heart skips a beat at the thought that I could have turned down the offer. How would everything have worked out then?

One afternoon in March 1977, I got home from work and Rita told me I'd had a call from Don Revie, the England manager. I knew Don because he and his assistant, Les Cocker, had come and put on a session for coaches when I'd set up the Lincoln and District Coaches Association, but the England manager wasn't in the habit of giving me a ring. Don had told Rita he'd call back later and so I had a restless afternoon wondering what the England manager wanted to talk to me about. After all, it was very unlikely he was going to tell me he was calling up one of my Lincoln players for the England squad.

The phone went and I let it ring a couple of times before picking it up, just so I didn't appear too eager. Don got straight to the point, as he usually did: 'Are you under contract at Lincoln?'

I told him I had just signed a new three-and-a-quarter-year contract.

'That's a shame,' he said, 'because I've just recommended you to a chairman.'

I could feel my chest swell a bit and I stood up a little bit straighter. It felt good to know the England manager was vouching for me.

'Oh yes, who's that?' I asked.

'Elton John. At Watford.'

At that moment, my shoulders slumped and my ego deflated. I had done well at Lincoln and we were on course to finish in the top ten in the Third Division. I was making a name for myself as a young manager and I was confident that my next move would be upwards, perhaps straight into the First Division if the right circumstances presented themselves. Watford, meanwhile, were in the Fourth Division and were owned by a pop star whose music was not to my taste because I much preferred Vera Lynn.

I tried not to let the disappointment show in my voice but I couldn't believe Don was doing this to me. Why would he think I would want to take a step backwards? Suddenly my confidence dipped. If this is what the England manager thought of me, was it how others felt?

A few weeks later, Elton called me. I still didn't know much about him apart from the pop-star image I'd seen on television, the big glasses and the outrageous outfits, and so his voice and calm, understated manner on the phone were not quite what I expected. Our call was not all that long but his passion for Watford and his knowledge of the Fourth Division did surprise me. I realised in that short call this wasn't just a daft pop star with too much money messing about with his plaything until he got bored and moved onto something else. But, despite Elton's persuasive words, it didn't feel like the right move for me and so the call ended with me saying: 'I'm sorry, but I'm not interested.'

Lincoln finished the season in ninth position, their highest placing for fifteen years, and before I went off on our first foreign family holiday (caravanning in France), I met with Heneage to talk about the following season. I believed that with a couple of new players we could push on for promotion but I could sense from him that he recognised my ambition was greater than Lincoln's and that it was time for me to move on. It's not that Heneage didn't want to be successful, but he knew there were limits to how far Lincoln could go.

Shortly after we'd got back from holiday, the phone rang and it was Elton, calling out of the blue: 'I know you said no, but I won't feel I am doing my job properly unless I meet you and explain to you what it is we want to do,' he said. 'I can't just say to my directors, "I rang him up and he said no and that's the end of it."'

I told Elton that he needed to speak to Heneage. Now, Heneage was a very clever man because when I'd signed the new three-and-a-quarter-year contract just a few months earlier, he had insisted on including a clause that said that if I left to join another club, that club would have to pay Lincoln City £20,000. That was a lot of money when you consider that Lincoln had only ever sold one player, Andy Graver, for more than that. I had been a bit concerned about this clause because I thought it might discourage clubs from taking me but my solicitor, Ray Ingram, told me not to worry about it because if it came to it we could argue that it was a restraint of trade and that it was not enforceable. When I raised my concerns about the clause with Heneage he assured me he didn't have any intention of actually enforcing it to prevent me from leaving. He promised he wouldn't stand in my way if a really good club made me an offer, but he was trying to look after Lincoln's interests as best he could. My view was that if someone was prepared to pay Lincoln £20,000 for me, good luck to them.

Heneage gave me permission to speak to Elton, but I still wasn't sure about Watford or about dropping back down to the Fourth Division. Before I met him, I went to Vicarage Road to have a look at the stadium and I was not impressed by what I saw. There seemed to be more life in the allotments that spread out behind one end of the ground. I also needed to be convinced that Elton John was focused on at least the medium term and wouldn't get bored after a year or two. I was worried that if it didn't work out my brief period of success at Lincoln City would be forgotten and I'd be seen as just a Fourth Division football manager who'd had one good season. I was also nervous about moving my family down south, moving the girls from their school and about the house prices. Dear me, a look in the estate agents' windows nearly persuaded me to get back in the car and drive straight back to Lincoln. The property prices concerned me for two reasons. Firstly, would I be able to afford to buy a house? And secondly, how hard would it be to persuade players at clubs outside the south-east to move to Watford?

In the meantime, I had heard that another club was interested in me. George Kerr, my assistant at Lincoln, said someone from West Bromwich Albion, who were in the First Division, had been in touch to say that their chairman Bert Millichip wanted to meet me. West Bromwich Albion – now, that was more like it.

Rita and I headed down to London where I planned to meet Mr Millichip at a Football League dinner at the Café Royal after the league's annual general meeting, stay over in London and then travel out to Windsor to see Elton the following morning.

After the meal I was invited over to West Bromwich Albion's table and Mr Millichip introduced me to everyone. I sat down and listened as they enjoyed their brandies and cigars.

'Graham, you've never played in the First Division or managed in the First Division, but I like to think we know all about you and we're prepared to take a risk,' said Mr Millichip. I have to say, I couldn't have felt much less welcome at their table.

Mr Millichip started talking figures and the salary he proposed, £9,000 a year, was less than half the figure Elton had mentioned on the phone. Then came the matter of Lincoln City's £20,000 release fee. Mr Millichip was aware of the clause and, as a solicitor himself, knew it could be got around. He said: 'We'll agree to it but we'll offer to pay it in instalments. We'll give them £5,000 up front but then we won't pay any more.'

I couldn't believe he was saying this and it immediately turned me off. I just didn't like the attitude of the people sitting round the table. For a start, they'd not asked Heneage Dove's permission to speak to me, and now they assumed I would agree to join them just because they were West Bromwich Albion.

'I should tell you, I've been speaking to another club,' I said.

'Do you mind telling me who it is? Mr Millichip asked.

'It's Watford.'

Mr Millichip scoffed. 'Watford! But they're in the Fourth Division. You'll have to go to places like Rochdale, Halifax and Workington.'

'Excuse me,' I said. 'Workington have not been voted back into the league. At your meeting this afternoon, you all voted on who should stay in and Workington didn't keep their place.' (This was before there was automatic relegation at the foot of the Football League and each season the bottom four teams in the Fourth Division had to apply for re-election and the chairmen of all the other clubs in the league had a vote to decide their fate.) Mr Millichip appeared to not even know the result of the vote he'd participated in that afternoon or, if he did, it hadn't registered with him and that really irritated me. I felt it was disrespectful towards another professional football club, even if it was one that was a lot lower down the ladder than West Bromwich Albion. I thought to myself: 'I'm not coming here, that's for sure.'

Mr Millichip said: 'You should give your right arm to join this club,' and I told him my right arm was staying exactly where it was – attached to my right shoulder.

The next morning, Rita and I headed to Elton's house. I knew I had been right to turn down West Bromwich Albion but nevertheless I worried about the wisdom of rejecting a firm offer from a First Division club.

Arriving at Elton's house was like stepping into a different world. I say house but it wasn't a house, it was a mansion, and a beautiful one at that. The driveway must have been a quarter of a mile long. We pulled up to the gate and there was a buzzer, which I pressed. 'Hello, it's Graham Taylor. I'm here to meet Elton John,' I said. The gate swung open and we headed up to the house where we were met by a lady I assumed at first to be his housekeeper.

She went off to make us all some lunch and when she returned she introduced herself as Elton's mum, Sheila Farebrother, just about as big a Watford supporter as you could meet. I suppose you might think it's a bit strange that I took my wife along to what was effectively a job interview and even stranger that the person doing the interviewing had his mum there, but it was clear to me that this was not an ordinary interview. I wanted Elton to know that I would commit everything to whichever club I worked for next but that my family was important to me. I wanted him to meet Rita and for Rita to meet him.

Elton's enthusiasm for football was obvious. He told me how he had supported the club as a boy, had first got involved as a director and now owned it and wanted to take it upwards. He told me it wasn't going to be a passing fad for him and that his commitment was total, although he was up front about the fact that his career would sometimes take him away from day-to-day involvement either to record an album or go on tour. Because of that, he wanted a manager who could not just shape a successful football team but build and run a club. That appealed to me immediately.

I have to hand it to Elton, he had done his research. He knew all about what I'd done at Lincoln City, including the community work I thought was so important. He also knew about Heneage Dove's £20,000 release clause.

Although I couldn't fail to notice the size of Elton's house – the beautiful furniture and vases, the artwork on the walls, the cars in the drive, the expansive grounds outside – the penny had still not quite dropped with me that £20,000 wasn't really a great deal of money to Elton, and I was nervous it was going to be a sticking point. But Elton made it clear the money was not an issue and that he was happy to pay it to Lincoln. That impressed me too because he could easily have got his lawyers to argue his way out of it if he'd wanted to.

Then he offered me a salary of £20,000 a year and a five-year contract. This was the sort of offer most First Division clubs might think twice about but Elton barely batted an eyelid. Don't get me wrong, it wasn't all about the money for me, but bear in mind my playing career had been cut short, when I was twenty-eight, and I had only a small Professional Footballers' Association pension and a long working life ahead of me with a family to support. There were far more secure lines of work than football management, even in those days, and so the opportunity to earn well was undoubtedly important.

I sat and listened to Elton speak quickly and excitedly about what he wanted to do with Watford Football Club. The more he spoke, the more he won me over but I still wanted to know if he had any idea what he was letting himself in for. Watford was a medium-sized town, close enough to London that people would be attracted to bigger clubs. Hertfordshire was not a footballing hotbed and the club itself had very little pedigree to speak of. They had spent three years in the Second Division under Ken Furphy about a decade earlier and had played in one FA Cup semi-final and that was about it. I decided to ask him exactly what he expected to achieve.

'I'd like to get into Europe,' he said.

I thought: 'This fella is crazy.' For the first time since we'd started talking, I thought my initial fears were founded. Perhaps Elton really was just a pop star with his head in the clouds. But there was something about the look in his eyes that told me he wasn't joking, and his ambition did excite me.

'OK,' I said, 'what do you think it will cost you to do that?'

Elton threw the question back at me. I thought I'd really try to frighten him by putting a big price on it: 'Well, I don't think you'll get much change out of a million pounds.'

Without missing a beat he said: 'Right, we'll give it a go,' and stretched his hand out to shake mine.

I thought to myself: 'That'll do me.'

What I didn't know at the time, although I pretty soon learned about it, was that there was a lot more going on in the background than I had realised. I gathered that Elton had already offered the job to Bobby Moore, the captain of

England's World Cup-winning team in 1966. I am sure it had made perfect sense to Elton to hire the Rolls-Royce of footballers, but three of Watford's directors – Geoff Smith, Jim Harrowell and Muir Stratford – had raised their concerns. They asked Elton if he thought Bobby Moore knew enough about the Fourth Division. So Elton asked them who they suggested instead and they recommended me. And so, when Elton decided to get some advice from the England manager, Don Revie, everything fell into place. He asked Don a very simple question: 'Give me the name of the best young manager in the lower divisions,' and Don said: 'Graham Taylor.'

It can't have been easy for Elton to change his mind but he did. I gather he offered Bobby more than his apologies, which he didn't necessarily have to do. I also know Elton paid Lincoln the £20,000 up front and I later heard that Heneage had walked into his next board meeting, knowing the money was safely in the club's account, and said: 'Yes, we did it.'

The next time I met Elton, it was to sign contracts. He was so excited he was practically bouncing up and down in his seat.

'Do you know,' he said, 'this is the first big decision I've made on my own in years.'

Elton John was already an industry. He had scores of people looking after his career – people at his management company, people at the record company, people who organised his tours. He couldn't necessarily make decisions about his own career any more. It suddenly dawned on me why Elton enjoyed owning Watford Football Club so much. It was his passion and his project.

What I hadn't yet realised was that Elton still had a lot to learn about running a football club.

8

'Either the dogs go or I go'

I was sorting through all the stuff in my summerhouse at home in Little Aston one day when I came across an old red notebook. I opened it up and found it was a book of notes I had made in June and July 1977 when I started work at Watford. By the looks of it, I kept a diary for about the first week, probably before the demands of the job took over, but it makes for interesting reading.

Keeping notes was part of the process of learning about the club. I wanted to know who everyone was, how long they'd been there and what they did. I made a list of everyone connected to the club – from the chairman, Elton John, to the tea lady, Mollie Rush. I wanted to know who got on with whom, and who didn't. I wanted to know if there were any trouble-makers or stick-in-the-muds but, most importantly, I wanted to form relationships with these people because they were going to be important if I was to make a success of things.

It would be easy to look back now and assume that because we rose from the Fourth Division to the First Division in five years it was all plain sailing, that I made the decisions and Elton signed the cheques and we went on our merry way without putting a foot wrong. But reading through a few pages of my notes reminds me how much work there was to do at Vicarage Road in 1977. It also reminds me of not only the fierce energy and burning drive the thirty-two-year-old me had but of how much power and responsibility I had been given. Elton had appointed me as the club manager, not just manager of the football team, and that meant I was in charge of every aspect of the club and had permission to make any changes I felt were necessary.

Wednesday 22 June 1977

Fact-finding visit to Watford prior to signing contract on Friday and before taking over officially as manager on Monday 27 June. Decided to arrive by train and took the Met Line from Euston. Pleasantly surprised on arrival to see parts of Watford I had not anticipated. Very residential area – first impression was that I could live here but would these people get 'excited' about their football club?

I am conscious that I am pre-judging the playing staff but I don't think they are good enough. They come from all over and are not readily on call.

Administratively, life could be a bit difficult as my office is situated in the wrong position and Patsy Gledhill is the only member of staff. She's overworked anyway and I'm sure the club suffer because of this.

Met with Ron Rollitt (general manager and secretary) and the chairman (Elton) came down. First impression of the club was that organisation and discipline was sloppy. On seeing the wage structure it was obvious that there had been no real policy.

There's a lack of lead from the board, who are immature and don't really know how a football club should be run. All very nice people though and the chairman is very sincere in wanting the football club to be successful.

At the end of the meeting – some two-and-a-half hours – I was just about as confused as I could be and still hadn't discussed half of what I had wanted to. There's a great deal to find out about a lot of the people and I am going to upset quite a number in order to get this club on its feet.

Reading that now it sounds quite harsh because I certainly didn't intend to upset people for the sake of it, but I knew that not everyone would be able to come on the journey with me. Some wouldn't be good enough and others would not want to challenge themselves or change enough to be part of it. I suppose I was treading a fine line between confidence and arrogance and I accepted that some people might think I had a bit too much of the latter for their taste. But I did have confidence in my ability to make big improvements and I was going to demand the same level of commitment from those around me.

Friday 24 June 1977: Board meeting

Elton John – chairman. Thirty-year-old multi-millionaire pop star. Watford supporter all his life. Local boy made world star. Wants success, doesn't really know how to get it. No grip of board meetings and yet has a mind of his own and is no fool. A lot of advantages but also disadvantages and simply because of who he is there are people who want him to fail.

The board is not stable in thought or policy at the moment and very reliant on chairman from a financial point of view, but they are prepared to work and are interested.

I had a good feeling about the directors because I could sense they had the club's interests at heart and they weren't just in it for themselves. I was determined not to be reckless with Elton's money; it had to be spent carefully and at the right time. There was certainly no point spending it to build a First Division team in the Fourth Division, and at the start I felt I had to earn Elton's trust and show that I could make improvements without spending a fortune.

Saturday 25 June 1977

A lot of mess still about from the greyhounds and this is obviously going to be a problem. The club evidently gets £12,000 per annum from them.

Equipment: We have a weights room, in which David Butler, the physiotherapist, organises a circuit – he is very keen on body work. Apart from that there are only a few cones and absolutely nothing else at all.

Kit: No one seems to know who is in charge of it. We have a lot spare because of a new colour scheme which started last season, and consequently a lot of the old kit is still available. Not impressed with how the kit is packed and would hazard a guess that no one really knows what we have got or not.

Medical: Dr Vernon Edwards is associated with the England party – probably this is how Dave Butler got his chance with the England youth team. Dr Edwards will obviously play a leading part in the development of the club and can be an influential figure. His philosophy is the same as mine – the treatment of the injured player should be as uncomfortable as possible!

Scouting: No scouting system at all. One local scout – Bob Croucher – and I think Bill McCracken is still on the staff (aged ninety-five). It's the traditional thing in football and evidently because of prior work he's been promised a job for life. No one watches [opposition] games and there seems to have been no work done in this direction at all. Will have to look into the whole system.

Youth policy: Almost non-existent.

Ground: There's a feeling that you are in the makings of a stadium and yet it is short of atmosphere. Has the greyhound track round it and that is used two or three times a week. Makes for untidiness and certainly a lot of the ground needs tidying up. Ground staff is Les Simmons with two or three part-time helpers. He pays a lot of attention to the pitch, even to the extent of not liking the players to go on it.

Les Simmons was a lovely man, and a real character, and his pride in the pitch was exactly what I was looking for. Back in those days it was not easy keeping a pitch playable through the winter and I knew how hard he worked on it, but having to give him two days' notice that I wanted to use the pitch for a first-team training session was just not on. He used to complain partly because he didn't want me blaming him if the pitch was in poor condition and partly to persuade me to let him hire a full-time assistant.

But one thing was clear: the greyhounds had to go. The situation had quickly become an issue, not least because of the dog mess on the track, but also because it meant three days a week there were people milling around at Vicarage Road who were nothing to do with the football club. The final straw came after I'd been at the club several weeks. One of the players was sitting on a chair outside the physio's room, waiting for some sort of treatment and I asked him why he was waiting.

'There's someone in there,' he said.

'Really?' I said. 'Who?'

The player shrugged.

As I swung the door open Les, who was mad keen on the greyhound racing, span round with a look of surprise on his face. Up on the physio's table was one of the bloody dogs.

'What the hell's going on in here?' I said.

'We think he's pulled something,' said Les, absolutely seriously, as if this was all quite normal.

It's quite funny when I think back to it now but I was livid at the time. I went straight up to see Elton, who happened to be in the office at the ground that day. 'Are we running a football club or a bloody greyhound stadium here? Because it's got to be one or the other – either the dogs go or I go.'

Thursday 30 June 1977

Spent three days interviewing the playing staff and, whilst interviews were conducted on a friendly basis, it's obvious to me that changes will have to be made. There are question marks for various reasons against Rankin, Garner, Horsfield, Sherwood, Joslyn, Bond. Many of the players don't live in or around Watford. Those players who live far away will eventually have to be replaced. There isn't a feeling of commitment to the club at all – more a feeling that it is being used.

It just goes to show that I don't get everything right because, of those players I was not too sure about, Alan Garner ended up as Player of the Season and Steve Sherwood stayed at Vicarage

Road for all of the ten years I was there, leaving in the summer of 1987 at around the time I moved to Aston Villa.

A look at the league table told me that the squad I was inheriting was not good enough because they had finished seventh in the Fourth Division the year before. I knew that I'd be able to improve some of the basics fairly quickly, but in order to do that I needed to be totally hands-on in terms of coaching the players. That meant there was no room for any contradictory messages. If I was going to knock the side into shape, I had to take every session and work on each department in the team until they were able to do what I asked of them. That meant I had to come to an agreement to release John Collins, who had been coaching the team. This also sent a message to the players that there was going to be only one voice that mattered: mine.

I had written to all of the players, making an appointment to meet with them one by one before I saw them kick a ball, and these meetings told me a lot about them. You can work out quite quickly who has a spark in their eyes and fire in their belly and who doesn't. Some of them had been bumping around in the lower divisions for years and had lost any sense of direction; others were young players who had a lot to learn. I told them that I intended to take the club upwards and I asked if they thought they were good enough to be part of it. I told them what I expected from them in terms of attitude and application as well as the type of behaviour I expected on and off the pitch. I wanted them to realise that I did not see footballers as mere employees but as representatives of the club and the town but, most of all, that the way they conducted themselves told others who they were as people. We had players who lived all over the place and some of them were spending an hour or more in the car getting into training. That had to change. The players would have to move closer, so they were within a certain distance of the town. Partly this was because I didn't want them sitting in their cars for so long because I believed it compromised their training and made them more vulnerable to injury, but mostly I wanted the players to be a part of the community. I wanted them to live among supporters and be available to visit schools and workplaces as my Lincoln City players had done. I was quite blunt in telling them that if what I was saying didn't sound like their cup of tea, we'd help move them on as quickly as possible.

Two players made enough of an impression on me during our meetings that I remember them today. One was a nineteen-year-old player who had a positive energy about him that I liked straight away. He sat down in front of me, looking eager but also a little nervous. I leaned across my desk towards him and looked him in the eyes.

'Luther. Blissett,' I said quietly.

He looked back at me, now a little confused as well as nervous.

'Looother. Blisssss-iiittttt,' I repeated, a bit louder, stretching out the words. The poor lad didn't know what to say, so he said nothing.

I stood up and said, even more loudly, and with my arms spread wide for emphasis: 'Loooooooo-thuurrrrr. Bliiissss-ittttt.' I paused as he looked up at me, clearly wondering if I was completely mad. 'With a name like that, son, you're bound to be a star.'

I'd never met the lad before and I have no idea where it came from but I think it made an impression on him.

The other player who impressed me was a Welshman called Tom Walley, a midfielder who had started at Arsenal and had played in Ken Furphy's Watford team that reached the Second Division before he went off to Orient. He'd been Elton John's first signing after taking over as chairman and was still only thirty-two but it was clear his playing days were as good as over.

As soon as he sat down, he said: 'I'll be honest, gaffer, my knee is fucked.'

I liked that he was being straight with me because plenty of footballers in his situation would have tried to squeeze another year out of their club. We talked about the squad and he told me there were a few gems in the squad but that they needed work. As I listened to him talk I recognised there might be a place for him after all, not as a player but with the youth set-up. We didn't have a youth system to speak of and I was adamant that we would develop a reputation as a club that spotted talent and produced its own players. It was absolutely vital for a club of our size that we were able to develop our own young players because it would save money on transfer fees and make us money if we sold on players who had not cost us a fee. I was going to have my hands full with the first team, so I needed someone who shared some of my values and ideas and Tom seemed perfect. He was direct, blunt, no-nonsense and a disciplinarian. If I'm honest, he frightened the life out of me, and I was his boss.

When I offered him a job developing the youth set-up, he said: 'I have to go home and check with my missus because if I take this on, it's going to be a twenty-four-hour-a-day job.' That was exactly what I wanted to hear.

As Watford supporters will know, both Luther and Tom played a huge part in what we achieved over the next ten years. Luther broke the club's goalscoring record and Tom ran a youth system that was the envy of most in the country. He spotted and developed numerous international players including Kenny Jackett and, when he went to Arsenal later, Ashley Cole.

When pre-season training started, the players were in for a shock. I was determined to make us one of the fittest teams in the division, just as I had done at Lincoln, and that meant running and weight training came before ball work. Sometimes we ran in Cassiobury Park, up through the golf course and back. Sometimes we ran at Vicarage Road. I'd get in early and set out a course with cones that went round the pitch and up the terrace. Other times we ran from Vicarage Road to Cassiobury Park and back, and the stopwatch was always running and the times were recorded.

On the first morning, when I had explained to the players what they were going to do, the two goalkeepers Andy Rankin and Steve Sherwood, who had been stood a little bit apart from the rest of the group of players, didn't move when I blew the whistle.

'What do you two think you're doing?'

They looked at each other and then at me.

'We're the goalkeepers,' said one of them.

'And?'

'Well, do we have to do this as well?'

'Do you want to be in the team?'

'Yes.'

'Well, you'd better catch them up then.'

More than once I heard someone say: 'This is ridiculous. Are we a football club or an athletics club?'

I liked to listen out for who was the first to moan and watch out for anyone trying to take shortcuts because this told me something about the players and their personalities too. I was not impressed with the general level of fitness. I joined in with the longer runs and was finishing ahead of some of them and I had a bad hip.

After a week or so of double training sessions, morning and afternoon, of long-distance runs and 'doggies' – the shuttle runs back and forth at speed – one of the senior players came to me and said the lads were tired and asked whether an afternoon off might not be a good idea so they could recover. My answer was simple: 'No.'

I pushed them to the point of rebellion before explaining my thinking. As they finished one of their runs I gathered the players in the centre circle on the pitch at Vicarage Road. I made them stand up while I was talking, even though I knew they wanted to sit down.

'Do you think it will be easy to win promotion this season?' I asked.

They mumbled and murmured: 'No, I guess not.'

I explained that there was no way to guarantee we could be the best team in the division but we could be the fittest and that might be the difference in some tight games when the opposition tired in the last ten minutes because tired players are more likely to make mistakes. Many footballers expect to get 'match fit' by playing football but I believed a greater level of all-round fitness was a benefit because it helped players avoid what I thought of as avoidable injuries. I agreed with Dr Edwards that I didn't want players who thought that picking up a 'knock' was a way to an easier life. I didn't want the treatment room to be a comfortable place. That's not to say I was unsympathetic to injured players, but the harsh reality is that a player who is not fit for selection is no use to the manager. It's also the case that in professional football there are players who cope better with the minor knocks and strains and will train and play on without complaint, and others who can't step onto the pitch unless they are one hundred per cent fit in their own minds. In my experience, the players who fit into the first group are the ones who have long careers and are most valued by the clubs they play for.

It wasn't long before I was ready to make my first move in the transfer market, and on 7 July I signed two players I knew and trusted: my captain at Lincoln, Sam Ellis, and Ian Bolton, who I had taken on loan at Lincoln but was at Second Division Notts County. George Kerr at Lincoln managed to get £6,000 out of us for Ellis, and Bolton cost us £12,000, which was arguably the best signing of my career in terms of value for money. I tried to get Dennis Booth from Lincoln at the same time but that would have to wait.

I felt we were ready to give it a go.

9

Total commitment

The task in front of me in August 1977 was to take a bunch of Fourth Division players who had barely set the world alight and mould them into a team capable of winning promotion at the first attempt. I was absolutely determined not to hang around in the bottom division any longer than necessary because I felt it was essential to establish a sense of momentum right from the start. Elton was paying me well, and that fact was in the public domain thanks to the *Watford Observer*. Their cartoonist, a man called Terry Challis who often seemed to hit the nail on the head with the nib of his pen, had drawn a picture of two Watford supporters reading a newspaper with the headline: 'Watford sign Taylor'. In the cartoon, one of the supporters is saying to the other: 'Blimey, when I saw the terms, I thought they'd signed Elizabeth.'

Although I could handle that – partly because I knew I wasn't on film-star money – I was aware that if we had a bad couple of months people might start to wonder what all the fuss was about. I wasn't so much worried about the supporters turning on me as not turning up at all.

I began by laying down the law in such a way that left no one in any doubt who was in charge and what we were going to be about. There would be no room for the lazy and lackadaisical. Training would be challenging, professionally run and it would start on time. I wanted total commitment in every training session, concentration and application. That didn't mean we were going to work in a heavy, serious atmosphere all the time because I believe that laughter and fun play a crucial part in helping people to perform to the best of their ability. But I wanted the players to understand my tone of voice and recognise when it was time to pipe down and pay attention.

I brought in a few little rules that may seem insignificant on their own but which all built up to bring in a code of discipline that everyone would follow. For example, as a team, we would all play in long-sleeve shirts or we'd all play in short-sleeve shirts, and the decision would be made and that would be that. It irritated me to see my team with half of them in long sleeves and the other half in short sleeves. I wanted the players to tuck their shirts into their shorts properly and fold the tops of their socks over in a consistent way so that the stripes were all the same.

The players needed to know that it was important to respect the club and its facilities. I didn't want them parking in the spaces reserved for the directors – and especially not the manager – even if they were available. I wanted them to present themselves smartly and be polite when they were at the club. These are not radical ideas – people who go to work in offices are expected to dress smartly and behave well because they are representing their employer. In my opinion, a footballer should be no different.

Before the season started, I went round as many of the local pubs and clubs as I could to introduce myself to the landlords and landladies. While I had no problem with the players enjoying a drink or two, I wanted to know if anyone was overdoing it and so I gave all the publicans my card and asked them to contact me if any of my players were misbehaving. I didn't want the pub owners to tell tales, and I wasn't interested in players who were having a couple of pints, but if anyone was drinking the night before a game or making a nuisance of themselves, I wanted to know. Every so often I did get a phone call and once in a while I did need to remind a player of his responsibilities.

Now, you might wonder why I made a fuss about these small, seemingly irrelevant details when they cannot possibly help you win a football match, but I happen to think that a club and a team is built by paying attention to the little things and making sure they are all in order. Once they are, you can begin to work on the bigger things.

As we worked to get fitter, I asked the players to recognise how much better it felt to be in good physical condition, how it required less effort to complete their runs and how it could help them perform better in matches. Some of my players might think I was too strong with them at times, but I did try to encourage and convince people rather than dictate to them. It sounds patronising, like the sort of thing a schoolteacher tells a reluctant child, but the work was for their benefit. Of course, none of this was compulsory. As I told them when they started grumbling, if they didn't fancy it, they could always ask for a transfer to another club. That usually worked a treat.

Once I had imposed my way of working, I had to figure out what the players were capable of and test them to see what they were made of. Did I have enough in the squad to win promotion? The funny thing about footballers is that almost all of them think they are better than the level at which they are playing. In a way, that's a vital quality to have because you want players who think they can operate at a higher level. But thinking it and showing it on the pitch are very different things. At one of our early training sessions, I asked them: 'Who here thinks they are a Fourth Division footballer?' None of them put their hand up. 'But you finished seventh in the Fourth Division last year, so that makes you Fourth Division players. If we believe we are better than that, we have to prove it by winning enough matches to win the Fourth Division champi-onship. Then we can call ourselves a Third Division team.'

There was some potential in the squad but I didn't get a sense that they had been coached to play as a unit. This may sound a daft thing to say, but did they know how to win football matches? You might think: 'Well, they were professional players, of course they did,' but I'm not so sure. For example, did they look at the game from any other perspective than their own?

Did they understand and appreciate the roles of each of their team-mates and know how the team fitted together?

A good example was Ross Jenkins, who was a bit like Percy Freeman, one of my favourites at Lincoln City, in that he was tall, naturally good in the air and people had a habit of underestimating his ability when he had the ball at his feet. As a youngster, Ross had played for Crystal Palace in the First Division. He'd been transferred to Watford just after they had been relegated to the Third Division – presumably signed to score the goals to fire the team to promotion back to the Second Division, but it hadn't worked out like that. During his time at Watford, Ross had endured some very lean spells and, because centre-forwards are judged on their goalscoring record, he had been criticised. It hadn't helped that Watford had also been relegated to the Fourth Division in that time.

By the time I met Ross, he was twenty-six, almost twenty-seven, and if he wasn't careful he was going to find it difficult to stay in the professional game. When I canvassed opinion about him, people would turn the corners of their mouths down and scrunch up their faces. They didn't write him off, but they didn't give him a ringing endorsement either.

Ross was the archetypal ugly duckling in that he was six feet four inches tall, all arms and legs and he had a running style that didn't make people fall in love with him. He was tall and strong but he wasn't a bully either because he didn't have a nasty streak. I asked one of my defenders what he found most difficult about marking Ross in training and he said: 'He's all sharp elbows and he has a knack of finding space and getting away from me even though he's that big he should be easy to mark.' I felt Ross could be coached to use his assets and ability more effectively. And that, in a nutshell, is the essence of football management.

I watched Ross closely in those early weeks and I recognised that, although he was good in the air and could flick the ball on with surprising accuracy, he was also excellent at bringing the ball under control with his chest, thighs and feet. Sometimes it took him two or three touches to get the ball down from a height but he could use his body tremendously well to shield the ball from opposing defenders. Ross could get the ball under control when we had no right to expect him to do so. In fact, I sometimes thought that if we fired the ball out of a cannon at him he'd have a better than fifty-fifty chance of bringing it down. He was good under pressure and he could lay the ball off to a midfielder or a wide player and then move to take up a new position, all the while keeping the central defender who was marking him occupied and on his toes. I felt we had something we could work with.

I used many of the same strategies and techniques that had worked for me at Lincoln City. Jim McGuigan's 'shadowplay' training sessions may have bored them senseless at times, but it worked. We developed a style of play that was about attacking quickly and with purpose. It was exciting play but I suppose this is where my reputation for so-called 'long-ball' football started. But at that time no one was critical of our style because we were a winning football team. We won thirty of our forty-six league matches and scored eighty-five goals.

We won the Fourth Division championship with a 1-0 win at Scunthorpe United. My dad was working that afternoon and it was one occasion where he didn't have to be shy about reporting on one of my successes. After the game I climbed up the steps to the little wooden press box and sat beside him, just as I had done when I was a boy, and we had a little chat and shared the moment.

One of the most enjoyable achievements of my career was winning over that group of players and helping them to make the most of the ability they had. If I had sat them down during the early days of the 1977-78 season and told them that we would not only win the Fourth Division championship at the first attempt but that a significant number of them would go straight through the Third Division the following season, and that four of them – Steve Sherwood, Ian Bolton, Ross Jenkins and Luther Blissett – would go on to play for Watford in the First Division, I think they'd have thought I was mad, equally as mad as I had thought Elton John to be when he said he wanted to take Watford into European competition. But we did it, and when the season was over I invited everyone to our house for a party where we celebrated together.

I don't want to give the impression that I had inherited a bunch of no-hopers who hadn't worked hard in their lives and didn't have a clue about how to play the game – because that wasn't the case at all – but I do think I raised standards to a level many of them had not been asked to aspire to before and I introduced ideas that challenged them. Some of them may have been hesitant at first but they soon realised that by training the way I asked them to, by doing the simple things effectively and supporting their team-mates on the pitch, they would win many more matches than they lost and that meant win bonuses and a little bit of adulation. And they realised that a winning dressing room is a wonderful place to be.

10

A guiding influence

One day, not very long after I had started work at Watford, an envelope arrived in my office addressed to 'Mr Graham Taylor, The Manager, Watford Football Club'. There was nothing particularly unusual about that, but the stiffness of the envelope and the gently sloping lettering, written in rich blue ink with a fountain pen, caught my eye. Inside were a couple of sheets of high-quality, watermarked writing paper and, as I saw the name of the sender, Bertie Mee, I wondered why he could be writing to me.

I got to the end of the letter and I still wasn't too sure because Bertie wasn't writing to me asking for a job – I think he would have been too proud for that – he was simply making me aware that he was available. I must be honest here and say that it crossed my mind to gently place Bertie's letter in the wastepaper bin because I still remembered how he had spoken to me when I was just starting out at Lincoln City and I'd phoned him to ask if he would loan me one of his Arsenal reserve-team players. But I knew that double-winning football managers did not grow on trees and that if he was available, I might be able to take advantage of his experience and knowledge, so I mentioned it to Elton and asked if I could invite Bertie in for a meeting, warning him that it might cost us a few quid to offer him a job. Not for the last time, Elton said: 'You're the football manager, Graham, it's your call.'

I am so glad I picked up the phone and called Bertie because he turned out to be such a huge influence on the club, and a tremendous help to me. His official title was assistant manager, but he was so much more than that to me. Often you hear people ask who motivates the manager and who picks him up when he's down after a bad defeat. Well, I like to think I didn't need much motivating but Bertie was, in many ways, my manager. At Lincoln I'd had a good relationship with Heneage Dove, the chairman, as well as Bert Loxley, the physio and coach. Both men were older than me, more experienced than me, and could offer a different perspective. At Watford, my boss, Elton John, was younger than me and – although I didn't consciously go searching for an older man to join my staff – I think on some level I understood that I needed someone to keep me in check and to question what I was doing from time to time. So I appointed Bertie Mee as assistant manager.

A Fourth Division club hiring one of the greatest managers in the history of the English game caused a bit of a stir, but it was beneficial straight away because of the influence Bertie had on everyone at the club. His arrival showed people we were not messing around, that we meant business, and it sent a message to the players that we were serious about improving the club on all fronts.

I've often wondered whether Bertie ever felt tempted to interfere in what I was doing. I am sure he didn't agree with every decision I made, but I am so grateful he stood back and let me work my way. Having been manager at Arsenal for ten years, he knew far more about management, particularly at the top level, than I did, although it could equally be said he didn't know all that much about the Fourth Division. It must have been a culture shock for him but he adapted brilliantly. He inspired us to strive to be the best we could be and was never snooty about some aspects of the club we couldn't afford to improve. How easy it would have been for him to start every sentence with the words: 'When I was at Arsenal, we did it like this…,' but that wasn't in his nature at all.

Bertie was only fifty-eight when he joined us, which surprises me when I think about it now, but I suppose people in their late fifties seemed older then than they do now. He was quite a stern man and he certainly lived up to his reputation as a disciplinarian. He probably frightened the life out of the younger players – and some of the older ones, for that matter – because he had a very sharp tongue at times. He could bring someone down not just a peg or two but half a dozen rungs with a sentence if he thought they were getting ideas above their station. It was never malicious but there was an edge to him if he thought standards were not being met. He hated poor time-keeping and untidiness and his values and ideals were exactly the ones I wanted to establish at the club. He had the authority of a military man, which probably shouldn't be a surprise because he had been in the Royal Army Medical Corps as a physio. He believed in physical fitness and mental discipline and he had such an economical way with words that he could get his point across very concisely. It wasn't easy to misunderstand Bertie.

Now, as I reflect on our relationship, I appreciate his work even more than I did at the time and I wonder whether, in my later years, I could have done for a young manager what he did for me. Somehow, I doubt I could have. Back then, I was full of energy and enthusiasm, in a hurry to make my mark on the team and the club, and far more concerned with making progress to worry too much about any mistakes I might be making. Bertie was the calming influence I needed. He would force me to slow down a bit or force me to think about a situation from more than just my own perspective, but he did that by asking questions of me rather than by giving his own opinion. It must have taken a lot of discipline on his part but he rarely offered an opinion until he was asked. Of course, when Bertie was asked to give his opinion he would do so without holding back.

I have to smile now, realising how full of myself I must have been, hiring a man who had won the Football League championship and the FA Cup to work as my assistant. That's not to say that I didn't occasionally do things just to make sure Bertie, and

104

everyone else at the club, knew who was in charge. We used to schedule our staff meeting for 8.30 a.m., before the players got in, and I sometimes turned up at 8.40 a.m., deliberately late, just to reinforce the point that I was the boss. I knew it drove Bertie mad but he never said anything – he didn't even say to me in private: 'You know, the manager really should set an example by turning up on time.'

There was never any doubt that Bertie was on our side but I do ask myself what he thought of Elton and me, the flamboyant rock star and the tracksuit manager. I can't imagine Elton's dress sense – which was at its loudest in the late 1970s – was Bertie's cup of tea at all. There was one match away from home in those early days, when Elton was dressed as Elton, and there was some discussion among our hosts' directors whether Elton's clothes complied with the dress code for entry to the boardroom. Bertie overheard this and nipped it in the bud before there was a problem.

'Gentlemen, I gather there may be a problem with our chairman's attire,' he said. 'Can you please confirm your dress code?'

After they ran through their requirements, he paused and replied: 'Mr John is wearing a jacket, necktie, trousers and shoes. Now, they may not be to your taste, and they may not be to mine, for that matter, but they do not bar him from entry.'

11

Elton and me

My friendship with Elton has lasted nearly four decades and I consider him to be the younger brother I never had. In recent years whenever we speak on the phone we still just pick up where we left off. He asks how my family are doing and I ask about his, and then we invariably end up talking about football and that usually involves reminiscing about our time together at Watford.

I often think back to my first match as Watford's manager in August 1977. It was a League Cup tie against Reading at Vicarage Road and as I took my seat on the bench just before kick-off I looked along the touchline and saw an unmistakable figure in platform shoes striding towards me. Turning to whoever was sitting alongside me, I said: 'Where does the chairman think he's going?'

I watched as he walked in front of me and took a seat on the end of the bench a few places along the row. Elton sat down as if it was the most natural thing in the world. I think my mouth was probably wide open in surprise but I didn't say anything because I didn't want to create any kind of scene by asking him what he thought he was doing.

At that time, we didn't have a dugout at Vicarage Road. In fact, for many years we had nothing more sophisticated for the managers, coaching staff, physiotherapists and substitutes to sit on than the sort of bench you'd see in a school gymnasium. As the years went on and we rose through the divisions, I was asked if I wanted a proper covered dugout to be built in front of the main stand but I refused because the home end was still uncovered and I felt that if the supporters were going to stand out in all weathers to watch their team then the least I could do was experience the conditions with them. When we played the top sides in the cups and later reached the First Division, I did chuckle when the opposition managers realised they'd be sitting out in the rain all afternoon. There was one memorable day when we played Manchester United in the FA Cup third round and Ron Atkinson came out of the tunnel, clocked where the bench was, looked down at the sodden turf and his expensive handmade Italian shoes and took a deep breath before stepping into the mud. To make things worse for him, we beat United 1-0 that afternoon. We probably still owe Ron a new pair of shoes for that.

I was a little surprised that Elton had chosen to sit alongside me for my first match in charge, not least because the worm's-eye view gave such a poor impression of the play. Once or twice, he stood up to face the supporters in the stand behind us and clapped his hands, imploring them to get behind the team. Every time we made a mistake, or when the referee gave a decision against us, Elton's body language drew attention.

After all the players had gone home, Elton and I were in my office talking about the game, which we had won.

'Do you usually sit on the bench?' I asked.

I told Elton that I didn't have a problem with him sitting on the bench, although I must admit I'd have preferred him to sit in the directors' box. But it was his club, after all, although I thought he had to be aware that if we were to experience any kind of success, all eyes would be on him. If the supporters or the press saw him throw his arms in the air because we missed a chance to score, what sort of impression would that make? I appreciated that he was a lifelong supporter of the club and he desperately wanted it to be successful but – if we were going to do this properly and if we were to be taken seriously – Elton needed to take on the role of chairman and be the club's figurehead in boardrooms up and down the country.

To be fair to Elton, he was as good as gold about it and at the end of the conversation we agreed that he would sit in the directors' box. I can't say he never ventured down to the touch-line again, because on a few occasions in those first couple of seasons he did, but he always behaved impeccably.

You might think I was very naïve but when I first met Elton, I had no idea he was gay. As I said, I didn't keep up to date with the pop charts let alone the gossip columns. Rita might say: 'Come on, Graham, how could you not know?' because Elton had come out as bisexual in a magazine interview a year or so earlier, but I genuinely didn't know about his sexuality when I accepted the job and it would not have made any difference to me if I had.

Having said that, I had worked in the game all my adult life and, to my knowledge, had never met a gay footballer up to that point. I talked earlier about the culture shock of going into a football club's dressing room as a teenager and seeing naked men getting in and out of the bath with everything swinging away. The conversation could be very macho and so I imagine being a gay footballer would have been very, very difficult in those days. I'm not all that certain it would be much easier nowadays. People talk about the abuse an openly gay player might get from the supporters but I happen to think the dressing room can be a far harsher environment.

Elton told me about the abuse he got from supporters at some away matches. He told me about one particular song chanted at him the previous season as he walked across the car park after the match at Rochdale. The song started with the words: 'Don't bend down when Elton John's around…' I won't dignify it by going any further but it goes without saying it was offensive and well beyond what anyone should have to put up with. Back then perhaps people thought it was funny, or saw it as a harmless joke, and it's certainly the case that attitudes at the time were different.

'Don't worry,' I told him, 'we won't be going to Rochdale too many times.'

I tried to lighten the situation with a joke but the fact of the matter was that this problem was not confined to Rochdale. Having half the people in a football ground chanting anything about you can be unpleasant, but as a player or manager it goes with the territory from time to time. If a team's performance is bad, the supporters are entitled to let you know about it, although they should stop well short of being abusive and using foul language. Being singled out for your footballing or managerial shortcomings is one thing, but being abused for your sexuality is quite another and it struck me immediately that there was simply no place for this sort of thing in the game. As with racist abuse, which was a serious problem at some grounds, it would take time to change people's behaviour and make them realise that it was unacceptable to abuse others because of the colour of their skin or their sexuality. It was one of the things I wanted to try to change and I made it clear that at Watford I wanted them to be vocal in their support of the team but that I would not put up with swearing or abuse.

Elton's ability to brush off the chants of a crowd amazed me but it also saddened me. There's something about the anonymity of a crowd that gives people the impression they have the security to say things they would never dream of saying if they were on their own. In no way does that make it right, of course, but back then it was tolerated. No one was arrested for shouting obscene things in Elton's direction and there was no outrage. Elton just had to sit there and put up with it.

What did hurt him was when he overheard individuals saying unpleasant things about him. In my second season at Watford, we lost an important away game and we were all very disappointed after the match because we had not played well. It was one of those days where we had to take a deep breath and go into the bar with our heads high and our lips tight because there was an atmosphere of jubilation from the opposition directors. They were enjoying rubbing it in, possibly because we were at the top of the division and they weren't. Elton was particularly annoyed by the defeat and he had gone to the toilet to sit in one of the cubicles to compose himself when two of the opposition directors went in to use the urinals. One said to the other: 'We showed that poof today, didn't we, eh?'

I'd rarely seen Elton so angry as when he told me what had happened. He wanted to confront the man he thought had made the comment but I said: 'Here's what we are going to do. We're going to go into the bar, have a drink, look them in the eye and congratulate them on their victory, then wish them the best of luck for the rest of the season and get out of here. Now, we may not mean it, but we're going to say it. Let them have their victory today and at the end of the season we'll see where we all finish. We are not going to give them the satisfaction of knowing they've hurt you. You're not going to change minds like that by confronting them here. Instead of thinking of you as a poof, they'll think of you as a poof and a bad loser so let's not give them that opportunity.'

Looking back almost forty years, I don't know if that was the right thing to say to Elton or not. Was rising above their behaviour actually giving them the right to think it was OK to say those sort of things about other people? I don't know. Perhaps attitudes might have changed sooner had people been tackled for their choice of language back then. However, I do know that at that time it would not have helped to have started an argument in the boardroom.

As far as I was concerned, Elton's sexuality was his business. I do remember very early on making a joke and then, as the words left my mouth, holding my breath because I suddenly realised I wasn't sure how the joke would be taken.

'I don't care what you do, Elton,' I said, 'as long as you don't try to kiss me.'

'Don't worry, Graham,' he said, as quick as a flash, 'you're not my type.'

My working relationship with Elton was first class from the beginning because, although he was passionate about making Watford successful, he did not interfere in how I ran the club.

He was a very, very wealthy man and with the way football was in those days, he could probably have afforded to buy Arsenal, Tottenham, Manchester United, Liverpool or any of the top clubs in the country. But Watford was his club.

Owning the club gave him something to focus his energy on away from music and a way to escape the demands of record-company executives and tour managers. During those first couple of years, he was always around because he had decided to take a break from touring and that gave us a chance to work together and to get to know each other well.

We were very successful right from the start, winning the Fourth Division title and following it with immediate promotion from the Third Division. Elton came to almost every game and he learned to become a football-club chairman and director, leading from the front and setting an example without ever stepping on my toes. He gave me tremendous power and I was in a position where I had the final say on everything. On plenty of occasions I left decisions to others but, if I had an opinion, I was free to express it and if I felt strongly something should be done a certain way, that was the way it was done. Occasionally there was opposition from others around the boardroom table but Elton would always step in and remind the directors that he was paying me to make these decisions. To be fair to our directors, Jim Harrowell, Geoff Smith and Muir Stratford, and the senior management team of Bertie Mee and Eddie Plumley, who came in as chief executive at Bertie's suggestion, they rarely stood in my way, they always listened and they aimed to help by offering their own experience and advice rather than imposing it upon me. I really was tremendously lucky to have such a collection of people at the club, and if there was ever resentment at this young upstart from Lincoln coming in and taking over they hid it well.

When I look back at what we achieved, it's very difficult to separate the outcome from the journey and it's too easy to assume that we felt confident in ourselves every step of the way. But I remember the long conversations I'd have with Elton about the club, the team, the opposition and certain players, and what comes to mind is the energy we both had and our drive and determination to take the club forward. I loved talking to him because, although he wasn't what I call a 'football person', he was very knowledgeable and he always had an interesting point of view. He always wanted to know my thoughts but he left the football management to me and he never, ever blamed me for wasting his money if a player I'd signed turned out to be a dud, which did happen every now and then. I'd told him it would cost him a million pounds to take Watford to the First Division and when we finally achieved promotion in 1982, I totted up all the transfer fees and calculated that I'd spent about £750,000. I joked that I reckoned he owed me £250,000 – but when you take into account the amount spent on improving the ground and the facilities, Elton had put a lot more than a million into Watford Football Club.

Elton wanted to get to know the players and, more importantly, he wanted them to know he was a supporter of the club. He was very down to earth and he disliked formalities so if it had been up to him the players would have called him Elton, but I said to him right at the start: 'To them, I am the gaffer and you are Mr Chairman and that's the way it's going to be.'

Elton was not just a pop star, he was one of the most recognisable people in the world, but at Watford he was just Elton and he relished being in an environment where people treated him normally. They respected him, of course, but they didn't defer to him, and I think he liked that. He had an excellent sense of humour and was very sharp, but he was the butt of the jokes just as often as anyone else and I don't think he'd have wanted it any other way.

He cared about my family because he knew how important they were to me. When I arrived at the club he had made sure we'd been able to buy a nice home in Mandeville Close in Watford so that I could bring Rita and the girls down south as soon as possible and didn't have to live in a hotel by myself for too long. Elton's stepfather Fred was a painter and decorator and he made sure the house was spruced up so we could move in. He arranged for me to have a club car, a Jaguar, and as I think about all this now, it's remarkable how much faith he put in me right from day one. Put it this way, if it had been down to me, I'd have expected a promotion or two before giving the manager a nice car to drive around in.

Often he came round to our house for a meal and a game of cards, although that almost ended in tears once when I realised that he and Rita had been colluding with one another in order to ensure I lost. When I twigged what was going on, they giggled like schoolchildren, which made it worse, and I lost it, tipping the coffee table over and sending the cards flying. That just turned their giggles into roars of laughter and in the end I had to admit it was pretty funny. Between them they had a wonderful way of ensuring I didn't get too full of myself.

Those are the days I remember most fondly, when we were making our way and just beginning to ruffle a few feathers in the game. Elton loved the idea that it was us against the world, and he'd often say: 'Come on, Graham, we'll show them.'

12

'It's not real work, is it?'

There's no denying that Elton attracted attention that we would not otherwise have got as a lower-division football club, and the tabloid newspapers in particular enjoyed any opportunity to call us 'Elton's Rocket Men'. In October 1978, we put ourselves on the footballing map with our first big cup upset when we went to Old Trafford and knocked Manchester United out of the League Cup. Luther Blissett, who was still only twenty, scored with two fantastic headers, both from attacking moves and runs that we had worked on in training. We had already knocked a First Division side, Newcastle United, out of the competition in the previous round but that had been a home game. This was something quite different because it was at Old Trafford in front of more than 40,000 people – by far the largest crowd most of my team would have played in front of at that time.

We trailed 1-0 at half-time and, as a Third Division team, it would have been easy to have folded or, at best, to have shut up shop and got away with a respectable 1-0 or 2-0 defeat. But I had spent a year and a bit drumming into the players that we were to treat all opponents the same, we were not going to be over-awed by the badge on their shirts, or the stadium, the crowd, or the reputations of the players we were up against. That is far easier said than done, of course, because footballers are people and people can be easily affected by what's going on around them, especially if the experience is a new one. I obviously didn't want us to be given a hiding, but at half-time I told them that I'd prefer them to get hammered trying to win the match than to meekly slip out of Old Trafford without leaving a mark. They took my words in and they were magnificent in the second half.

What made it all the more pleasing was that Elton was there that night, and I remember seeing the pride written all over his face as he was interviewed by the television people. That made me feel good because I knew there were at least a couple of thousand Watford supporters who had made the journey up to Manchester and who would be travelling home with exactly the same feeling. I also remember getting back into the dressing room and seeing Dennis Booth sitting on the bench in just his shorts, talking through Luther's second goal, which had come from his cross. In fact, Dennis mentioned that goal quite a few times over the weeks that followed and the other players liked to tease him about it. I've watched it since on the internet and it was a perfect example of what we were trying to do. Brian Pollard, our little winger, got the ball on the right-hand touchline and ran into the space ahead of him but released the ball before the United defender had an opportunity to challenge him. He played it (on the ground, I should point out) up to Ross Jenkins, who had run towards the corner flag, bringing his marker, Gordon McQueen, with him. Ross controlled the ball neatly and played it back to John Stirk, the right full-back, who found Dennis Booth in space near the corner of the penalty area. Boothy took one touch and then crossed it for Luther to attack. Luther was arriving from deep, in between two United defenders, neither of whom was really sure who had the responsibility of marking him. And because Ross had pulled McQueen out of position, United's defence was all at sea.

Of course, everything worked out perfectly on that occasion and it led to a match-winning goal, but it was very satisfying because we had worked on our movement in training. It demonstrated to the players that what we were trying to do could be effective against one of the best sides in the country as well as down at our level. I'd been telling them that if we moved the ball with pace and purpose, if each player worked on his movement so that when he released the ball he took up a fresh position and tried to shake off his marker so he could be available to receive the ball again, and if we did all this while not leaving ourselves exposed at the back and vulnerable to a counter-attack, we could beat teams that were supposedly much better than us.

We went all the way to the semi-finals of the League Cup that season, but a 3-1 defeat at Nottingham Forest in the first leg proved to be too much for us to overcome at Vicarage Road, where we drew 0-0. We were underdogs, of course, but whenever I spoke to the players, or to the press, I made it clear that we were not just happy to reach the last four of the competition and that we wanted and expected to make it to Wembley for the final. I felt it could be too easy to exceed expectations and then settle for that rather than trying to press on and achieve something really special.

Once the League Cup run was over for us, our focus was on securing promotion from the Third Division and we did manage to do that, even if we stumbled a bit towards the end of the season. I look back at the results and I remember the jitters we all felt around Easter time, when we faced two games in two days. On Good Friday, we lost 3-0 at home to Colchester United, which was a very poor performance and result. We had to leave Vicarage Road by coach straight after the match so we could face Shrewsbury Town, our biggest rivals for promotion (and eventual champions), the following afternoon. We drew 1-1 there, which turned out to be a very important result but because we lost another couple of away games – to Swindon Town and Carlisle United, who were both on our tail – there was a lot of tension around the club as we approached the final four matches.

We'd spent a bit of money on a couple of players from higher divisions to try to get us over the line, and in a way that had changed things for us. Ray Train was a winger we signed from First Division Bolton Wanderers, and Steve Sims was a centre-half who had played in the top flight for Leicester City. Sims was an England under-21 and 'B' international, and the £200,000 we paid for him was a record for a Third Division club at that time. While Watford was not exactly a pressure cooker and the local press didn't shine the brightest spotlight on us, it was still a price tag that weighed on Steve at the beginning and it took him a while to settle. In fact, it proved to me that some very good players struggle in the lower divisions for a variety of reasons, some because the game is too slow for them and they're just not on the right wavelength. I'm not sure that was necessarily the case with Steve but in those first few months he was not the player I'd hoped I was signing – although he more than made up for it later on and he was absolutely superb for me not just at Watford but at Aston Villa, too.

Anyway, as the 1978-79 season drew to a close, there were half a dozen clubs bunched up at the top of the table and we were as likely to win the championship as miss out altogether. I hadn't really appreciated it at the time, but a decade or so earlier Watford had endured a few near-misses trying to get out of the Third Division before Ken Furphy finally achieved it, and people were thinking back to those times and fearing we were going to blow it again.

No matter how much I tried to reassure people and cajole people into thinking positively, I always felt that uncertainty creeping back in. I was also struggling to convince the players that they were capable of finishing the job. I tried a number of tactics to try to influence the way they were thinking and it was as big a test of my man-management skills as anything I'd faced since starting my career.

In the end, everything came down to the final game – a rearranged match against Hull City that had been postponed earlier in the season. We had to win to make sure we went up.

There were nine days between our final two matches and I can remember it felt like an eternity. Trying to keep training fresh was a challenge, especially as I didn't want to over-work them at the end of a long campaign or risk someone getting injured by playing full-blooded practice matches. Months earlier we'd arranged to go to France to play a friendly against Sochaux. The arrangement was that they would come to Vicarage Road the following season but we had this game planned and – even though it fell only a few days before the critical match against Hull – I decided to honour the commitment.

I decided to do something out of the ordinary, partly to amuse myself and the players and partly to give them something else to think about than the bloomin' Hull game. Before the game, I said: 'Right, lads. We're going to be playing in Europe in a few years' time so I want you to imagine that this is the first leg of a Uefa Cup tie and I want you to play for a 0-0 draw.'

They took the challenge seriously and there was a lot of sideways passing and very little attacking. It was probably the only time I'd ever sent a side out with the intention of not winning and it was also the most boring match I've ever sat through, but we got our 0-0 draw, although we didn't impress our hosts all that much. They were so annoyed with us that they refused to come to Watford for the second match, and I did feel a bit bad about that because it was a bit naughty of me.

The day before we faced Hull, as the players arrived at our training ground and got changed, I could sense the anxiety. I got them to jog round the pitch for quarter of an hour to warm up, then I told them to find a bit of space and lie down on the grass.

It was a sunny day with a few pretty, fluffy clouds in the sky. As they lay down, looking a bit puzzled, probably wondering what their mad gaffer was up to now, I walked between them and talked.

'It's a good life, this,' I said. 'All we've got to worry about is winning a game of football. That's all. It's not real work, is it? We're very lucky people, really. We've not got a care in the world.'

I could feel a few of them looking at me.

'But you know who's luckiest of all? I am, because I'm the gaffer and if I fancy the rest of the day off, I can just take it off.'

I paused for a moment.

'So I think I'll pop home, take the wife for a bit of lunch and then spend the rest of the afternoon sitting in the garden.'

I could tell the players were wondering if I was winding them up. Then I said: 'Come on, what are you waiting for? Let's all have the day off and I'll see you tomorrow.'

The following night we hammered Hull City 4-0 and claimed our place in the Second Division.

13

Time to take stock

We finished eighteenth at the end of our first season in the Second Division and, although we were never really in any danger of getting relegated, it was my toughest year in football management up to that point. We struggled for goals, particularly away from home (we scored only twelve on our travels in the league all season), and I think some of the supporters wondered if we were going to survive at that level, let alone push on upwards. I knew I would have to begin to change the team but I waited until the autumn for a couple of reasons. Firstly I wanted to give the players who had earned promotion a chance to show what they could do at the higher level. This was not a sentimental decision but a practical one. I had a feeling some of them might not make the step up, and others were getting older, but the thing about footballers is that you never know who might surprise you when they are challenged. The second reason for taking my time was that I wanted to have a good look at the players I was interested in signing to make sure I wasn't wasting the chairman's money.

I'd established a network of scouts when I started at Watford and we'd added people here and there to give us coverage of the whole country. I'd speak to our scouts on the phone regularly and I'd read their reports and I'd watch a lot of games myself so I was really plugged into what was happening at every level of the game. If someone was highly recommended, and was within our price range, I'd send Tom Walley to watch him and if Tom gave the player the thumbs up I'd go and see for myself.

This was a part of the job I loved, particularly in those days before I was a recognisable face. I loved going to watch midweek matches when I had my eye on a player. I'd finish up at the ground early and then drive into London and park up at one of the stations before taking the train north out of Euston or King's Cross. I'd never call the club in question and ask for a ticket – partly because I wouldn't want to give them any hint I was interested in one of their players, but mostly because I wanted to watch the game from the terraces where the supporters stood. I'd get off the train, buy some fish and chips on the walk to the ground and then watch the game, keeping my ear on the conversations to see if I could pick up what people were saying about the player I was there to see. I'd move around a bit and watch the game from different areas of the terraces and it always surprised me what a different impression I'd get of a game of football standing behind the goal compared to sitting on the halfway line. By standing up high, near the back, or down low at the front I'd notice different things about the match. Supporters can often be very revealing about their team, especially when they have no idea they're being overheard by a football manager, and I liked to listen out for their comments. If I was watching a winger, for example, I could work out very quickly if the supporters were frustrated by the lack of delivery from crosses or by the player's refusal to drop back and help out on the defensive side of the game. The supporters would have been watching the player every week and they'd be well aware of his shortcomings. I'm not saying I based my transfer policy on what supporters said about players, but it was an interesting part of my research.

After the game, I'd head back to the station and get on the overnight sleeper train back to London. I'd have a little glass of something to help me sleep, then I'd wake up and head to the diner's car for a cooked breakfast before getting off the train and driving my car back to the club for the morning's training session. Those trips were so valuable because on the train I had time to clear my mind and think about things without anyone else around. I must have done a dozen or so of those trips and one of my favourites was to go up to Newcastle, so if there was a chance to watch a player at St James' Park, I'd take it. I know I signed Wilf Rostron after having watched him play for Sunderland at Newcastle one evening.

No one at the club would know I'd gone on my overnight trip and when I got back in to work the following morning I liked to have a chat with Tom Walley or Bertie Mee about who I'd seen. 'I think I've got one if we can afford him,' I'd say. It was exciting and the buzz of signing someone was what I imagined it felt like to be a shopaholic let loose in a department store.

Before signing a player, I liked to watch him play a handful of times, and at least one of those times had to be away from home because there are plenty of players who are very good at home but tend to disappear a bit away from home. But of course, no matter how much you watch someone play, you also need to know they will fit into the dressing room and so I'd like to find out about the player's character too.

When I was happy the player would add something to the squad, I then did my background research on the person I was signing. One of the things supporters tend to overlook a little bit is that footballers are just like the rest of us. They have personal lives, families and friends. Moving from one area of the country to another can be disruptive. I knew I was not just signing the player, I was signing his wife and children too. A good player can be easily unsettled if his wife is unhappy or if the children have difficulty at school. I wanted to get to know a player's family and show them what sort of club we were running and what sort of man I was. I couldn't promise a family indefinite stability because footballers move on, but I could make sure that a footballer's wife knew I had her husband's interests at heart. I also asked around to find out what sort of person a player was and what he was into. Was he popular, was he a joker or a moaner? Did he like a drink? Did he spend his afternoons in the betting shop? I can't say I never signed a drinker or a gambler but I had to be confident they had things under control. I'm not saying I was unique in this respect – I'm sure most managers did their homework on the players they were signing – but it was an aspect of the job I took very seriously because when you make the decision to spend money on a player there should not be too many doubts in your mind.

Of course, I didn't get every decision right either. I'd say over the course of a manager's career if you could say that roughly a third of all signings worked out well and added real value to the team, a third did OK and a third didn't make the grade, then you'd be talking about a manager who had done pretty well. The key to being successful in the transfer market is to make sure the flops are the cheap ones. With transfer fees the way they are now, I use the word 'cheap' relatively, but even back then I was aware that we were spending money that wouldn't be easy to come by.

There was one moment that autumn that convinced me I had to bring in a bit more know-how. The coach pulled up outside Stamford Bridge before our match against Chelsea and the players didn't budge. Usually they would be up and off the coach straight away but I looked round and realised they were waiting for me to make the first move. It wasn't that none of them had played at Chelsea before, but as a group they seemed hesitant. Perhaps they weren't certain where the dressing rooms were. I'm not sure I knew where they were at that time either but it struck me that there wasn't a leader among them who had a great deal of experience at this level. Chelsea were a big club – although they weren't the club they are today, of course – and I think they represented territory that we weren't all that familiar with. I have thought about that game a lot over the years and wondered whether I am exaggerating in my own mind the significance of it, but I can remember it being a day when I realised something about my squad. We didn't perform that afternoon. We lost 2-0, which wasn't a terrible result for a newly promoted team, but we lost in a very meek manner. We didn't close the Chelsea players down or make life uncomfortable for them, and after the match

I heard one of my players, Roger Joslyn, say something that confirmed what I was thinking. 'They weren't as good as I thought they'd be,' he said. I loved Roger because he was as honest as the day is long and he would give everything for the team. He had played almost every game for two seasons, but I think even he would admit that he was a very good lower-division footballer. When I heard Roger, of all people, say that, it made me realise that we couldn't afford to think of ourselves as the underdogs in the Second Division.

Between October 1979 and January 1980, I spent almost £600,000 of the club's money on five players who all had experience of playing in the top two divisions. There was a goalkeeper from Brighton and Hove Albion called Eric Steele, who went on to be a goalkeeping coach at Manchester United for many years; a right-back called Mel Henderson and left-winger Wilf Rostron from Sunderland; Martin Patching, a midfielder from Wolverhampton Wanderers; and Malcolm Poskett, a striker from Brighton. They each improved the team in their way, but as the season ended I wondered if I had turned away from my own ideas about the game too much. Had I let the Second Division alter me too much? We won just about enough games to stay in the division and we had a good run in the FA Cup before losing to Arsenal in the quarter-finals, but I didn't enjoy our play. We weren't scoring goals or creating enough chances for my liking. Was it because we were playing in the way we thought we should be playing, rather than getting at the opposition and trying to beat them?

At the end of the season, I felt rather flat. Elton had been away for much of the year, results had not been all that good and there were murmurings among the supporters that perhaps I'd reached my level or we'd been found out, which was an understandable response because it's what supporters often think. Elton's reaction to all this was to offer me a new five-year contract, which I suppose was the vote of confidence I needed. Having said that, it was smart on Elton's part because if he'd waited, it would have cost him a lot more money.

I wouldn't say I had a period of soul-searching that summer but I did make a conscious effort to evaluate what it was I wanted from my team. I wanted to keep moving forwards rather than settle for Second Division survival, and a letter I had received earlier in the season was to give me the confidence to back my instincts and the impetus to push on again.

Back in October 1979, Vicarage Road had hosted an under-21 international between England and Denmark and I had watched from the stand as England won an uninspiring game 1-0. Luther Blissett played in the match and I barely recognised my own player as he was reduced to a peripheral figure by England's ponderous play. It was almost as boring as our friendly match against Sochaux. Just as I would sometimes wonder later that season whether my Watford team had seemed to play the way they were expected to play, I had the same feeling about the England youngsters that night. They played what they thought international football was supposed to be, rather than making the most of their natural gifts and playing to their strengths. The pace of the game was slow as they passed the ball from side to side and backwards rather than looking to attack and hurt the Danes. After the game, a journalist asked me what I had thought and I was perhaps a little too honest. I said that if international football was going to be played that way, I could do without it. My remarks were reported by the local paper and picked up a couple of days later by the national press, and shortly after that a letter arrived on my desk from a man called Charles Reep.

Reep had been a wing commander in the RAF and was now a statistician who had watched thousands of football matches and had analysed the games, using a system of shorthand he had devised to note down every pass, every cross and every shot. From these notes he had drawn a few conclusions about the game, the most notable being his assertions that most goals were scored from moves consisting of three passes or fewer, that there were an average of ten shots on goal per goal scored, and that if a team had twenty shots in a match they had an overwhelming statistical chance of winning the game.

I later found out that in the 1950s, Reep had worked with Stan Cullis, the manager of Wolverhampton Wanderers, and Wolves had won the league playing a direct, fast-paced game that relied on getting the ball forwards quickly and trying to create as many goalscoring chances as possible. At the time I read Reep's letter, I didn't know that, but I was interested in his analytical way of looking at the game.

The dossier Reep sent me had sat in my desk drawer for months simply because I had not found the time to look at it properly. After the season finished I took it home and one night I sat up in bed and read through it. As I read, I found myself thinking there was something in it, because it chimed with many of the things I was already doing. It just provided some statistics to back up some of my own theories. Remember, this was in the days before any detailed computer analysis of football matches. There were no Opta statistics. Nowadays we can all watch a match on television and the graphics will come up saying that the home team has had fifty-six per cent of possession and seven shots on target. But back then, the only televised football were the highlights on *Match of the Day* and *The Big Match*. There were perhaps two or three live matches shown on television each season – the FA Cup final and a couple of England internationals. At Watford we had just started videoing our home games but all we had was a camera on the roof of one of the stands, which offered a fairly basic view of the game.

I went to meet Reep at his home and, although I found what he said very interesting, I didn't agree with all of it. What did strike a chord with me was his conviction that the more shots on target a team had, the greater the probability they'd win the match. When I was at Lincoln, I had made a note of where each goal was scored from and how many passes were in the move leading up to that goal, but Reep had analysis of thousands of games at every level which reinforced my own thoughts.

Where I disagreed with Reep was in his rigid interpretation of his analysis and the set of targets he later devised to work to. For example, he wanted us to win the ball back in the final third a certain number of times in a game, but he also wanted us to play the ball into the final third a certain number of times. My argument was that it would be very hard to achieve both targets in a single match and, in fact, in order to do so we'd have to deliberately lose the ball in the final third in order to win it back again, which was a daft idea. He wouldn't take my point and so we had to agree to differ on that. He also wouldn't come to meet the players and explain his theories face to face, which I found interesting. I concluded that he did not want to be challenged by players.

I used Reep's information the way I would have used any technique I'd learned on a coaching course: I took the bits I agreed with and incorporated them into our training and our play, and I discarded the rest.

We continued our progress upwards in 1980-81, finishing ninth, and I felt that we made a big step forwards that season. I made three key signings, bringing in Pat Rice, who had played in Bertie Mee's double-winning Arsenal team, a midfielder from Oxford United called Les Taylor, and Gerry Armstrong, a centre-forward from Tottenham Hotspur.

At the same time, we were just beginning to enjoy the benefit of investing so heavily in our development of young players. When I arrived at Watford it had been one of the areas I had identified for improvement and Tom Walley had put together a first-class youth system, with teams across all the age groups making us a very attractive club for young players in the area. We were close to London and so we were competing with Tottenham, Arsenal, West Ham, Chelsea and so on, but we finally had a set-up that could compete with them – and arguably we offered a talented young player a greater chance of breaking into the first team than those bigger and more famous clubs. Our first crop of youngsters included Steve Terry, Kenny

Jackett and Nigel Callaghan, all of whom established themselves in the first team as teenagers and went on to have successful careers. The work Tom Walley did was incredible because when he started in 1977 he had barely more than a set of cones that he laid out in the car park outside the stadium and a few footballs. Little over two years later his youth team was among the best in the South East Counties League (the league for junior teams in the region). He had scouts watching games everywhere. If there was a talented lad in Yorkshire or Yeovil, Tom would know about him. All the more remarkable was the fact that when he started we were in the Fourth Division and he knew there was no point discovering boys who could make the grade at that level because by the time they were old enough to challenge for a first-team place we might be in the First or Second Division. So he had to develop youngsters who would be capable of competing with the best in the country when the time came, while the first team itself was nowhere near that level yet. The fact that we clinched promotion to the First Division in May 1982 and two days later our junior team beat Manchester United to win the FA Youth Cup just proves what a great coach Tom Walley was. I must give credit to Steve Harrison and all the others who worked on building our youth set-up into one of the best in the country, too, because it wasn't a one-man job.

By the start of the 1981-82 season, I believed we were ready to challenge for promotion, and the discovery of a seventeen-year-old called John Barnes perhaps proved to be the final piece in the jigsaw.

We'd been tipped off about John by a Watford supporter – a taxi driver, I think he was – who had happened to see him play for Sudbury Court in north-west London. Now, supporters are often contacting football clubs, claiming they've spotted the next Pelé playing for a local pub side, but this guy was insistent and said that Queens Park Rangers had been watching him, so we sent a scout to watch a game and Bertie Mee decided to go along too.

Bertie liked what he saw, got a phone number and called to speak to John's father, Colonel Ken Barnes, who was working as a military attaché at the Jamaican embassy in London at the time. It worked out perfectly for us because they got on very well. As a military man, Bertie was exactly the sort of person Ken Barnes would have related to. As they spoke they realised they had met before, when Ken was manager of the Jamaican national team and Bertie had taken his Arsenal side to Kingston for a friendly match. Bertie said that he felt John had the talent to make a very good career for himself, but Ken explained that the family were due to move back to Jamaica that summer when his posting in London came to an end. So we had to convince Ken Barnes to trust us with his son and allow him to stay in England.

We invited Ken to the club and told him what we stood for and how we worked, assuring him that John would not be left to his own devices. The way we ran the club and the discipline I talked about appealed to Ken and, fortunately for us, he agreed to let his son stay in England for the season to see how it went. We were lucky because other clubs had started to show an interest but by then it was too late because we had already made a very good impression on John's father. John moved into digs with Steve Terry and very quickly became a part of the first-team squad.

People ask me how we found John Barnes playing for a team on a public park in London and I always say that it was partly luck. But when we saw him play it was obvious he had talent. John was a fabulous athlete. He was tall and strong, he had good coordination, great balance and quick feet. When he first did our regular cross-country runs through Cassiobury Park he was faster than everyone else. He was excellent at pretty much anything that involved hand-eye coordination too, whether it was tennis, table tennis or ten-pin bowling. The fact we managed to sign him by giving Sudbury Court a set of football kit makes it the best transfer deal I ever did.

With John Barnes on one wing and Nigel Callaghan on the other, the team had a wonderful balance to it. They were both exceptional wingers but quite different to one another. John could twist a defender inside-out with his skill and beat almost anyone for pace, while Nigel could cross a ball with incredible accuracy even when very tightly marked. I always maintain his delivery was better than David Beckham's.

Midway through the season, with promotion within our grasp, I persuaded Wilf Rostron, who had been in and out of the team as a winger, to try playing at left-back. He'd never been a defender before but I just had a feeling that he was one of those players who would be more effective with the game in front of him. He could also support Barnes and, because he'd been a winger, could overlap him and put in a very good cross. I remember calling Wilf at home on a Thursday evening, two days before we were to play Chelsea at Vicarage Road. I asked him if he thought he could play at left-back and he said yes.

Wilf was a manager's dream. If I put up on the noticeboard that we were all to meet at the ground at 3 a.m. and there would then be a 2,000-mile coach trip to the game, Wilf would be there on time and he wouldn't say a word about anything. He was so professional. His attitude was: 'If that is what we are doing, that's what we are doing,' and in that respect he was a great role model for the younger players. He never looked further ahead than the next game. If I asked him who we were playing a week on Saturday, he wouldn't know and I was fine with that because he concentrated on the job in front of him and trusted the management staff to let him know what he needed to know.

Converting Wilf into a defender turned out to be one of my best decisions because he went on to win the Player of the Season award a couple of times and later became my captain. He never had a bad game and you could rely on him to always turn in a performance worth seven out of ten, even when he wasn't at his best. Years later, I wanted to take him to Wolves as part of my coaching team but he had set up a furniture business and it was going well. He'd been at Brentford as assistant manager when he and the manager got the sack and I think he'd fallen out of love with the game a little bit. I had such respect for Wilf and that was football's loss.

On the other side was Pat Rice, who kept the sometimes wayward Callaghan focused, particularly when it came to his defensive duties. Up front we had Luther Blissett who was equally happy partnering Ross Jenkins or Gerry Armstrong. In midfield were two holding players (although no one called them that back then), Les Taylor and Kenny Jackett, or a Dutchman called Jan Lohman when Kenny got injured halfway through the season. In the centre of defence were Ian Bolton, who – like Luther, Ross and the goalkeeper Steve Sherwood – would complete the journey from the Fourth Division to the First with us that season, and either Steve Sims or Steve Terry. And that was the team that took Watford into the top flight for the first time in the club's history.

Promotion was secured with a 2-0 win over Wrexham at Vicarage Road on a Tuesday evening in early May 1982. The supporters ran onto the pitch when the final whistle blew. Then we went up into the directors' box and the celebrations went on for a while. I was making my way to my office when someone told me that the Argentinians had sunk *HMS Sheffield* that day during the Falklands conflict. To this day I cannot separate those two events and I remember stopping in my tracks and taking a moment before rejoining the others. I couldn't help thinking about the people who had lost their lives serving their country while we were here celebrating winning a football match and enjoying our success. I was delighted for everyone at the club, and for myself, but it did remind me that, when all is said and done, football was just a game.

I headed to my office because I knew Elton was on the phone. He was in the middle of a tour and had been performing in Norway that evening. He'd apparently come off stage early so he could listen to the last few minutes of the commentary by telephone. Now the players and staff were taking it in turns to speak to the chairman. Eventually it was my turn. I took the receiver. I'll never forget Elton's words: 'We did it, Graham. We did it.'

14

The family club

By the summer of 1982, we could consider ourselves a First Division football team, but there was still a lot of work to do before we could claim to be a First Division club. When I look at how much Vicarage Road, Villa Park, Molineux and indeed most grounds have improved in the past twenty years, it's easy to forget what a poor state English football was in back in the late 1970s and early 1980s. There was hooliganism, racist and obscene chanting, and the type of abuse that Elton had to deal with at many grounds, but we were determined to stamp that out at Watford.

One of my favourite phrases has always been: 'family first, except on matchdays'. What I meant by that was that my family took priority and I wanted my players and staff to enjoy time unwinding with their wives and children because I felt it helped everyone when it came to focusing on the work that had to be done at the football club. In exchange, I expected football to be the top priority on a matchday until the final whistle. Our boardroom became a happy, vibrant place because Elton would allow my two girls, Joanne and Karen, and other children in on matchdays rather than preserving the dusty, austere atmosphere we encountered at some clubs.

In order to thrive and grow, I believed Watford had to appeal to a wider section of the public than just men. We wanted to encourage parents to bring their children to games because if we could attract local youngsters to Watford before they had a chance to support Arsenal or Tottenham, then we would be able to build the next generation of supporters. But in order to convince parents to bring their children we had to prove that our football ground was a safe, comfortable and enjoyable place to visit, and that meant working very hard to eradicate foul language, aggression and violence. I am not saying Watford supporters were all angels but we did not have a reputation for attracting troublemakers, and I do remember the atmosphere in the ground soured when some of the London clubs – Chelsea and West Ham, for instance – visited us when we reached the Second Division. There were a couple of occasions when there was fighting on the terraces, but fortunately we were not affected as badly as some other clubs.

I was reading through some of my old programme notes recently, which I always used to write myself in those days, and I came across this one from the Chesterfield match on 3 March 1979:

My initial reaction to the news that we have been chosen to stage the England under-21 international against Denmark next September was one of delight, but I could not believe that Vicarage Road had been picked because of good ground facilities.

Facilities at football grounds up and down the country, including the National Stadium at Wembley, are generally in a woefully poor state and it is more than time that something was done. I was at Wembley for the recent match between England and Northern Ireland and quite frankly what I had to put up with in getting to and from my seat and using the toilet facilities was deplorable.

I found no pleasure at all in going to that ground. It is a fact that people are turning away from football and that gates are dwindling and I can't say that I really blame them, bearing in mind the lack of consideration that is given to the spectator in terms of catering, seating, toilets, entrance, stewarding etc.

Money has to be found to improve facilities in the hope that people will take some form of pleasure in visiting football grounds, apart from simply watching the game.

Vicarage Road needed a lot of work to be ready for the First Division. I remember the day a group of engineers came to test the strength of the crush barriers on the Vicarage Road end's terrace. Our chief executive Eddie Plumley looked quite pale when he realised every single barrier had failed the stress test and needed to be replaced at the cost of a very decent centre-forward.

At one stage, there were plans to rebuild the stadium and add other facilities, such as a sports centre, a restaurant and possibly a bowling alley – things that could generate an income when the football team was not using the stadium. When those ideas were rejected by the local council, we looked at moving away from Vicarage Road and some plans were drawn up by a firm of architects and the club began looking for suitable sites. The council weren't keen on that either, and when plans for a new stand and a roof on the home end were also rejected it was clear the local authorities had no interest in helping us help ourselves. Football wasn't flavour of the month with politicians and planners at that time. Although I wasn't deeply involved in the plans, I knew that we had to look to improve the ground if we were to establish Watford as a First Division club. With a bit of cooperation from the council, we could have been trail-blazers with a new all-seater stadium with leisure and shopping facilities next door.

Even though the ground was old and inadequate, our sense of pride meant we tried to make the most of what we had. Sometimes just making an effort to improve how things look can be all the difference. Shortly after I had arrived at Watford, I had suggested introducing red to our shirts and shorts as a third colour. There were other clubs that played in yellow and black, but yellow, black and red would be unique in the Football League. A couple of years later we switched from black shorts and socks to red and it transformed the look of the team, making us much more vibrant. There's been debate among Watford supporters ever since about which combination looks best but I will always be firmly behind Team Red when it comes to the shorts and socks. Again, this might sound like a trivial detail but it gave the club a sense of identity.

We put a lot of effort into producing merchandise for the supporters to buy. We encouraged them to buy a scarf or a hat in the club's colours, we expanded the club shop, which had previously been a hut, and had outlets at Watford market and, eventually, a second shop closer to the town centre. We hired a marketing manager, Caroline Gillies, who never gets the credit she deserves for the work she did in taking Watford Football Club out into the community.

We began to be proactive in going out and marketing the club to potential supporters. We tried to raise our profile in neighbouring towns and counties. The players did a tremendous amount for us too. We tried to get it written into their contracts that they had to do a certain amount of appearances or events each season but we ran into difficulties with the Professional Footballers' Association, so we did it on an informal basis and whenever I signed someone, I explained that they would be expected to visit schools or the hospital or start fun runs in their spare time. To be fair to them, they all bought into that. Almost every club now has a community section, and I had done this sort of thing when I was at Lincoln City. I also remember Lawrie McMenemy taking his Grimsby Town players to the docks in the early 1970s, so I am not claiming we invented this sort of thing. But I do think we took it to another level.

There were so many great events. I remember John Barnes taking part in a charity pancake race in Watford High Street, or the annual fireworks display set to music that we held at Vicarage Road, or Elton giving out Easter eggs to children. We established an end-of-season tradition with an awards night and cabaret at the nightclub in the town. The players and staff would put on little sketches, many of which were making fun of yours truly, of course. I'll never forget Steve Harrison dressed up in flares, platform boots and outrageous glasses, miming along to the chairman's hits. We invited the supporters to buy tickets to these events and they helped to create a bond between the club and the people who followed the team.

The young supporters were absolutely vital to us and we formed a club, the Junior Hornets, so they could feel a part of the broader club. There were junior discos (Nigel Callaghan DJed at a few of these), an open day where the children could play against the players on the pitch and get their autographs afterwards, and gift packs we sent out when the children celebrated their birthdays. All this work was done by people who understood and shared the vision we had for the club and its future. We established a seating area for families and made it even clearer that bad language would not be tolerated in this part of the ground. I remember Ann Swanson, who ran the Junior Hornets, telling me I had to have a word with Pat Rice because he'd use fairly industrial language when talking to Callaghan. 'Just tone it down when you're on this side of the pitch, OK, Pat?'

In 1983 I ran the London Marathon to raise money to construct the family terrace, and suddenly Watford was a friendly place to visit. In fact, we started calling ourselves The Family Club. We began attracting crowds of 20,000 or more for big matches and there was not a perimeter fence in the ground. I am not saying there was never an arrest or any incident but, by and large, we did not have many problems.

We were committed to improving the matchday experience for supporters. In my programme notes from the Blackpool game in August 1978, I wrote: 'While success on the field remains our first priority it has also become a matter of great importance of how you win. No club can guarantee success all the time, but a club can try, and by improving the facilities and the attractiveness of its football, endeavour to continue to draw people to them should they encounter difficult times.' I was convinced that dwindling attendances at matches up and down the country and across the divisions was partly down to the appalling conditions supporters were expected to put up with but also because the game lacked a sense of drama and entertainment. One thing you cannot guarantee a supporter when he or she parts with his money is a victory. You can try your best, but draws and defeats are part of the game. You can try to entertain, and we did that by playing an attacking game and by attempting to have plenty of shots on goal. But every now and again, there will be a dull game no matter how hard you've tried. However, you can do things to make the afternoon or evening enjoyable in other ways.

We were one of the first clubs to install an electronic scoreboard – although after one of the early games I had to have a word with the man operating it to make sure nothing inappropriate appeared on it. I seem to remember text scrolling across asking the referee if he needed glasses after he'd disallowed a goal and I didn't think that was the proper use of it.

In 1981 we invited Vancouver Whitecaps over to play a friendly and we introduced some American-style excitement to the game. There were cheerleaders and drumming majorettes before the game and a shoot-out with a difference afterwards, with the players taking turns to dribble the ball from thirty yards out before trying to beat the goalkeeper. During the match we had a gentleman's agreement to ban back-passes to the goal-keeper – or rather prevented the goalkeeper from picking up the ball from a pass by a team-mate – eleven years before that rule was introduced by FIFA. It was just an experiment and a bit of fun but it showed that we were trying to be forward-thinking about the game. The Taylor Report and the creation of the Premier League eventually took football in that direction, with all-seater stadia, big screens and other sorts of entertain-ment and, when they're pumping the music out so loudly before kick-off, I sometimes wonder if it's gone too far the other way, so I suppose I ought to take some of the blame for that.

15

Not bad for a side that can't play

I was never too worried about whether or not we'd be good enough to survive in the First Division because we'd had some excellent cup results against top-flight opposition that showed we could handle some of the best sides on a one-off basis. For example, in September 1980 we'd hammered Southampton 7-1 at Vicarage Road in the second leg of a League Cup tie, having lost the first game 4-0. I sent the players out saying that I'd like to win the first half. I told them if we could come in 2-0 up we might have a game on. It was one of those days when we had absolutely nothing to lose and we played with such fierce determination. Once we'd gone a couple of goals up, the doubts started to set in for Southampton. When we got the third, they were panicking. Eventually we scored enough to earn the chance to finish them off in extra-time. In the end they just couldn't live with us because we were a very fit side. After the match I saw their manager, Lawrie McMenemy, in the corridor outside the dressing rooms and he was as white as a sheet. Later that same season, we thrashed Nottingham Forest, who were the European Cup holders, 4-1, and at the start of 1982, midway through our promotion season, we knocked Manchester United out of the FA Cup on the afternoon Big Ron ruined his bespoke leather shoes walking across the wet, muddy grass to the bench.

Those results meant I was confident we would win our fair share of matches, but I didn't want to take any chances, so over the summer I decided we would increase the workload during pre-season training. We didn't have much of a break because two days after the season ended in May 1982, we flew to Australia for an end-of-season tour. We played one game in Melbourne before heading to New Zealand to face their national team as they warmed up for the World Cup. Then it was on to Malaysia for another couple of matches and it was early June before we got back. After a month or so off, we flew to Norway for a pre-season trip that the players still tell me was more like an army boot camp. Even thirty-odd years later, the players who were there remind me about it.

I was absolutely merciless and I chuckle to myself when I think back because I don't think I ever made a team work as hard as the Watford squad did that summer. We were staying in very basic accommodation, a bit like an army barracks, and in some respects it probably was like being in the army. We did three sessions a day, except on days when we had a match in the evening and I'd let them off with only two. Before breakfast we'd run up to the training ground, which was about a mile away, complete some drills and then run back for something to eat.

Norway was experiencing a heatwave that summer and so I made sure we avoided the hottest part of the day, but there's no doubt we worked hard. We also played four games in eight days against Norwegian sides and I insisted we treated them like league matches, making it very clear I wanted to see us play at a high tempo, not at pre-season pace. The Norwegian sides were not all the best but they were in the middle of their league season so a couple of them gave us a good test.

The reason for all this work was simple: I didn't want the First Division to catch us out. Pat Rice aside, we had very little experience of the First Division in the squad. I thought we were a good football team but I accepted that we might not be the best. However, I also knew that if we couldn't be the best, we could certainly be the fittest. I thought we had to be fantastically fit – fitter than we'd ever been – and that if we were, we could catch a few teams by surprise. That didn't mean I wanted us running round like headless chickens, by the way, but if we could close down opposition players, win the ball back from them high up the pitch, and pressurise them in every position, we could force the top players to make mistakes. I told the players that we were going to start games imagining that we were already a goal down so we would play hard and look to score right from the kick-off.

I was determined that we wouldn't be in awe of the other teams. If they were better than us, that was fine but we would push them hard to prove that they were rather than look at the names of the teams we were playing – Liverpool, Manchester United, Arsenal, Tottenham and so on – and take for granted that they would beat us.

Another thing that helped us, I think, was that I felt people would have spent the summer watching the World Cup, which was played in the heat of Spain, and had been seduced by the idea of slow, patient football with steady build-up play from the back. We were going to stick to our guns and play attacking football from the first minute to the last. I accepted that once in a while we might get our bottoms spanked, particularly away from home, but I could live with that because I felt we could win more than we lost by being true to the team we were.

My instincts proved to be correct. We started the season very well, beating Everton 2-0 at home, then going to Southampton and winning 4-1, which was very satisfying because it enabled me to remind Alan Ball of something he'd said a couple of months earlier. Alan had been on the same flight as us when we travelled to Australia the previous May. He was going over there to play in their league to earn a bit of extra money over the summer. Alan was enjoying a few beers on the flight and, egged on by him, I suspect, a couple of my lads had too much to drink, which didn't please me greatly. It was all good natured but Alan was winding them up a bit, taunting them about how we supposedly played the long ball. 'Wait until you get into the First Division,' he said, 'we'll show you how to play proper football.'

I got a bit wound up by it, but I didn't say anything, and I'm glad I didn't because it made my comeback even sweeter. I waited on the touchline for Alan as the players came off the pitch. It was typical of me, really, I couldn't let it go. 'Not bad for a side that can't fucking play, are we?' I said it with a bit of a smile on my face and, to be fair, Alan took it well. 'Hey, credit where it's due,' he said. 'You played very well and if you carry on like that, you will shock a few people.'

Although we lost at Manchester City, we really should have won. They scored early and then lost their goalkeeper, Joe Corrigan, through injury. There was only one substitute, and no sub goalkeeper, in those days so they had to put an outfield player in goal but even though we created chance after chance we couldn't get one past him. A 3-0 win over West Bromwich Albion at Vicarage Road on 11 September put us top of the Football League on goal difference. That evening, Rita and I went with Bertie Mee and his wife Doris to the Royal Albert Hall for the Last Night of the Proms. Bertie was very good at organising things like this, and that night is one I remember so fondly. I was so happy signing 'Rule Britannia' and 'Jerusalem' at the top of my voice, knowing we were top of the league and everything was going well.

Two weeks after that we demolished Sunderland 8-0. We were 4-0 up at half-time and the players always remind me that I refused to let them sit down during the break and instead made them jog on the spot. It's true we went through our pre-match warm-up routine again because I didn't want us to let up. If we'd relaxed, we might have let Sunderland get back into the game. OK, we were unlikely to lose the game from 4-0 up, but if Sunderland scored twice and we won 4-2, our supporters would go home slightly disappointed. I told them to try to repeat what they'd done in the first half and they did.

It was a magnificent season because every time I felt we were running out of steam the players found something to keep things going. What made it so special was that this was exactly the same group who had won promotion from the Second Division because I only signed one player all season, and that was young Richard Jobson from Burton Albion. People could say with some justification that the gap between the top two divisions then was far smaller than the gap between the Championship and Premier League now, but it was just as true in 1983 as it is now that the league table does not lie.

On the final day of the season, we welcomed Liverpool to Vicarage Road. They had already been crowned champions a few weeks earlier and the occasion was special particularly for them because it was Bob Paisley's last match as manager before retiring.

We won the game 2-1, which meant we guaranteed ourselves a place in the Uefa Cup. Then we heard that Manchester United had lost at Notts County, which meant we had clinched the runners-up position.

The Liverpool players and staff were all due to fly off for an end-of-season tour either late that evening or the next morning so we invited them into the boardroom for a drink. We sent someone off to get fifty portions of fish and chips and we all sat round eating chips out of the paper and drinking champagne.

Elton's dream of qualifying for Europe had come true just five years after we'd set out on this adventure.

16

The Watford way

Not everyone enjoyed the Watford fairytale. On our way up through the divisions we'd had a certain amount of attention, most of which had been very positive, perhaps because people were curious about us and we were still something of a novelty. Once we started beating the big teams there was quite a lot of criticism about our style of play, and I think one or two journalists who took it upon themselves to be guardians of the game went over the top.

When we beat both Tottenham Hotspur and Arsenal at their own grounds, there was a lot of critical press coverage. They dismissed us a kick-and-rush side but, as I'd said to John Motson on the BBC's *Match of the Day*: 'If it is as simple as that, why doesn't everyone kick and rush it? But you know as well as I do, it's not as simple as that.' People talked about the 'right' and 'wrong' way to play the game but as far as I was concerned, the only 'right' way to play was within the laws of the game. Other than that, people were free to play the game in any way they wished.

Wimbledon followed us up through the divisions a few years later, and in many ways their achievements were all the more impressive than ours because they came from non-league, they won the FA Cup and they stayed in the top division a lot longer than Watford did. But where I take exception to any comparisons with Wimbledon is that at times they broke the laws of the game with their aggression. They could be a dirty side and, in my opinion, they singled out talented players for

143

special treatment. In fact, when they got into the First Division and we played them for the first time, Dennis Wise kicked John Barnes in such a way that I am convinced it was deliberate. Now, there are two things to say about that: firstly, it's up to the officials to spot and punish foul play and plenty of players will try to get away with as much as they possibly can; and secondly, Dennis Wise was a good player who I later picked for England and who didn't need to go round kicking people to have a positive impact on the game.

I felt Wimbledon crossed the line too often, whereas one of the things I pride myself on was that Watford's discipline was very good season after season. We played hard and tackled hard but we were a fair side. We did not try to con the referee and we didn't speak back because if there was one thing I couldn't stand it was dissent. I wanted them to play to the whistle, as we are all taught when we're children learning the game, and to respect the referee's decision because you are never going to change his mind once he's given a decision. I felt the officials had a hard enough job without twenty-two players giving them grief all match long. We all have to accept that they are only human, they only have two eyes and they can only take up one position on the pitch at any one time. That means they are going to make mistakes, but I felt it showed good character if we could accept those mistakes without going red in the face about them.

It annoyed me when people said that Watford's style was setting the game back twenty years because I felt we were playing attacking, exciting football. During our debut season in the First Division we scored seventy-four league goals and conceded fifty-seven. We won twenty-two matches and lost fifteen. If you look at the negatives, you could ask how a side that lost fifteen games and let in fifty-seven goals could possibly finish second in the league. Well, we won more than we lost and we scored more than we conceded, and that is what I felt football was all about. I know that a 4-3 win is worth the same number of points as a 1-0 win, but if you gave me the choice I'd rather be involved in the 4-3.

We played with four forwards – John Barnes and Nigel Callaghan were on the wings and Ross Jenkins and Luther Blissett were in the middle – and we tried to get the ball to them as much as we could. Our midfield players, Kenny Jackett and Les Taylor, pressed the opposition hard and closed down the space – qualities that are, quite rightly, valued very highly nowadays.

The critics really started hammering their typewriters in November 1982 when we beat both north-London clubs in quick succession. We played very, very well at Tottenham and it was still goalless going into the final few minutes. The ball was up in Tottenham's half and, as I saw Les moving forwards to support our attack, I was up off the bench shouting at them not to over-commit themselves. Then the ball broke to Les on the edge of the box and I shouted at him to hold it but he took a shot instead and it flew into the net. I took a bit of stick for that afterwards: 'Didn't you hear the gaffer, Les? He said to hold it.'

This was probably one of the first times I had faced the full pack of national newspaper journalists afterwards and a lot of the questions surprised me. They were all about the way we played and I could tell that some of the journalists thought it was fine for us to come up to the First Division as long as we didn't try to spoil things for the big London clubs. The Tottenham manager, Keith Burkinshaw, was asked what he thought of our game and he answered honestly. The next day, the papers quoted Keith as saying: 'I wouldn't play the Watford way.' Keith rang me to say that, although he had said it, he'd meant it in the context of being Tottenham's manager and that he had nothing against us if that was how we wanted to go about things.

Tottenham had Glenn Hoddle, who was one of the best long passers in the country at the time. Hoddle could pass the ball forty or fifty yards with great accuracy and people commended him for it, and rightly so. But our centre-half Ian Bolton could do that too and yet we were the ones who were criticised for it. I knew from Charles Reep's analysis that Liverpool played as many long passes as we did but – because it was Alan Hansen or Mark Lawrenson or Ronnie Whelan playing the ball for Ian Rush or Kenny Dalglish – people viewed it differently.

My view has always been that there are two types of passes: the one that goes directly to someone and the one into space for a player to run onto. One thing I can say for sure is that our plan was not to simply thump the ball from one end of the pitch to the other and hope for the best, as our critics suggested. We weren't hitting it long to try to gain yards like a rugby team, we were trying to get the ball forwards quickly, often into wide positions, so that we could engineer a goalscoring opportunity by getting the ball and a player into that sweet spot in the opposition's penalty area.

If you ask any defender what makes him uncomfortable, he will say that he never likes it when the ball or the man is behind him and he's facing the 'wrong' way, towards his own goal. And he particularly doesn't like it when both the ball and the man are behind him because then he knows he's in trouble and there's the possibility of conceding a goal.

I will happily admit we practised certain moves because we worked very hard in training so we could execute them well, but we were not formulaic or robotic. We worked very hard on restarts – throw-ins, corners and free-kicks – because they were opportunities when you had the ball and the opposition had to wait until you played it. Think about how many restarts there are in a game. All of them are a chance to dictate the play. Free-kicks and corners are an opportunity to put the ball into the penalty area unchallenged, and so if you can work on your team's movement and on the delivery of the ball there are so many scoring opportunities to be had, especially if you also work on the second 'phase' of play by anticipating where a clearance might fall. I've got notebooks with diagrams of corner, free-kick and throw-in routines in them because I knew they could be such good opportunities for us.

The fundamentals of the game have not changed all that much in the past thirty years either. Watch all the goals from one weekend of the Premier League and count how many of them come from a set-piece and how many come from a mistake. We all remember the shot that flew in from twenty-five yards or the wonderful piece of individual skill that led to a goal, but they are still in the minority. A lot of goals are what you might consider 'ugly' but they all count the same.

Reep's statistics told me that a large percentage of goals came from one-touch finishes and, in fact, that the chance to score diminished the more touches a striker took. That makes sense, of course, because the longer the clock is ticking the more chance the defenders and goalkeeper have to recover, close down space or put in a block or a tackle. So I drilled into the players the importance of shooting early on the basis that if you don't shoot, you can't score.

A lot of what we were trying to do sounds simple but we became very good at doing the simple things well.

I could handle the criticism and I expected opposition managers to focus on our style when we had beaten them because it deflected attention away from the result, but I think some of the comments blew things out of proportion. When we beat Arsenal 4-2 at Highbury I was so happy because the focus had been on our style of play, everyone was talking about it and how basic it was, and yet Arsenal had been unable to stop us. After the match I decided not to go and speak to the press because I realised all the talk would be about our style and I already recognised that a few of the journalists weren't going to change their minds in a hurry. The journalists were perfectly entitled to their opinions, of course, but they didn't seem to want to find out what we were all about. I invited two of the most persistent critics, Jeff Powell and Brian Glanville, to come and watch us train and talk to the players but they never came.

Because I had been asked by Bobby Robson, the England manager, to coach and manage the England youth team through to the European Under-18 Championships, people paid even more attention. But once people had decided there was nothing to our game except the long ball, I knew I was fighting a losing battle trying to explain otherwise, so I stopped bothering. I do wish that right at the beginning I had nipped the phrase 'long ball' in the bud and referred to it as a 'long pass' though because it was a phrase that came back to haunt me over the years. Sometimes perception is far more powerful than reality.

Of course, I do smile to myself when I watch a game on television nowadays and the pundits all look at the statistics and talk about how much possession one team had and how many shots the other team had. When I revealed that we employed one of Reep's people – a chap called Simon Hartley – to take detailed notes of every pass, tackle and shot and compile a report on each Watford game, I was told I was a slave to the statistics. Now everyone has them at their fingertips.

17

European adventure

I don't like to single out individuals for praise too often because football is a team game, but if one man symbolises what we achieved at Watford in those five years, it is Luther Blissett. Here was a boy who clearly had some talent – he was quick, strong and he liked to shoot at goal – but he was very raw when I first met him and he needed guiding. Our journey through the divisions gave him the time and opportunity to develop into a very good striker. Each time we made a step up, he proved himself and when we got to the top he took the First Division by storm. He scored thirty goals that season – twenty-seven of them in the league – which earned him the golden boot as the top scorer in the division. From the turn of the year onwards, I knew we might struggle to keep hold of him because a number of clubs had shown an interest.

At the end of our debut season in the First Division, we went on a tour to China and everybody came – Elton and the directors, many of the staff, the players, of course, a group of people from our sponsors and some supporters. Luther and John Barnes joined us later because they were representing England in the Home International matches against Northern Ireland and Scotland. Nothing gave me a greater sense of pride than seeing Watford players representing their country, whether it was Luther and John for England, Kenny Jackett for Wales, Gerry Armstrong for Northern Ireland or any of the young players who played at under-21 or youth level. Seeing Luther's transformation from a young Fourth Division striker uncertain whether he would make a career in the game, into an England international was so special for me and for the club. He was a very easy player to coach because he wanted to learn and was always so enthusiastic. We talk about players who are prepared to put their bodies on the line, well, Luther was one of them. If there was a chance of scoring a goal, he'd put his head in where there was a risk of getting hurt.

While we were in China, it became public knowledge that AC Milan were interested in signing Luther. We'd known about this for months because the Italians had come to Vicarage Road a number of times to watch him. When Milan finally made an offer, Elton asked me what I thought and I said that, although there was no way we could stand in Luther's way, we should hold out for a million pounds.

Our chief executive Eddie Plumley and I did the negotiations with two men from Milan – at least, they said they were from Milan, but we weren't always sure who we were talking to because each time they sent different people over from Italy to talk to us. Eddie and I were on our way to Lord's to watch the World Cup final between India and the West Indies and so we all met at an Italian restaurant in London where the talks went back and forth for hours. Milan wanted to pay half up front and half later, but we were adamant we wanted the full fee in one go. Then there were discussions about the exchange rate from lira to pounds because we wanted to make sure we got the full million. They wanted to pay £999,999 and Eddie said something like: 'We'll say it's a million pounds anyway, so you may as well give us the extra pound.' Luther was sitting in the middle of all this and I suddenly became aware that we were losing so much more than a footballer. It felt like we were selling our son.

When we finally agreed the deal, Eddie and I had missed a good deal of the day's play, and I felt a sort of emptiness I had not felt when selling a player before. There's little room for sentiment in football, particularly when it comes to selling players. Part of a manager's job is to make decisions that are in the best interests of the club, but losing Luther did feel different.

There was no way I would have denied him the opportunity to go and experience a completely different type of football that would make him a better player, and to earn money that we could not possibly offer him. If you looked at it from another angle, you could say that Luther not only helped us go from the bottom division to the top but his transfer fee also covered the cost of that journey, so it was a fantastic deal for all of us. As I stood outside that Italian restaurant somewhere in north London and shook Luther's hand, I promised him I would travel over to Milan to watch him play, which I did a couple of times.

Luther was not the only player I needed to replace. We let Gerry Armstrong join Real Mallorca. Gerry had been great for us and he had made a name for himself in Spain the previous summer by scoring Northern Ireland's winner against them in the World Cup, so when a Spanish club came in for him it made perfect sense. Gerry had scored Watford's first-ever goal in the top division, so his place in the club's history was assured, but I felt he was making less of an impact on matches. I also released Ross Jenkins, who was now thirty-two, because I felt we were not going to get much more from him. Pat Rice was thirty-four but I offered him a coaching position, although he was still registered as a player, and Ian Bolton was coming to the end too, so when you look at the team that finished runners-up to Liverpool, more than half of them had to be replaced.

The million pounds we'd got for Luther had to be spent wisely but that turned out not to be easy because every club we approached thought we had that money burning a hole in our pockets. I tried to get Gary Lineker as a direct replacement for Luther – and I would have been prepared to spend a big chunk of the Luther money on him – but Leicester City refused to sell. Gary eventually went to Everton, then Barcelona and Tottenham, so he did OK for himself, didn't he?

I replaced Ross Jenkins with George Reilly from Cambridge United. George was similar to Ross in many ways in that he was tall and a lot better with the ball at his feet than people gave him credit for. My other signings were Paul Atkinson, a midfielder from Oldham Athletic, who broke his ankle in a pre-season game and didn't play for the first team until Christmas, and Lee Sinnott, an eighteen-year-old defender who had been in my England youth squad.

At the start of the season, we had a terrible injury crisis. At one point there were more people in the treatment room than on the training pitch, and so I had to bring in players from the reserves, fill the team with teenagers and ask Pat Rice to carry on for a few weeks while we got people fit.

It really was an extraordinary situation because we were in the Uefa Cup and I was determined to try to represent the country as well as we could. In the first round, we were drawn against Kaiserslautern and travelled to West Germany for the first leg. They were a good side and they beat us quite comfortably. But it was 3-1 and I felt the away goal might give us a slim chance at home.

When the Germans arrived for the second leg they sauntered into Vicarage Road in their tracksuits and I saw an opportunity to get the players fired up: 'Hey, lads, look at them. They think they've already won.'

What followed was quite magical. Vicarage Road had a real European atmosphere that night because our marketing department had done a great job of encouraging people to bring flags and horns. We had nothing to lose and I had no right to expect anything of the team because half of them were youngsters from the reserves. The star on the night was Ian Richardson, who was making his first-team debut. He scored twice as we won 3-0 to make it through to the second round.

When we drew 1-1 at home to the Bulgarians Levski Spartak in the first leg of the second round, I thought it was the end of the run, but the performance in Sofia has to be up there with the finest I've ever witnessed.

The Bulgarians did what they could to intimidate us. The night before the match we were allowed into the stadium for a training session. Uefa rules said that we should have the place to ourselves but our hosts had let in at least 10,000 people and they were booing, hissing and whistling at us as we worked through our session. In a way it might have done us a favour because we knew what we would be in for when the ground was filled with 60,000 people the following night.

I have rarely felt so up against it as we were in that match. Levski were given two penalties in about the first twenty minutes. They scored one and hit the bar with the other. Fortunately, between those two penalties, Nigel Callaghan scored with a sensational long-range shot but that was almost our only serious attack of the first half.

The Levski team tried to bully us and I spent most of half-time reminding the players not to retaliate because I felt the referee would not take much persuading to send one of our lads off. We survived to take them to extra-time and then scored twice against the run of play. A few minutes before the end, Nigel Callaghan was standing waiting to take a corner as the Levski supporters threw glass bottles from the terraces. The glass was shattering close to him and he turned to the bench and gestured as if to say: 'Can you see what they're throwing at me?' I stood up and shouted: 'Well, get on with it then, Nigel.'

In terms of a team pulling together to get a result against all the odds, that was as good as anything in my career. We were an inexperienced side, with some very young players, and we stood up to everything the Bulgarians chucked at us, both on and off the pitch.

Shortly after that match, I placed an advertisement in the classified section of *The Times*. It read: 'Wanted: Professional Footballers. Many vacancies now available at First Division football club for men (or women) aged between eighteen and eighty and prepared to work on Saturday. Some playing experience desirable but preference will be given to those with two arms and two legs in good working order. Apply in writing to G Taylor, Vicarage Road Stadium, Watford.'

It was my attempt to make light of our situation but also to draw attention to what was happening at the football club. We had signed new players but because they joined after the Uefa deadline, they were not eligible for the European matches.

When we came up against Sparta Prague in the third round, we met a side that was more than a match for us. They won the first leg at Vicarage Road 3-2 and I knew that would make the game in Czechoslovakia very difficult for us. We were into December by now and the conditions over there were ridiculous. The pitch was frozen solid and heavily rutted. Because of our travel arrangements there was no way the game could be called off and rescheduled. Besides, the pitch would have been exactly the same the next night. I did hear a rumour that they had some sort of undersoil heating system at Sparta Prague's stadium but that they switched it off to give themselves an advantage, although I have no idea if there's any truth to that. What I do know is that we were expected to play on a surface that was like an ice rink.

By kick-off it was absolutely freezing. There was a bit of a confrontation in the dressing room between our young left-back, Neil Price, and Roy Clare, our kit man. Roy was a lovely man and he knew I was a stickler for details and that I liked all the players to be in the same type of shirts. I overheard Neil politely asking for a long-sleeve shirt and Roy snapped at him: 'You're soft, you lot. We're in short sleeves tonight.'

I went over to Roy and said: 'It's pretty chilly out there, so I think long sleeves will be OK tonight.'

Our lads went out to warm up and realised they couldn't wear studded boots because of the frozen surface, so they changed into the boots with rubber soles that they'd usually wear for games on the plastic pitch that Queens Park Rangers had at the time. Unfortunately they weren't much use either and our players struggled to keep their footing. I couldn't swear to it but I strongly suspect the Sparta Prague players had studs that had been filed into a point so they would dig into the icy surface. I never managed to get a clear enough look to be certain but they were able to move quite well. Either way, they were used to the conditions and we weren't and so they beat us very comfortably.

With a couple of minutes remaining, we were 4-0 down in the match, 7-2 down on aggregate. For some reason, our regular doctor Vernon Edwards had been unable to make the trip and his assistant Dr Peter O'Connor was with us. I turned to our physio, Billy Hails, and said: 'Well, Bill, it looks like our European adventure is over.'

The doc said: 'Oh, I don't know, Graham. There's still a couple of minutes left.'

He meant it in the best possible way but we burst into laughter. I often think about that moment and how it embodies everything we were about. We had a member of staff who wouldn't rule out the possibility of scoring five in two minutes. He refused to admit defeat until the final whistle blew. That was the Watford way of doing things. I wonder what would happen these days, with every game filmed, if the camera cut to the bench and spotted the manager and his staff rolling with laughter while their team was 4-0 down away from home in Europe. I'd have probably been criticised for not caring or taking it seriously enough.

By the time we were knocked out of European competition, the spotlight fell on our league form and the supporters were beginning to get a bit concerned about our position at the bottom of the table. I could understand their worries. We'd come up through the divisions rapidly and the feeling was we might easily return just as quickly if we weren't careful. I received quite a number of letters from supporters fretting that we might go back down again, but I was confident we would be fine once the new players settled in.

Things improved dramatically when I signed Maurice Johnston from Partick Thistle because he struck up a great partnership with George Reilly both on and off the pitch. Maurice had been recommended to me by Jim McGuigan, my old manager at Grimsby Town, who had become part of my scouting team. When our home match against West Ham United was moved to a Friday night, I had the opportunity to go and watch Maurice play. I took Rita with me to see Partick Thistle play Airdrieonians in the Scottish First Division, which was one below the Premier Division. Yes, that really was my idea of a romantic weekend away in those days. I've had to look it up in an old copy of the *Rothmans Football Yearbook* to see that Partick won 2-1, but I know that Maurice was the outstanding player on the pitch and that he scored after about five minutes. Midway through the first half, I asked Rita what she thought of him. 'He's got a small bum,' she said.

'Oh, I see, that's why you come to matches, is it?'

'It means he won't put on weight,' she replied.

Maurice was one of the most instinctive goalscorers I ever worked with. He was every bit as good as Gary Lineker was at his best. Sometimes his movement in the penalty area seemed illogical. He might drop back a bit when the obvious move would be to go towards the ball. I'd think: 'Why is Maurice going there?' and then the ball would be deflected or half-cleared and it would fall to him and he'd score. There was nothing I could teach him about forward play, his movement or the art of scoring goals; he just had an instinct and a hunger for putting the ball in the net.

In terms of coaching, Maurice was a joy to work with, but he was also one of the most challenging players I managed because he pushed the boundaries I had set more than most. I'd done my research before I signed him and I knew he liked a night out in Glasgow and I also knew that he would soon be on first-name terms with the nightclub bouncers and bar staff in and around London too. Don't get me wrong, Maurice was not a bad lad at all, but he was a twenty-year-old boy who enjoyed going out and he encouraged the other players to join him. He had blond highlights in his hair and he'd wear a white leather jacket, so he couldn't fail to be noticed.

Although I laid down the ground rules, Maurice didn't think they applied to him. In the end it was pointless fining him because it didn't make any difference. The thing was, Maurice could handle the nights out and still perform, whereas some of the others could not. But they would see what Maurice could get away with and think they could do the same, which caused me problems.

More than once Maurice came to training straight from a night out without having had a wink of sleep. Steve Harrison had to sober him up with a cold shower in the dressing room before sending him out onto the pitch for training. Maurice thought I didn't know, but I did.

Just after New Year 1984, I took the squad to a gym off Tottenham Court Road in London for a series of fitness tests. This was the start of sports science coming in, and the players ran on treadmills, blew into something that measured their lung capacity, and had a blood test. Afterwards the doctor came to me with the results.

'Mr Taylor, one of your players has performed very well but he is officially drunk.'

'Who is it?' I asked, already knowing the answer.

'Mr Johnston,' he replied.

But – just as Rita had predicted – Maurice didn't put on weight, his times in our running sessions weren't affected, and he scored goals, so it was hard to argue that his nights out were ruining his performances. For six months, he and George Reilly were unstoppable and they scored the goals that lifted us away from the bottom of the table and took us to the club's first FA Cup final.

18

The last thing I want to watch

I've had a video of the 1984 FA Cup final for more than thirty years and I've never once watched it. When a recording of the match came out on DVD a few years ago, someone sent me a copy and I thought: 'What have you sent me this for? This is the last thing I want to watch.'

We lost 2-0 to Everton and I feel very disappointed we didn't win the cup because I felt we didn't do ourselves justice on the day. The second goal, the one that killed us off, was a foul by Andy Gray on Steve Sherwood and nothing anyone says will convince me otherwise.

From the turn of the year, I'd had a feeling our name might be on the cup. Before the third-round draw was even made, I'd told Elton not to make any concert plans for Saturday 19 May – FA Cup final day – just in case. Talk about confidence.

We got a horrible draw in the third round, away to our rivals Luton Town, and when we went 2-0 down in the first half-hour, I was feeling a bit silly. Watford supporters will know that we managed to drag ourselves level, then won the replay, before getting past Charlton Athletic and then Brighton and Hove Albion with relative ease.

I expected a tougher match from Birmingham City in the quarter-final but we won that 3-1 to set up a semi-final against Plymouth Argyle of the Third Division. We were the favourites, which was a slightly unfamiliar position to find ourselves in. We won the game 1-0 and, although there were some nervous moments at the end, we deserved to go through.

Three weeks before the final, our captain Wilf Rostron was sent off in a league game against Luton Town, which meant he would be suspended for the FA Cup final. Before the match the referee, Roger Milford, came into the dressing room, as the referees often did in those days. He had a quick word with the players and he made it clear he wouldn't stand for any dissent. I said: 'We've got a cup final coming up so you'll have no trouble with us.' I regret that to this day because it was a stupid thing to say. I was either tempting fate or putting an idea in the referee's head. I always felt Milford was one of those referees who liked to be the centre of attention.

Wilf and Luton's Paul Elliott went in for a tackle and they went down to the ground together. It was a clumsy challenge by both of them and when they got up they went chest to chest, presumably each thinking the other had gone in a bit too high or with his studs showing. At the most I thought it was worth a caution apiece, but Milford sent them both off and I knew immediately that Wilf would miss the final.

After the match, I came the closest I've ever come to laying a hand on a referee. I blocked him in the corridor and wouldn't let him past. 'Do you know what you've done?' I shouted. 'You've cost our captain the chance to play at Wembley.' Milford should have reported me to the Football Association for that because I was really out of order.

That evening, Rita and I went to Stratford-upon-Avon to see a Shakespeare play. For the life of me I can't remember which one it was, but I do know it was a miserable night because I was so upset for Wilf. We thought about appealing to the FA but there was no video of the incident and we knew that the previous year Brighton's captain Steve Foster had been in a similar position and had appealed to the High Court to over-turn the FA's decision, without success. So we accepted that there was very little chance the FA would change their minds.

A couple of weeks before the final we had a visit from the FA's secretary Ted Croker to run the players through the protocol for cup final day. All the players were sitting round, including Wilf, and Croker turned to him and said: 'This doesn't concern you because you won't be playing. Don't worry, my brother missed a cup final but he got there the following year, so make sure you do it again next season.' It may only have been a joke but it was a terrible thing to say and I could see the hurt in Wilf's eyes. It annoyed me too and I knew it would hurt our team in the match. I know they were the rules but it seemed unfair to me that you could be dismissed in one competition and miss the final of another.

If I made one mistake in the build-up to the FA Cup final, it was that I named the team too early. We had the problem of how to replace Wilf at left-back and we were also missing the experience of Steve Sims, so I knew we had to field a young defence. Against Plymouth, Kenny Jackett had been injured, so Wilf moved into midfield and I brought Neil Price in at left-back. That meant our back four was Lee Sinnott, who was eighteen, David Bardsley, who was nineteen, twenty-year-old Price, and the daddy of them was Steve Terry, who was still only twenty-one. I'd been so impressed with how they handled the occasion at Villa Park and everything that went with playing in an FA Cup semi-final, and that played a big part in my decision to go with the same line-up at Wembley. Our final league game, seven days before the cup final, was against Arsenal and we gave Pat Rice the chance to end his career against his former team. Pat had been in my thinking for the cup final because he was still registered as a player, but I had my doubts because it was almost six months since he'd played a league match. Pat would have given his all but he made my decision for me when I sat down to talk to him.

'I'd be honoured to be picked,' he said. 'I've played in five FA Cup finals but I've barely played this year. If I play badly, you'll get the blame for picking me. And I don't want to deny one of the younger players who has been in the team their chance.'

Pat was absolutely right and I appreciated his honesty so much because he could have thought: 'Here's a chance to play in another cup final and I'm going to take it.'

After the Arsenal match, which we won 2-1, I knew in my mind what the team should be. We knew Bardsley would recover from the knock he'd had and so, as the players sat in the dressing room, I announced the team for the FA Cup final. Of course, if someone had picked up an injury I'd have changed it, but I told them that if everyone was fit that would be my starting eleven.

Almost as soon as I'd done it, I realised I'd made a mistake and, as the week wore on, I wished I hadn't backed myself into a corner. It's not necessarily that I would have started with a different team – maybe I would, maybe I wouldn't – but I had denied myself the time to think and the opportunity to change my mind. I saw things over the week leading up to the match that I wasn't happy with but how could I go back on what I'd said? Perhaps I could have done, but would there have been even greater consequences to changing my mind? I just don't know and I have thought about it from time to time.

Basically, I ignored a great piece of advice from the great Liverpool manager Bill Shankly, who said: 'Never pick your team for the next match on the way home from a win, a draw or a defeat.' He was absolutely right, so why had I done it? I thought it might settle them down and help them relax if they knew they weren't fretting over their place in the side all week. I felt they needed that sense of security but perhaps I was wrong. Let's face it, two-thirds of the side would have been very confident of their place no matter what, but even a player who is a fixture in the side isn't entirely sure until they see their name on the teamsheet. On one hand players like to know they are in the side but, on the other, that sense of uncertainty is a part of a footballer's life and it's what keeps them sharp and on their toes from Monday to Friday.

I can't say that anyone let themselves down in training that week but there was so much else going on that I felt perhaps if they had not been sure of their places they would have kept their minds on the match more. Some of the distractions were just part of the FA Cup final build-up, such as finalising all the tickets for friends and family – which is always more fraught for big matches than you think it should be – and going for the final suit fitting. There was a lot of interest from the media, but of course the reality of that is that the newspapers and broadcasters all want to speak to the same few players and so there can be a bit of an issue, not least in that you've got two or three players spending a lot of time doing interviews.

One problem we could have avoided was that we had to find a new training ground for the week. The lease on our regular ground expired at the end of the season and, although we went to great lengths to try to extend it by a few days, it was impossible because the place had been hired out and apparently the arrangements couldn't be altered. It seems absurd now that a First Division football team would be left without a training ground for the week leading up to the FA Cup final, but that was the situation. Although we found an alternative and the pitches were fine, the facilities were not great and sometimes there wasn't any hot water. It all added to the sense that the week was different when I was trying to establish a routine that was as close to normal as possible.

On the day itself, we had a television crew in the hotel and part of the build-up for the broadcasters was for us to have the comedian Michael Barrymore doing his routine while we were having our pre-match meal. That wasn't particularly to my taste and I'm sure there were as many players who enjoyed it as found it a bit embarrassing, but it was different to what we were used to. Perhaps I should have been stronger and said to the television people: 'No, I'm sorry but we're going to prepare our way,' but that was what FA Cup final day was all about. It was expected that you opened the doors and participated in these things.

Everyone remembers Elton's tears when 'Abide With Me' played before kick-off and I wasn't immune to the emotions either because when I got into Wembley stadium and I saw all of our supporters, it suddenly hit me just how far we had come. I am just sorry that in the match itself we didn't do ourselves justice. I can't be critical of the players because they tried their best, but they just couldn't reproduce their best form and it has to be acknowledged that they came up against a very good Everton side who were just beginning to turn themselves into the best team in the country. The following season they won the league championship and the European Cup Winners' Cup, after all, but the two cup-final goals were unfortunate. The first was a Graeme Sharp shot from the edge of the penalty box that hit the inside of the post and went in, and the second was Gray's header that needs no further discussion. I felt our goalkeeper Steve Sherwood was unfairly criticised though, because we lost the game as a team. We had one or two good chances, especially early on, but as the game went on we faded.

That evening there was a party at John Reid's house and, although it was wonderful to be able to invite everyone connected with the club to join us, I didn't feel much like celebrating. Elton and Kiki Dee sang a duet and there was champagne and laughter and, while I didn't exactly sit quietly in the corner, I couldn't mask my disappointment because I had gone to Wembley fully expecting to win the cup.

19

Time for a fresh challenge

Did reaching the FA Cup final represent the summit of the mountain? It would be wrong of me to say that I regretted finishing runners-up in both the league and the FA Cup in our first two seasons in the top flight, but in a way it left us nowhere to go and made life difficult for us in a way I had not anticipated.

To improve on those performances, we would have to win the league or win a cup. If we were honest with ourselves, winning the league would be very difficult. Winning either the FA Cup or the League Cup was within reach but I had to keep reminding the supporters, and myself, that we had no right to expect success. The challenges I now faced were very different when compared to the one of trying to steer the club upwards.

After the cup final, the players' expectations rose as well and I remember a period when they were talking about bonuses and wages a little too much for my liking. One day at the training ground I was heading into the meeting room and I overheard them all talking about money and I flipped. I pulled out a ten-pound note from my pocket and waved it at them. 'Here you are,' I said, 'is this all that matters to you?' I ripped up the note and let the pieces flutter to the floor before I stormed out, my point made.

At Christmas that year, John Ward and the other coaches gave me a present. I unwrapped it and it was a little picture frame. I turned it over and saw it was the ten-pound note they'd picked up off the floor and Sellotaped back together. I had to laugh and, in fact, I put it on the wall of our downstairs loo as a reminder to myself not to get carried away by money.

Keeping our best players was always going to be difficult. It started the morning after the FA Cup final, when I opened the newspaper to see reports saying that Maurice Johnston wanted to go to Celtic. We'd just lost the cup final and none of us had covered ourselves in glory and this was the last thing the supporters wanted to read. Stories kept appearing in the press and although I knew Maurice wasn't responsible for them – he had a couple of advisers who I suspected were feeding the papers – I had to put a stop to it. So when Maurice had been selected to play for Scotland in France at the end of the season, I asked the Scotland manager, Jock Stein, if he would mind me flying over to watch the game. After the match, I asked to see Maurice and his jaw nearly hit the floor when he realised I was there to give him a telling-off.

'Look,' I said, 'we will get you your move to Celtic because I know we can't keep you, but we are going to do things properly and that means I want you to put a stop to all these stories in the papers.'

Later on that summer we had a short trip to Majorca and faced Barcelona and Real Mallorca on consecutive nights. It wasn't the ideal trip for us because it was very hot and we didn't need to be playing back-to-back matches late in the evening. We flew home on the Sunday and as we got off the coach at Vicarage Road at the end of our journey, Maurice handed me an envelope. I knew it was his formal transfer request. 'Thanks, Maurice,' I said. 'It's Sunday today and I don't work on Sundays, so I shall open this tomorrow.'

A few weeks into the season, we did sell Maurice to Celtic and I was sorry to see him go. He'd been with us less than a year but he had made such an impact. I liked managing Maurice. It can get a bit boring if you've got a whole squad of good chaps, and I had learned that some of the best players were also the biggest characters. He kept me on my toes and, although he had me pulling my hair out at times, I couldn't stay cross at him for long. When he was called up for the Scotland team, he gave me his first cap, which I really appreciated. I still have it, although I'd like to return it to him because it's something that he should have in his collection.

Losing Maurice was made easier by the fact we had brought Luther back from Milan for about half the money we'd sold him for. I had kept my promise to go and watch him play in Italy, and each time I did I'd felt so sorry for him because I could see how hard he was working and how little the Milan team were doing to exploit his strengths. I had such admiration for him because he went there, took a risk and spent a year of his career well outside of his comfort zone. I felt that when he came back to us he was a better all-round player than he'd been when he left.

I improved the team by bringing in some very good quality players. The goalkeeper Tony Coton from Birmingham City was one of the first. Tony will be the first to admit he had a reputation as a drinker and a bit of a brawler, and when I agreed to sign him I hadn't realised how much trouble he was in. He'd got involved in a situation with a taxi driver and was facing an assault charge. I spoke to people who knew him and they told me he was not a bad lad but that he needed to get away from Birmingham and some of the bad influences that were around him in his personal life. We signed Tony with a court case hanging over him and when I introduced him to the squad I explained the situation he was in and I asked his team-mates to look after him and keep him out of trouble.

When Tony's case came up, I asked the court if I could appear as a character witness for him and I made this speech saying that it was a one-off incident and that we had signed Tony because we believed in him, that his character had been second to none since he'd joined us, and that now he was away from unhealthy influences he was a new man. At the end of the hearing, the judge said: 'Mr Coton, you have been found guilty and will go to prison for six months…,' and as I heard those words my heart was in my mouth and if I'm honest I wasn't thinking of him, I was thinking of the £300,000 we'd paid for him going down the drain. Fortunately for us, and Tony, the sentence was suspended for two years. Later on Tony told me his sister had said she didn't recognise the man I'd been talking about but, to his great credit, Tony never caused me any trouble at all and he was one of the best signings I made.

As we began to establish ourselves as a First Division club, the calibre of players we were able to sign improved. John McClelland joined us from Glasgow Rangers and had a big impact, and later on I signed the centre-forward Mark Falco from Tottenham Hotspur, and Kevin Richardson, who had played for Everton against us in the FA Cup final and later went on to win the league championship with Arsenal. We continued to develop young players as well and in five years in the First Division we were never outside the top twelve places. Every now and then we would beat the top sides – we beat Tottenham Hotspur 5-1 away and Manchester United 5-1 at home in the space of three days in May 1985, for example, and we always seemed to get the better of Arsenal, but we were not consistent enough – particularly away from home – to challenge for the very top places.

After the crowd trouble at the 1985 European Cup final between Liverpool and Juventus in Brussels, English clubs were banned from European competition and that narrowed our horizons further. It meant that the FA Cup and the Milk Cup or Littlewoods Cup (as the League Cup was called then) were our most realistic chances of winning a trophy and, although we had some very good results, we fell short each year. In 1986 I felt we had a great chance when we got a very good 0-0 draw away at Liverpool in the quarter-final of the FA Cup and then led 1-0 in the replay at Vicarage Road. But Ian Rush won a penalty as Liverpool fought back to win. He ran onto a through-ball that had been played into the box, Tony Coton came out to meet him, Rush went over, and Roger Milford (him again) pointed to the spot. Tony swears he didn't touch Rush.

As a club, we had become self-sufficient, certainly in the sense of not relying on Elton to buy players for us, but he still footed the bill when we finally got permission to build the new stand on the west side of the ground, and as I look back now it was then that things started to change a little bit for me. The 1986-87 season was my tenth season as Watford manager. The first seven years had been about constant improvement and adventure. The next three were different and I suppose some of the fun had gone out of it. I am not saying that I wanted the job to be thrills and spills the whole time, but the challenge of trying to keep the team halfway up the First Division, with the possible excitement of a run in one of the cups, felt very different. Watford had arrived as a football club to the extent that some time around 1985 Elton and our chief executive Eddie Plumley had been invited to join the chairmen of the top six or seven clubs for talks about establishing some kind of breakaway Super League. Our community work and the fact we had a stadium where supporters could watch in a friendly atmosphere without having to look through ugly metal fences designed to stop them running on the pitch had been noticed, and in many regards we were seen as an example to follow. Of course those talks came to nothing at that time and by the time the Premier League, as it was eventually called, was established in 1992 Watford had slipped away from the top flight. But the fact we were involved in those discussions at that time shows what we had created in a very short space of time.

In 1987, we had another very good cup run and beat Arsenal at Highbury in the quarter-final on one of those days when the team defied the odds to win. We went 1-0 down, battled to get 2-1 up and then, in the dying moments, Arsenal appealed for a penalty and we broke away, got the ball up to Luther and he scored at the second attempt after John Lukic had blocked his first shot. The whole of the Arsenal team had stood still, shouting at the referee to give them a penalty, and I was up off the bench waving at my lads to keep going and play to the whistle. After Luther scored all hell broke loose. The Arsenal players surrounded the referee, our players were celebrating with our supporters, and the Arsenal supporters were banging on the back of our dugout calling us cheats, which was strange because we were the ones who'd played to the whistle rather than try to intimidate the referee. The protests carried on as the final whistle went, and my priority was to get our players off the pitch because their celebrations were only inflaming the situation. The coins were raining down on us and it threatened for a moment to turn really ugly but fortunately everyone cooled down just enough. It was one of those days where we felt on top of the world, having gone to one of the biggest clubs in the country and turfed them out of the cup when they'd expected to get through.

We were drawn to face Tottenham Hotspur in the semi-final, which was always going to be a tough game, but ten days before the match our task got a lot harder when Tony Coton broke his thumb during a training session. It was a bad break and we knew he'd be out for the season. Then, two days before the semi-final, his understudy Steve Sherwood dislocated his little finger while we were training at Lilleshall. He dived to save a shot and caught his finger in a divot on the pitch and it came out of the socket. Steve Harrison tried to get it back into place but it wouldn't go, so Steve had to go to hospital. In the end, his finger was out of position for at least a couple of hours and the swelling was bad. I called all the staff together and we ran through our options in case Steve was not fit to play.

We only had one other goalkeeper on the books and that was the youth-team player David James. Now with the benefit of hindsight, I've been asked over the years why we didn't put him in because David went on to have a very good career at the highest level and played for England at the World Cup. But at that time, David was still four months short of his seventeenth birthday and, although he'd played a few reserve-team games, the idea of putting him into an FA Cup semi-final against Tottenham Hotspur in front of 40,000 people just never crossed our minds. It would have been irresponsible of me to put a young boy, with his whole career in front of him, into a position where he might have such a traumatic experience it could be detrimental to his development. You might say that it could have been the making of him, or you might cite the old saying: 'If you're good enough, you're old enough,' but I happen to think that goalkeepers are slightly different. Whereas I would always give young players an opportunity when I felt they were ready, bringing in a player at the age of sixteen because we had no one else would not be fair on him. If it went well, fantastic, but if it went badly, he would always be the goalkeeper who conceded four on his debut in an FA Cup semi-final. So the idea of selecting David James was never considered.

As I remember it, the problem we faced was that we couldn't sign anyone who'd played in an earlier round of the FA Cup because they would be cup-tied. That ruled out every first-choice goalkeeper in the country. And because the transfer deadline had passed, we couldn't sign anyone who was registered with another club either in England or elsewhere, which ruled out pretty much everybody else. I know we contacted Pat Jennings – the legendary Northern Irish goalkeeper who had played in the 1986 World Cup at the age of forty-one but had not played a serious game since – but he was not interested, not least because Tottenham was one of his former clubs.

In my view, we had to have a plan in case Steve was unfit to play and, after a brainstorming session that went nowhere, it seemed our only option was the chief executive's son, Gary Plumley. Gary had been a professional goalkeeper, had played in Europe for Newport County, but now ran a wine bar down in South Wales where he'd also been playing non-league football. So I called Eddie and asked him whether he could get his lad to sign the forms to ensure he was eligible to play, just in case. At that stage I didn't think in a million years we'd need to use him.

The decision weighed heavily on me over the next couple of days. We gave Steve as much time as we could to recover and gave him a thorough fitness test on the morning of the match but, although he insists to this day he was fit enough to play, there was a nagging doubt in my mind. The medical staff told me there was a risk Steve could suffer a serious injury if he dislocated his finger again in the match. In the end, I went for Eddie's son. Perhaps I was guilty of thinking we could pull off another miracle but I genuinely believed it was the best decision, although it turned out not to be the case because Tottenham took shots whenever they had the opportunity and they quickly went 3-0 up and eventually won 4-1.

People will say I made the wrong decision, but at the time it felt like the correct one. Looking back, I wonder if subconsciously I was in the right frame of mind because somewhere between that magnificent win at Arsenal in the quarter-final and the semi-final against Tottenham, the fight went out of me. I certainly don't want to give the impression that things went sour, because they didn't, but I do want to explain why I came to the conclusion it was time for a fresh challenge, and to shed light on a few of the things that happened in that period to help me make up my mind.

In the week before the FA Cup semi-final against Tottenham, we had sent back almost 1,500 unsold tickets. Three years earlier – before the semi-final against Plymouth and the final against Everton – we'd been inundated with letters from supporters who had missed out on tickets, pleading that they were a special case and asking if we could arrange a ticket for them. There were so many letters that I had to say something to the local press and write in my programme notes asking for people to stop writing to us because the allocation was sold and there was nothing more we could do. Three years later, we were in another semi-final and there wasn't the same energy and excitement or sense of occasion and, although it perhaps shouldn't have mattered to me, the fact we sent tickets back to the FA did hurt me and make me wonder whether we were all getting a bit too cosy and complacent.

I could accept the criticism I took for deciding to play Gary Plumley in goal, but what I didn't like was that I received a letter from a supporter accusing me of nepotism by picking the chief executive's son. I was so angry about that. He put his address and phone number on the letter and I suspect he was hoping I'd give him a call. It was well known at that time that I replied to letters that were sent to me and sometimes I would call a supporter who had written to me if they had the wrong end of the stick about something or other. I called this chap and I was angry with him, which I didn't take any pleasure in at all. I tried to set him straight on what had happened and why I'd made the decision but, whatever anyone might think, I did not pick Gary Plumley as any sort of favour for Eddie – absolutely not.

My relationship with the supporters over the years was very good and I tried to be as honest as I could with them about things that were going on at the club, although there were obviously times when things had to be kept private. Once or twice I got things wrong and there was one famous occasion where I had to apologise to them. We were fighting for promotion to the First Division and were just entering the final part of the season. We'd beaten Bolton Wanderers 3-0 and played very well but we had only 12,000 or so in the ground and the atmosphere had been very quiet. Rather unwisely I made some comments asking if Watford supporters really wanted promotion and whether they shared the passion for success that I had. It was a big mistake because I got a lot of letters and so did the local paper. I knew I'd got it wrong and so before the next home game, against Crystal Palace, I went onto the pitch before the players ran out and held up a sign which read: 'I'm sorry.'

As we established ourselves as a mid-table side, I felt that the novelty wore off for some people. I do want to be very clear that I am not blaming the supporters at all because they were first-class, but finishing second in our first season did not necessarily help us. Some of them might have thought: 'Give it a year or two and we can win the league,' and that is absolutely fantastic, that is what I wanted the supporters to dream about. But if we were being brutally honest and realistic about our chances, were we actually going to be able to deliver that for them? There were times, too, when the crowds did dip, and some nights in 1987 we had only eleven or twelve thousand in the ground.

During the spring of 1987, there was another issue rumbling on in the background and that was the future of one of our star players, John Barnes. John had consistently shown what a talented footballer and athlete he was, and had scored and created goals for us over the course of six seasons. He had become an England international and played a role in the 1986 World Cup when he came on as a substitute in the quarter-final against Argentina and put over the cross for Gary Lineker to score a goal and then put over another very similar cross which almost resulted in an equaliser. There had been a lot of interest in John from the big clubs over the years but we had always managed to convince him to stay and continue his development with us, but now he was twenty-three years old and it was time to let him go. When you consider how football is now, there is no way a club like Watford would keep a player of John's ability for six seasons because the interest in him and the money on offer would be impossible to resist.

Over the years, people have asked me why we sold John so cheaply, because the fee of £900,000 that Liverpool paid was a bargain, particularly when you consider the players who moved for £2million that summer. But as I have always explained, it wasn't as simple as that. John's contract was due to expire and he wasn't going to sign another one but – because this was before the days of the Bosman ruling, which entitled players to move for free – Watford would be able to retain the player's registration until a fee had been agreed with the buying club. If we couldn't agree a fee, then an independent transfer tribunal panel would get involved, hold a hearing and decide on a fair fee based on a range of factors. Those factors included: how much did we pay for the player when he joined? In John's case, that was the price of a set of football kit. What was the player's salary and what sort of contract had we offered him? We had offered John a very good contract, one that would have smashed our wage structure if he'd signed it. We knew he would almost certainly turn it down, not because he was being greedy but because we knew he wanted a new challenge at a big club. It was all part of our attempt to demonstrate to a tribunal, if it came to that, how much we valued John. We could have said to the tribunal that we wanted £3million for him but our valuation would carry very little weight at the tribunal.

Our other problem was that the bidding war we hoped would drive up the price never materialised. Initially, John wanted to go to Italy but – other than a tentative enquiry from Sven-Göran Eriksson, who was about to go from Roma to Fiorentina – there was no interest and certainly no bid. In fact, the only club that was serious about John was Liverpool, the reigning league champions. They had contacted me back in January, asking if we were interested in selling and I told them to wait until the end of the season. I have to hand it to their manager, Kenny Dalglish, and their chief executive. They played a very smart game because they knew John wanted to join them and they could afford to wait. John's agent was Atholl Still and he knew what a strong position Liverpool were in. We did try to make other clubs aware that John was going to be available so there might at least be a bit of competition, but someone had done their job well and the football grapevine knew that Liverpool were the only club John wanted to join.

Before one home match towards the end of the season, I spotted a banner being held up on the Vicarage Road end terrace. It said: 'Don't sell Barnes.' I walked up the touchline and onto the terrace and I had a chat with the supporters because I felt they were not in possession of all the facts. How could they be? I said: 'You have to understand, it's not a case of us "selling" John Barnes. We have had six very good years out of him – more than we could have had the right to expect. He is now one of the best players in the country, and an England international, and his contract is expiring. We have no right to hold him back if one of the top clubs are interested in signing him.' I promised them that we would work very hard to do the best we could for Watford and in the end that meant accepting that if we dug our heels in and tried to play hardball with Liverpool, we might end up with much, much less money. We'd been on the receiving end of the transfer tribunal system once or twice – when we signed Paul Atkinson from Oldham Athletic we actually ended up paying more than Oldham had even asked for in the first place – so we knew it was an imperfect system. If the tribunal set a fee of £400,000 they might very well say: 'You paid the price of a set of football kit for him, so that's a fair price.' Liverpool offered us the choice of a million pounds, with half up front and half a year later, or £900,000 all in one go, and we opted for the £900,000. It wasn't what John was worth when compared to the fact Ian Rush was leaving Liverpool to join Juventus for £3.2million, but given the set of circumstances we faced it was as good a deal as we could do.

While all this was rumbling on, there were reports in the newspapers saying that Elton was trying to sell the club. Elton had underwritten the share issue that we hoped would cover the cost of the new stand (the one that now bears my name) but it fell well short and he ended up paying the bulk of the bill himself. I can't speak for Elton but I think he possibly felt that, although the club had become self-sufficient in some regards, everyone still looked to him when really serious money was needed. We never talked specifically about that but it's the feeling I got in those final months.

Recently, I happened to read through my programme notes for the Tottenham Hotspur game in May 1987 – what turned out to be my final league match in charge of Watford (for the best part of a decade, at least). My final line in those notes read: 'Whatever my future, Watford will always be a part of me for the remainder of my life.' Reading those words now it sounds almost as if I knew I was leaving, doesn't it? Perhaps my mind was made up. I do remember after that game, which we won 1-0, a journalist from one of the national papers took me to one side and said: 'Is that your last game here, Graham?' I said: 'Look, I can't tell you, but it probably is, yes.'

That was subtle of me, wasn't it? But a week or so earlier I had been contacted by a man called Dick Taylor, who had made me aware that there would be a job for me at Aston Villa if I wanted it. He had played for Scunthorpe United as a centre-half and was one of the players I would see running past the window during their training sessions when I was at school. He knew my father and always kept an eye on my career. In the 1960s, Dick had been manager of Aston Villa, and by 1987 he was running a sports shop around the corner from Villa Park and supplied the training kit to the club, so he was very well connected. Aston Villa had been relegated from the First Division a couple of games before the end of the season and had sacked Billy McNeill as manager. When Dick called me, it was the first time the idea of leaving Watford had seriously crossed my mind. Over the years, there had been a few approaches from other clubs but nothing that appealed to me. Crystal Palace and Sheffield Wednesday both sounded me out when Watford were still in the Second or Third Division. I'd been linked in the press with Manchester United (when they eventually opted for Ron Atkinson) but I don't remember any contact from anyone at the club. Ken Friar, the secretary at Arsenal, had been in touch at one stage but that never went anywhere and I often wondered why not.

There was something about the thought of going to Aston Villa that interested me. They'd been league and European champions within the past six years and they had the potential to be one of the very biggest clubs in the country. Having just been relegated they would no doubt be in need of a good shaking up but perhaps that was just what I needed. I had given it a bit of thought and the idea stayed in my mind, but it wasn't until the season ended that I made my mind up to go.

The day after our final league game, I was back at Vicarage Road to present trophies to the winning teams at a corporate five-a-side day the club had hosted. By the time I'd handed out the cups and posed for the photographs, practically all the staff and directors had gone home. I was more or less left to lock up the ground and, although I was well aware I had created the situation where I had the final say and responsibility for almost everything that went on at the club, I felt that I was being left to it more than I had been previously.

We had another tour to China coming up and, whereas in 1983 everyone wanted to go, this time there was only lukewarm interest. All these factors were playing on my mind when, three days after the final game of the season, we gathered for a board meeting at Vicarage Road in the afternoon before the first team were due to play Heart of Midlothian in Steve Sherwood's testimonial match.

My memory of that board meeting was that it was a bit tetchy, as if more was going unsaid than was being said. The cost of the new stand was weighing heavily on everyone. After the meeting, I had a quiet word with John Reid, who more or less confirmed that Elton wanted to sell the club. So I told Elton about the approach from Aston Villa and he said: 'We wouldn't stand in your way.'

No one got the pair of us together and said: 'Look, is this what the two of you want?' But even if they had, it wouldn't have made any difference because the truth is that it was time for me to go. I needed a fresh challenge before I got too set in my ways. I'd spent ten fantastic years at Watford and we had achieved everything we had set out to achieve, but even the very best things come to an end eventually. I had enjoyed such freedom to learn from my successes and failures and I'm sure by the end there were people who privately questioned the power and influence I had at the club and wished that perhaps the manager kept himself to football matters. It was, without doubt, the happiest ten years of my career but by the very end the buzz had gone.

Of course, Watford had to find a successor and I tried not to be too hurt by how quickly Elton approached Dave Bassett to take over from me. He offered Bassett the job before I'd officially resigned, in fact, and for a brief period of perhaps a day or so, Watford had two managers. At one point, Elton rang me at home. Rita answered and he asked her if I'd signed for Villa yet. 'No, he hasn't,' she said. 'Oh,' Elton said. 'Is he going to soon?'

My departure was a little bit messy but my friendship with Elton survived and, as I went on and learned the way other clubs operated, I only appreciated even more the relationship Elton and I had enjoyed. Because if there was a chairman who was the polar opposite of Elton John it was 'Deadly' Doug Ellis at Aston Villa.

20

Deadly Doug

Whenever I approach the Trinity Road stand at Villa Park it still causes me to pause, look up and just quietly take in the beauty of it for a moment. The steps seem to go on for ever and the red brickwork and the lettering 'Aston' and 'Villa' painted in gold on the facade give it a certain majesty that few other football grounds in this country have. Yes, Old Trafford is bigger and dominates its surroundings, and Arsenal, Manchester City and other clubs have very impressive modern grounds, but Villa Park – for me at any rate – has a sense of romance about it. I am so glad that as they have developed and improved the ground over the years, they have managed to preserve that entrance because it is special.

There was no doubting that Aston Villa was a big club. They had won the league championship and the European Cup only a handful of years earlier and yet had fallen from the top so quickly. From a distance, Aston Villa Football Club might have looked like a sleeping giant, but my first impression of the club was of one in complete disarray. If you examined the stadium too closely you could see parts of it were crumbling and the facilities had been left to deteriorate. From the carpets in reception to the cracked and missing tiles in the dressing room, the place was like a run-down stately home. I very quickly realised that the club was in trouble.

My first meeting with Doug Ellis was at his house only a couple of days after I'd told Elton of Aston Villa's interest in me. Rita had already planned to go up to Nottingham, where our elder daughter, Joanne, was at university. We were going to celebrate her twenty-first birthday with her but we stopped off to meet Doug and his wife, Heidi, on the way.

All that sticks in my mind of the conversation is this.

Doug asked me: 'Have you got a club car at Watford?'

'Yes,' I said.

'What is it?'

'It's a Jaguar.'

'You'll not be getting one of those here. And how much are you on?'

I told him whatever it was.

'Oh,' he said, 'we can't afford that.'

I was sitting there thinking: 'What am I even doing here?' That wasn't because Doug wasn't going to match my salary or give me a fancy club car but because the conversation was all the wrong way round.

At one point, I said: 'I will be dropping down a division to come here.'

I have to give Doug credit here because he was clever and he did have an answer for everything. Quick as a flash he said: 'Yes, so you will be a Second Division manager on a Second Division salary.'

I accepted that but I said that if we got promoted at the first attempt, I wanted the difference between my Watford salary and what Doug was offering me paid as a bonus, and he would then have to offer me a better deal. He was happy with that because I was effectively asking for performance-related pay, and I was happy because I saw moving to Aston Villa as an opportunity. If I could get them back to the First Division and if we could fill Villa Park on a regular basis, we would be able to attract good players and we might be able to challenge for the league title.

By the end of the meeting I had more or less agreed to become Aston Villa's new manager but, from that one meeting with Doug, I had worked out that I was going to have my hands full with him. I think it was Jimmy Greaves who came up with the nickname 'Deadly' Doug. As Villa's chairman, Doug had a reputation for being ruthless when it came to sacking his managers but by modern standards he was actually reasonably patient. Doug had been chairman of Villa for two spells but the unfortunate thing for him was that they had won the league and European Cup during a period when he was not at the club and I think that always irritated him, to say the least. When Tommy Docherty took over as Villa manager in 1968, Doug apparently said to him: 'I'll be right behind you every step of the way.' Tommy replied: 'Oh no you won't, Mr Chairman, you'll be in front of me where I can keep an eye on you.' That just about summed Doug up. I could never be quite sure what he was up to.

It was Doug's club, in the same way that Watford had been Elton's club, but I soon realised that Doug wanted to be the one running the show. He was a very successful man, as anyone who could afford a football club needed to be, and he'd made a lot of money running his travel companies, but he insisted on working at Villa Park every day, which meant he liked to get involved in what I was doing.

After I'd been at the club a few weeks, there was a board meeting, which I attended. As chairman, Doug sat at the head of the table, with the club's secretary, Steve Stride, next to him. I got on very well with Steve because he was excellent at his job and I found I could trust him, in as much as I could have a conversation with him and what I said would not find its way to Doug.

During this meeting, we got to Any Other Business on the agenda and Doug said to me: 'Graham, you have been here a few weeks now. What are your feelings about the club?'

I began to say that, in my opinion, the club was in a very poor state for one the size of Aston Villa. The ground, the training facilities, the complete lack of a scouting network, the way we treated guests who visited the club, the level of disorganisation. I rattled through these things and I was just starting to get warmed up but Steve, who was taking the minutes of the meeting, was struggling to keep up.

Doug leaned over and put his hand on Steve's hand and stopped him writing.

'Let's leave it at that, shall we?' he said.

'Mr Chairman, you asked me a question and I'm answering it.'

'I said, let's leave it at that.'

I can understand that he didn't want all the club's shortcomings to be highlighted in front of the other directors by his new manager who had only been there five minutes, but it did demonstrate to me that I had to be cleverer about making my point. I realised that I would have to play games with Doug and that they were games I'd have to win if we were to improve things at the club.

I don't want to give the impression that Doug was a bad man to work for, because he wasn't. If he had been, I'd not have lasted three years and I certainly wouldn't have gone back to Aston Villa when he asked me to become a director in 2002. But I had a constant battle of wits with him. On one hand, he owned the great majority of the club and he was the chairman, so he was perfectly within his rights to say Aston Villa was his club and that I was his employee. But I knew that if we were to sort the club out and restore the team to the First Division, I had to be able to exert my influence over all the things I felt were important – which was more or less everything that went on.

The other thing I had to be wary of was that Doug was not popular with the supporters. They held him responsible for the team's relegation, and when I gathered together a few weeks' worth of the local papers there was a lot of feeling that the club would be better off if Doug resigned as chairman and sold it to someone else – not that there was a queue of people waiting for the opportunity to buy it.

I had to make sure the supporters knew I was not Doug's yes-man and the way I did that was by getting up to address the shareholders at the Annual General Meeting, which happened not long after the season had started. An article about the AGM in one of my old Aston Villa programmes says I got up and spoke for fifty minutes, which I can well believe because that is exactly the sort of thing I would have done. I remember Doug was sitting alongside me and I could feel his eyes looking at me as I outlined all the things that were wrong. Because we were in front of the shareholders, he couldn't shut me up. He just had to sit there and take it, and I know he would not have been happy about that because when I said the club was badly run, I was basically saying it had been badly run by Doug. After the meeting, Doug could easily have been very angry with me but he let it go and from that moment on I felt we had a chance to sort things out.

The day the players reported back for pre-season training, I called everyone together and I invited the chairman, knowing that he would want to come. This was my chance to set out how things were going to work, knowing that everyone was going to hear it at the same time.

'I've asked the chairman to come and listen to what I'm telling you,' I said. 'We are in the Second Division and we are all going to be in this together. I can't do it on my own – in fact, it will be down to the players on the pitch to achieve promotion – but I will provide a lead and I expect things to be done in a certain way.

'What we don't want is a chairman who interferes in everything. We all want to get on, but I can guarantee that over the next ten months there is no way everyone is going to agree with everyone else. But what we're not going to do is go behind people's backs. If I have something to say to you, I will do so directly to you. If it's about the football, I will say it in front of the other players because it's for the benefit of the whole team. If you're not happy, I don't want you bothering the chairman, come to me.

'I am not interested in who did or didn't get us into this mess. I don't want you dwelling on what's gone wrong. I want you to be the group that is going to put things right.'

I knew the players would all nod along in the meeting and then go away and speak among themselves because that's what players always do. I wanted to make sure that everyone knew I was not going to be an easy touch.

I wanted to put together my own group of coaching staff but I had to tread carefully when it came to making one of my key appointments. When I left Watford, I had given them time to retain the coaching staff before I made an approach. I knew that Steve Harrison was out of contract because I had offered him a new deal at Watford and he had not signed it. He told me he had hesitated over signing the contract because he thought I would be leaving the club and he wanted to keep his options open. So I took him to Villa with me and I know it left a bit of a sour taste because Watford thought I was poaching their people. Having said that, Dave Bassett was bringing in all his own people, so I don't know if Steve would have stayed anyway. Shortly after arriving at Villa, I got in touch with Bobby Downes, who had been one of the players I had inherited at Watford in 1977 and since retiring had established himself as an excellent coach. Bobby was my youth-team coach. Dave Richardson, who had been at Villa when they won the European Cup, came back from Leicester City. And, together with the physio Jim Walker, that was my management team.

Sorting out the team that had to go onto the pitch was a different matter. As you would expect from a team that had finished bottom of the First Division, morale was very low. We'd also lost two very good defenders because Paul Elliott had already agreed to go to Pisa in Italy, and there was little chance of keeping Tony Dorigo, who went to Chelsea.

My first moves in the transfer market were to bring Steve Sims up from Watford and to sign Alan McInally from Celtic. I had lined McInally up for a move to Watford, and when I spoke to Celtic about taking him to Aston Villa instead they put about a hundred thousand on the asking price – even though we were a division lower than Watford – on the basis that they thought we were a bigger club and could afford it.

There was undoubtedly enough talent in the squad – we had Nigel Spink, who was a first-class goalkeeper, and a young centre-half called Martin Keown who Sims helped tremendously in that first season. We had two terrific wingers, Paul Birch, who sadly passed away from cancer in 2009, and Mark Walters, who we had to let go around Christmas time when Glasgow Rangers came in for him.

We also had Andy Gray, the centre-forward who had scored the second goal for Everton in the FA Cup final against Watford. I quickly made up my mind that I needed to move Andy on – and it was nothing to do with that goal, honestly. Andy had enjoyed an excellent career and he was very popular at Villa Park because of his first spell at the club, but I felt he had too much influence around the place. Don't get me wrong, I liked Andy, but I needed to demonstrate that I was the boss and that it was not optional to follow my rules. I wanted the players to enter the stadium by the players' entrance, not through reception and past the offices. Andy had a habit of going through the reception. Now, he may only have done it a couple of times but it was one of those things that I was not prepared to be flexible about. I didn't want the younger players seeing someone go through the main reception and thinking there was one rule for them and another for someone else. That wasn't the sort of club I wanted to be running.

Andy was thirty-one and had been at the top and I felt I needed players who had a hunger and desire to get there rather than someone who had been there already. Andy might bristle at the suggestion that he didn't have the desire, but I also had the words of the legendary Bob Paisley in my ears. He had once said: 'Make sure your player's legs go when they're on another manager's pitch,' meaning move them on before they start to fade. We got Andy a loan move to West Bromwich Albion and at the end of the loan they signed him.

My first home game in charge was against Birmingham City. We lost 2-0 and I found out then what a big-city derby game was all about. I mean no disrespect to Watford and Luton Town, because those derby matches could be spicy – although David Pleat, my opposite number at Kenilworth Road for several years, and I worked very hard to try to take the nastiness out of the fixture – but Aston Villa against Birmingham City was on a completely different level.

The reaction of the supporters that afternoon opened my eyes to what being the Aston Villa manager was all about. The atmosphere in the stadium was very, very hostile. At the end of the game, I wasn't sure who the Villa supporters hated most – Birmingham City or me. There was quite a walk along the touchline from the dugout to the tunnel and, dear me, I took some stick. I could feel that the goodwill towards me and all of the benefit of the doubt I'd been given evaporated that afternoon. Welcome to Aston Villa, Graham.

I knew it would take time to sort things out and to get everyone working the way I wanted to, but the pressure was on immediately. We didn't win any of my first six league games at Aston Villa. Fortunately, we were reasonable enough away from home to pull away from the bottom of the table, but the malaise at Villa Park went deep. The supporters stayed away. There had been 30,000 at the derby game but as autumn wore on and the nights drew in, we could attract only eleven or twelve thousand through the gates. That meant Villa Park was only a quarter full, and some days it felt like a club that was on its last legs. Although hardly anyone was coming to watch us, there were two newspapers in the city – a morning paper and an evening paper – plus a couple of radio stations, and all of them had something to say about the Villa.

I found the problems stemmed from a lack of leadership from the top. I don't want this to sound like I hold Doug responsible for everything that was wrong with the club and that I see myself as the hero who went in and sorted it all out, but when I think back to my three years at Aston Villa it is my relationship with the chairman that dominates my memories.

There was a lack of discipline at the club. There was a lot of gossiping, information leaked out when it shouldn't have, and no one seemed to know who was responsible for what so it was easy for people to pass the buck when things went wrong. It took me a long time to untangle all of that, but I went back to the basics that had served me so well at Lincoln City and Watford and, in the main, they served me well again.

One thing that couldn't work in Birmingham the way it had worked in Lincoln and Watford was that I couldn't take the club out into the community in quite the same way. I am not saying it would have been dangerous to do so but I was aware that not everyone in Birmingham supported Aston Villa. Half the city hated us and so we had to invite our supporters to us rather than go to workplaces, schools and so on. Early on, we organised an open day for children and their parents to attend and about 2,000 people turned up, which caught us by surprise. But I was generally unimpressed by the way the club engaged with the supporters. The club seemed to think that they would turn up no matter what, but it was plain to everyone that they had stopped turning up because the football results were not good enough. In a way, it was the downside of the 'big club' mentality they had at the time. What was heartening, though, was that when we made an effort the people did come back.

Doug was a businessman – and a very successful one – but I felt he had lost the willingness to speculate to accumulate. Perhaps the club had been losing money at such a rate that he felt it was like trying to fill a bottomless pit, but I always thought that if you spent a pound on something that benefited the supporters, you might get two pounds back from them in the medium term. What I found, by being open, was that people wrote to me about all manner of things. When we were doing badly in those early months, the supporters complained about the toilet facilities and the catering. I got a lot of letters about the team's kit too. We were playing in a strange shirt that was dark claret on one side and light claret on the other. The supporters wanted a traditional Aston Villa shirt with light blue sleeves. I have to admit I agreed with them but we were committed to a contract so we were stuck with it. What struck me was that when the team started to improve, the letters complaining about these things dried up. I am not saying that having a winning football team meant we could afford to neglect these details but I felt that we needed to improve all aspects of the club, on and off the field, if we were to be successful.

One thing I cannot doubt about Doug is that he badly wanted the club to be successful, partly because Aston Villa Football Club was his club and he wanted everyone to know it. So I had to demonstrate that what I was doing was for the benefit of the club, but it was always difficult to keep him from interfering.

When I first arrived, he would pop into the dressing room five or ten minutes before kick-off to wish the players good luck, and no matter how many times I told him to come earlier he wouldn't. I had no problem with him being in the dressing room but I wanted him in there no later than half an hour before kick-off because after that it was time for the players and staff to complete their final preparations for the game. It's when the nerves would be at their most intense, when players were starting to really concentrate on the match ahead and get themselves into the zone, and it was when I wanted to make my last remarks to them. No matter how well-meaning Doug was, I didn't want that time disrupted.

We were away at Huddersfield Town early in the season, ten minutes from going out onto the pitch, when I saw the door to our dressing room open. I got a glimpse of Doug and I leapt over to the door and slammed it shut saying: 'Not now!'

As I shut the door I trapped Doug's fingers – not on purpose, but I definitely caught them hard. The players were all looking at me, thinking: 'Has he just shut the chairman's hand in the door?' One or two of them started laughing. It was probably more disruptive than it would have been if I'd just let Doug come in to offer his best wishes, but the point had to be made.

The players went out and I headed up to the directors' box to watch the first half, as I often did. I sat down next to Steve Stride who said: 'The chairman says you've broken his fingers.'

'Well, Steve,' I said, 'if Doug says his fingers are broken I'd say they're badly bruised, at most.'

After that, Doug would make sure he visited the dressing room earlier.

I was engaged in this battle of wills and, if he is reading this, Doug might think that he won more than he lost. Perhaps I'm guilty here of only remembering my little victories, I don't know, but it was a difficult time for me because I was not used to having to play these kinds of games.

Doug used to like to know the team for Saturday's game and, while I had no objection to telling the chairman in confidence, I had a feeling that he didn't keep it to himself. I would work late at the training ground on a Thursday, ringing all the scouts and giving them their assignments for the weekend. Doug knew I'd be working late and he'd ring to ask what the team would be and I'd tell him. I then found that the team selection would be common knowledge around the club on the Friday. Usually I would not even tell the players the team until the end of Friday's training session or sometimes not until Saturday morning, but people – my secretary, staff at the training ground and so on – would know the team. I can't swear that Doug told people but I can't think how it got out otherwise.

After a few weeks, I'd give Doug the team but with two, three or four that I knew were wrong. And after a few weeks he realised he was not being given the accurate team line-up and he stopped calling. He never said to me: 'Hey, the team you told me on Thursday was wrong,' and I never said: 'Doug, people seemed to know the team line-up before I'd told the players.' I don't think there was anything malicious in it, I just think he liked to make sure everyone was aware that he was 'in the know'. But I couldn't have a situation where I couldn't trust the chairman with basic information.

The same was true when it came to discussing transfer targets. Doug would have his ideas about players, which is absolutely fine because it was his money we'd be spending, but he was reluctant to take my word. We'd have long meetings in his office discussing possible signings, and if he suggested a player I couldn't just say: 'No, he's not for me.' So I had to list all the player's bad points. If there was a player I liked, I'd get Steve Stride to drop his name into conversation with Doug so that it wasn't a surprise to him when it came up. I had to steer Doug towards my targets in such a way that he eventually thought it had been his idea. The risk was that he would be able to say: 'I suggested him to Graham,' but I could live with that.

In the main, the games we were playing were quite good fun and they kept me on my toes. I formed a good relationship with Doug's secretary at Villa Park and I got her to call the training ground whenever she knew he was on his way over. Again, I had no problem with the chairman coming to the training ground but I liked to know in advance that he was coming.

We had manual gates at Bodymoor Heath in those days and from one of the pitches you could see the cars that pulled up outside. One day I was out on the training pitch with the players when Dave Richardson came over and said: 'The chairman's here.'

I gathered the players round and said: 'OK, the chairman is coming to watch and I know he's going to want to get involved so, when he gets here, we're going to do some shooting practice, OK?

'I am going to ask the chairman to stand behind the goal and retrieve any balls that go high or wide of the goal.

'Now,' I said, 'I do not want anyone scoring a goal, OK? In fact, there's a five-pound fine for every goal scored.'

Doug came over and asked what we were doing. I told him and asked if he would retrieve the balls for us.

We started the drill and the lads were firing the ball as far over the bar as they could, trying not to burst into laughter as they were doing so. We did score a few goals, of course, but

Doug was running here and there, gathering the balls and kicking them back. He got quite a sweat on. After ten minutes or so, I wound up the session and said: 'OK lads, that's enough, in you go.'

As we were coming off the pitch, Doug came over to me and said: 'Good God, Graham, they are poor, aren't they?'

It was naughty of me but it was good fun and it made the point.

Sometimes, Doug would make me want to tear my hair out but at the same time I can't help but smile at some of the things I did. I had to be one step ahead of him. If I wanted some peace and quiet, I'd go and sit in one of the executive boxes up in the stand and work in there with the light off so he didn't know where I was.

Some of the things he did and said made me laugh too. We were talking about football in his office when he claimed he had invented the bicycle kick. He said he was playing for Tranmere Reserves during the War years and he said the ball came to him, he couldn't quite reach it so he leapt up and kicked it over his shoulder. What could I say to that? Maybe he did invent the bicycle kick, I really don't know, but that was Doug. He was always right.

21

Mr Chairman, it was never in doubt

One day, maybe a month or six weeks after I'd joined Aston Villa, I was down in London for a meeting and afterwards, instead of driving back up to Birmingham, I found myself heading towards Watford and Vicarage Road. I just wanted to have a look around the place and say goodbye, I suppose.

I parked in Occupation Road and got out of the car. Seeing a gate open, I walked into the ground and just took a seat in the stand and let all the warm memories come flooding back.

Over the next six months, I found myself making the same trip to Vicarage Road whenever I had the opportunity. I remember going to watch a Queens Park Rangers reserve game one afternoon and I made a detour to Watford on the way home. I must have gone half a dozen times or so, and sometimes I would go into the stadium if a gate was open but other times I would just sit in my car outside the ground. I told Rita what I'd been doing and I think she thought I was going mad.

There had been a few tears in the Taylor household when I decided to leave Watford, and I don't mind admitting some of them were mine. Ten years is a long time and I look back on the decade between 1977 and 1987 as the happiest time of my life – not least because Watford was the town where my two girls grew up and went to school. Thinking about it now, I was probably adjusting to more than just leaving Watford Football Club. It was also a time when I realised my daughters had grown up. Joanne was at university and Karen had left school and begun work at a bank. When she announced that she was not staying on to do her A Levels because she had got a job with NatWest, it never crossed my mind to tell her to carry on at school because my parents had never put any pressure on me to stay at school when I wanted to join Grimsby Town. It was her decision and we supported whatever she wanted to do.

In those first six months at Aston Villa I suppose I felt homesick. It certainly took me time to settle in the Midlands, but gradually it began to feel like our home. Rita and I found places to walk our dogs and the more I saw of Birmingham and the places surrounding it, the more I liked it.

Had performances on the football pitch been better, I expect I would have settled in more quickly but it was late October before we hit any sort of form and forced our way into the top few places in the Second Division. It felt like we had turned things around a bit but it wasn't until the New Year – when Steve Harrison left and went back to Watford as manager – that I really managed to shake the feeling that being at Aston Villa was a temporary sort of thing.

At the time I was a bit disappointed in the way Steve left but I couldn't really complain because he was being offered the opportunity to be a manager and I understood that he had to go and find out whether he was cut out for it. I think Steve would admit that it wasn't for him and that he was much happier as a coach, but until he went to Watford he couldn't know that. But, if nothing else, it stopped me from hanging around at Vicarage Road because I couldn't risk Steve spotting me sitting in the stand. That would have been difficult to explain.

Steve leaving for Watford also pushed me into making what turned out to be one of the best signings of my managerial career. We had played Huddersfield at home one afternoon over the Christmas period, and after the match I asked Steve to look after things because I was going to shoot off as soon as the final whistle went. I knew that Crewe Alexandra were playing at Newport County that evening, so I drove down to South Wales to watch their young midfielder David Platt. I paid at the turnstiles and stood on the terraces just as I had done in the old days, and I watched this player who had such excellent timing coming onto the ball from the midfield. When Steve joined Watford, I knew I had to move quickly because he knew of my interest in Platty and I heard on the grapevine that he wanted to make him his first signing. Crewe asked for £200,000, which was a bit more than I wanted to pay for him but – when you consider he played for England within about a year of joining us, starred in the 1990 World Cup and then earned Aston Villa £5.5million when they eventually sold him to Bari in Italy – it wasn't a bad signing. When I signed David I didn't really have room for him in the team and he didn't really break into the team until late February, but I knew I had to get him.

I have to give a great deal of credit to the players because the start of the season had been bad and they were getting a lot of criticism, but they stuck with what we were trying to do and they believed me when I told them that we would come good eventually if we carried on applying ourselves the way I wanted.

We hit the top of the table in the New Year but we made hard work of it during the run-in, losing three in a row and then drawing at Crystal Palace to slip out of the automatic promotion places and into the play-off spots. We beat one of our closest rivals, Bradford City, 1-0 at Villa Park in our penultimate game but it was a very, very nervy performance and it still left us needing results to go our way on the final day of the season. Millwall were already up, and had clinched the championship, and Middlesbrough were in the second automatic-promotion place, a point ahead of both us and Bradford City. Middlesbrough and Bradford had home games and we were away at Swindon Town.

We didn't play well. The pitch was bobbly and we were tense because we knew what was at stake and no one wanted to have to go through the play-offs having had such a great opportunity to win promotion outright. The game ended in a goalless draw but word had reached the dugout that both Middlesbrough and Bradford were losing. We heard the final whistle had gone at

Bradford, which meant everything hinged on the outcome of Middlesbrough's match against Leicester.

For some reason there was a long delay to the match at Ayresome Park and we had an agonising wait. According to reports it was only nine or ten minutes but it felt much longer. I was milling around in the corridor, waiting for the cheers from our supporters that would confirm we'd made it. Then came the cheers and the players started to run back out onto the pitch. But there was one man missing. I wondered where Simsy was.

Now, Simsy is not a religious man but when I went into the dressing room I saw he was kneeling on the floor, hands together, praying. 'It's worked, Simsy, we're up,' I said and we hugged and I let him go out to join the rest of the team.

We were up, but it couldn't have been much closer. We were level on points with Middlesbrough. We had the same goal difference but we were promoted because we had scored five more than them over the course of the season. My belief that the more goals you could score the better served us well.

As I got onto the coach, I sat down next to Doug.

'There we are, Mr Chairman. It was never in doubt,' I said, before leaning over and lowering my voice. 'I need to talk to you because I don't know if you know this, but I've heard a whisper that we might be able to get Gordon Cowans back from Italy.'

Within an hour of clinching promotion, I was planting the seed in the chairman's mind that we needed Gordon to strengthen the team for the First Division. Cowans had won the European Cup with Villa before going to Bari – the same club Platty would later join. Doug didn't know it but I'd been over to Italy to watch Gordon play a few times and I knew the club had first refusal on him if Bari decided to sell. When I'd been to watch Gordon, I sat with his wife Jackie – a lovely lady who kept feeding me chocolates throughout the match in an attempt to get me to sign her husband because she was desperate to come back home. On my final visit to watch him, I didn't tell her I'd already made my mind up to sign him, just in case she stopped offering me the chocolates.

When I first went to Aston Villa, I had had a conversation with Steve Harrison about how I was going to coach the team. 'Nothing is going to change except the way we talk to the players,' I said. 'I don't want to hear the words "long ball". "Long pass" is fine, but we'll change the language in case it causes us any problems.' When Steve went back to Watford, I brought in John Ward and I said the same thing to him.

I could be wrong about this, but I don't remember my Aston Villa side getting the same level of criticism as Watford had got, and yet I would say I changed very little in terms of my approach to the game. We were a direct side – I would not wish to deny that – and one that tried to create chances and win games. I liked the full-backs to play the ball up to the forwards quickly but, just as with Watford, we were not a team that hit it long and hoped for the best. There was a plan behind our play and, wherever they were on the pitch, the players knew what was expected of them. We had forward players who could win the ball in the air or hold it up effectively – Garry Thompson, then Alan McInally and later on Ian Olney, Ian Ormondroyd and Tony Cascarino – and we'd have been daft not to play to their strengths.

What I did do was change the way I delivered my messages. I used my coaching staff more because I felt that players needed to hear a different voice every now and then. No one likes to be bored in their work and, without a bit of thought, the rhythm and routine of the football season can quickly become over-familiar. Over the years, I employed various techniques to keep players entertained. Sometimes that was as simple as varying the training we were doing, but sometimes I'd surprise them by doing something completely different. I used to love going on long walks, and perhaps once or twice a season we would meet up at the training ground and instead of working on our football we'd go on a long cross-country walk and have a pub lunch. One time, when I was at Watford, I put up on the blackboard in the team room: 'Wednesday – bring in your dog (if you have one)'. The following morning I brought in our big red setter, Ben, and watched as some of the players got their own dogs out of the car. And that was us for the day, off on a long walk with our dogs. It was a chance to get to know each other as people, to talk and joke and generally grow to like one another because, although it's easy to assume footballers all get on famously, I can say from experience that a sense of togetherness has to be worked on and if you allow the players to think of themselves as individuals they will play like individuals.

At Aston Villa I told the players we were going away for a few days between matches and that they should report at the training ground with their passports. I'd done this before at Watford, but it wasn't something I could do often because they'd have known what was coming. Of course, they were all very excitable when they saw the coach pull up, like kids ready to go on a school outing, and they were speculating about where we might be off to. Spain, perhaps, for some warm-weather training. We got on the coach and headed towards the airport. There was a groan as we went sailing past the turn-off. Then they thought we might be heading to Heathrow and on to even more exotic climes, but we went past there as well. The bus driver was in on the joke, of course, and I remember we got to one of the ferry ports on the south coast and drove towards the check-in but went round the roundabout and came away again. 'Come on, gaffer, tell us where we're going,' they all said. Eventually we pulled up at Pontins holiday park, just as a coach load of pensioners from somewhere like Barnsley were arriving.

We'd train, of course, and I'd perhaps book a football pitch somewhere nearby so we could work on something or we'd do some fitness work, but it was about building a team spirit without forcing it to come together. One morning we went down to the beach and I said to John Ward: 'OK, Wardy, I want you to walk out into the sea, please.' Wardy looked at me as if I was mad – it was probably February or March and the sea would have been freezing. 'Off you go.'

Wardy started walking into the icy water.

'Keep going.'

The players were in hysterics by now.

'Keep going, Wardy...,' I said, until the water was up to his chest. 'That'll do you.'

I told the players they had to run into the sea, round Wardy and back. Then they jogged back to Pontins in their soaking wet kit.

When we got back we saw Steve Sims, who must have been injured, in his Aston Villa tracksuit with a bead of sweat on his brow.

'What have you been doing, Simsy?'

'Well,' he said, 'while you were gone, I entered the indoor bowls tournament and I'm through to the semi-finals.'

So that afternoon the whole Aston Villa squad was cheering on Simsy against a pensioner from Barnsley in the semi-final of the bowls competition. Sometimes it was the simplest of things that could bring a group of players closer together.

22

Even the best can have problems

Keeping Aston Villa in the First Division proved to be almost as difficult as getting them there in the first place. In 1988-89, we stayed up by the skin of our teeth after a very poor run of results in the spring. If the season had gone on another couple of weeks I suspect we might have gone back down, but fortunately we drew against Coventry City on the final day of the season which, combined with results elsewhere, was enough to keep us up.

I signed Derek Mountfield, a central defender from Everton, but he and Martin Keown did not get on terribly well. Both players had a lot about them – Derek was experienced, and Martin was not only quick but he was a quick learner. He'd been a youngster at Arsenal and I suspect he considered playing for Aston Villa a step down from that. I was quite strong with him and I wonder if he felt I picked on him a bit. I could see a very good defender in there but I also felt he had a lot to learn about the game. Like a lot of defenders who are quick, he used his speed to get himself out of difficult situations and I felt he could learn from the likes of Steve Sims and Derek Mountfield about how to read defensive situations and anticipate the play in order to cut out danger before it even happened. By making simple moves as the opposition start to come onto you, defensive players can spare everyone a lot of stress and anxiety before they even have to start defending. Eventually I sold Martin to Everton and he did get back to Arsenal and, of course, he played under Arsène Wenger for a long time and proved himself to be a top-class defender. I picked him for England, and when we played the Netherlands at Wembley I asked him to man-mark Ruud Gullit and he did an excellent job. In fact, that was his great strength – he could man-mark anyone in the world and keep them quiet for ninety minutes.

My problem was that, although Mountfield and Keown were both very good players, in terms of a partnership they could sometimes be like the opposite ends of a magnet in that they didn't go well together. We lost heavily at Nottingham Forest and I tore into both of them after the game. 'You two are letting each other down. You have to learn to play together.' As it turned out, they didn't because as I look at the Villa results from that season I can see that they only lined up together three more times because one or other of them was invariably out of the side.

But I could see there was the beginnings of a good team in there, even if results weren't going too well; it was just difficult to get everything to come together at once. I was getting to grips with the First Division again and trying to make the most of players we had. I didn't get everything right, not by a long chalk, but I was very confident in what I was doing and I wasn't afraid to make difficult decisions if I thought it would benefit the team. I remember at Middlesbrough we had Keown sent off when we were leading 2-1. I put Paul Birch on as a substitute and within about five minutes realised that I'd got the balance of the team all wrong. As far as I was concerned there was still time to correct it and get something out of the game so I asked Derek Mountfield to warm up. When the board went up with Birch's number on it, he looked amazed and must have thought it was a mistake. He was right over on the other side of the pitch, about eighty yards away, and he mouthed across to me: 'Who? Me?' I beckoned him off and I put my arm round him and said: 'I am really sorry but I made a mistake and had made the wrong substitution.' He was so good about it. I suppose it does happen from time to time but I wonder if you'd get away with that now, with all the television cameras at games. It would certainly get a lot more attention and would be used as evidence to suggest the manager didn't have a clue what he was doing, but I believe that a football game changes and evolves, particularly when the players on the pitch change, and that if the manager has the ability to make a change to try to get a result, it's up to him to do that even if it means looking a bit silly in the short term. Fortunately we managed to get a 3-3 draw there.

At the end of the season, we sold Alan McInally to Bayern Munich, which annoyed me because I learned about their interest very late, by which time Doug had more or less agreed to sell him. To be fair to Doug, it was a very good deal because we made almost a million pounds profit on Alan, and it was a very good deal for Alan because he was going to play in Germany for one of the top clubs in Europe, so it wasn't that I wanted to stand in his way but it did frustrate me that Doug thought he could make a decision without consulting his manager.

I didn't do too badly for Doug in the transfer market, though, because before I left I signed Dwight Yorke, although Doug always insisted he spotted him first. In fairness, you didn't need to know much to recognise that this boy had something special. In the spring of 1989, after we'd been knocked out of the FA Cup, we had a chance to take advantage of an invitation to Trinidad to play a couple of games and enjoy a bit of sunshine. Dwight played in one of the games and made such an impression that at half-time I went into the opposition's dressing room and asked if they'd let him play for us in the second half. They explained that they couldn't do that, saying it might not go down too well if he scored against his own team. It may only have been a friendly for us, but it was a big deal for the Trinidad team. Anyway, I spoke to his manager and arranged to speak to Dwight's family and we invited him to Birmingham for a trial. It was very similar to the situation we'd had at Watford with John Barnes in that I was being trusted to look after a teenage footballer who was away from his family. Although Dwight only made a couple of appearances for Villa before I left, he was a big favourite with the supporters for many years.

When I left Villa for England I said to him: 'If you ever need anything, give me a call. Just because I am going to take the England job does not mean I'll forget about my responsibility to you.'

I heard from Dwight once in a while and one day, several years after I'd left, he called me and said: 'Gaffer, I've got a problem.'

'Go on,' I replied.

'Aston Villa have just offered me a new contract that will make me their highest-paid player ever.'

'Yes?'

'But Manchester United have come in for me.'

I thought for a moment and then said: 'You have to ask yourself, who are more likely to win the Premier League and European Cup in the next few seasons – Aston Villa or Manchester United? The other thing is, I said you could call me any time you had a problem.'

'Yes,' he said.

'Well, you've called me to say that Aston Villa want to pay you more money than they've ever paid anyone, and Manchester United want to sign you. So my question to you, Dwight, is what's your problem?'

Manchester United paid Aston Villa more than £12million for Dwight Yorke and so if Doug is reading this, I'd like to say that no matter how much of a pain in the neck I was for him at times, I think I made it worth his while.

I don't know how I came to hear that Paul McGrath was available but I do remember my phone call to Alex Ferguson to ask why he was letting him go. It turned out that Manchester United weren't just trying to sell him, they were trying to persuade Paul to accept a testimonial and hang up his boots. In effect, they wanted to pay him off. I'd heard rumours about the drinking culture at Manchester United – everyone in the game had – but I couldn't believe they were prepared to just write off a player as good as Paul, so I asked Alex what was going on.

'If you can keep him sober and fit he's the best defender in the country,' Alex said. 'We've tried but I don't think it can be done, so if you think you can do better, good luck to you.'

That sounded like the sort of challenge I could take on. Paul may have thought I didn't know about his drinking but I did; I just didn't realise the extent of the unhappiness he was experiencing and I soon found myself wondering if I had taken on more than I could handle.

When he first arrived, I thought I was just dealing with a player who liked a drink. I thought the challenge would be to make sure he didn't drink on the eve of a match or miss training because he was hungover. After I'd signed him in July 1989 I rang round a lot of the popular pubs and clubs and asked the landlords and landladies to keep an eye out for McGrath and to let me know if he was overdoing it, but that wasn't anything I hadn't done before.

What I didn't appreciate was just how much physical and emotional pain Paul was in. He had a long-term problem with both his knees. He'd had so many operations that he barely had any cartilage left in the joints. A lesser player would have been forced to retire but, with careful management, we were able to keep him playing. He had to train differently to the rest of the players. On the first day, I got the whole squad to run laps round the pitch and Paul was very soon a hundred yards behind the rest so we realised we had to excuse him from the running, and much of his training was done in the gym on an exercise bike or with weights to spare his knees. We just needed him to do enough to keep his general fitness levels from deteriorating.

But he was also a vulnerable person who was struggling with things that I had absolutely no experience of. He was a mixed-race boy with an unmarried mother and it can't have been easy for him growing up in Ireland in the 1960s and 1970s. He had been from children's home to children's home. Paul didn't tell me this at the start, but I asked about him and his background and I pieced it together.

I couldn't begin to understand what all that must have been like for him, so my first decision was not to pretend that I could. It wouldn't help him if he thought I was being nosy or patronising or just treating him as a commodity I wanted to make the best use of. I don't like to use the word 'damaged' but Paul was hurting and I knew I had to handle the situation carefully. When I signed him, I promised him that I would help and support him. Of course, I had done that because I knew he could be an asset to the team, but also he was a human being who had problems and it was my responsibility to do everything I could to help him.

I didn't know him well, but I could see that he was a boy who needed to be loved, supported and encouraged. Football can be a tough world and showing weakness often does people no favours at all, and so I could understand when people resorted to drink either to bolster their confidence or forget their problems. So I told him that my office door was always open if he wanted to talk to me. At first, I didn't see him apart from in training. He didn't knock on my door but that was understandable. He didn't know me and he perhaps didn't trust me yet.

I knew he could play though. He could read the game so well I sometimes wondered if he could somehow see a minute or two into the future. He could pass, tackle and head the ball. He covered for his team-mates, he organised the defence and he dictated the play. Having said that, it's fair to say he did not show that in the first few weeks of the season.

I had persuaded Doug to pay a considerable fee for a player Manchester United were trying to put out to pasture. I'd convinced Doug to give Paul a considerable wage – much more than he had been on at Old Trafford, I think – and in the first six weeks of the season I was wondering if I'd made a mistake.

Shortly before kick-off at Villa Park one day, our physio Jim Walker came to me and said: 'I'm pretty sure McGrath is drunk.'

We'd handed in the teamsheets and, although we could probably have said to the referee that Paul had injured himself in the warm-up and made a change, I didn't necessarily want to draw attention to the situation if I could help it.

I walked round the dressing room and gave my final instructions to the players. When I got near McGrath, I could smell the drink on him. I couldn't swear to it, but I think he may have held his breath. 'You OK, Paul?'

He hesitated but replied: 'Yes, gaffer.'

'Sure?'

'Sure.'

'OK, well, just do what you do best. Keep it simple, help your team-mates and good luck.'

As the players left the dressing room, I watched Paul carefully. There's no doubt about it, he was drunk, but he played OK and didn't do anything to embarrass himself but I realised that I needed to get a grip of things. What I didn't appreciate was that things would get a lot worse for Paul before they got better.

A couple of weeks later he travelled to Dublin to join the Ireland squad before their match with Northern Ireland. Paul was actually injured and wouldn't play in the game but I agreed with the Ireland manager, Jack Charlton, that he could join the squad because the World Cup was only round the corner and he wanted all his best players with him. I felt that a few days away might do Paul good because it would keep him occupied.

He was due back with us on the Thursday to begin preparation for our game at Luton Town on the Saturday, but he didn't turn up for training that day or on the Friday. No one had mobile phones in those days, so it wasn't a case of giving him a quick ring to find out where he was and what he was playing at. I rang his wife, who hadn't seen him, and I rang Jack, who said they'd last seen him on the Wednesday night or Thursday morning. Paul didn't show up for the Luton game. I told the press he was injured and hadn't travelled with the squad, but the truth was we didn't have a clue where he was.

Eventually he turned up, after a bender that had lasted several days, and I resisted the urge to give him a telling-off because something about the whole situation told me it would do more harm than good.

One afternoon, Jim Walker got a call that confirmed to us just how serious things had got. Paul's children's nanny was on the phone in distress, saying that Paul had slashed his wrist with a kitchen knife. He went first to hospital and then we got him a place at a clinic and we were very careful who we told about what had happened because the last thing we wanted was the press finding out.

After that, Jim spent a lot of time with Paul and would travel with him to Ireland games to make sure he didn't disappear again. We did what we could to help him, but what we could not do was live Paul's life for him. All we could do was make ourselves available to him and hope that he would come to us. Gradually, Paul started to open up to me and we'd talk every now and then. It was clear to me he didn't want to carry on drinking as much as he was but that at times he found it very, very difficult to stay away from alcohol. I asked him how he felt about playing football and he said that he was at his happiest when he was at the club or on the pitch. I told Paul he could talk to me about anything at any time, that he was welcome to come and stay with Rita and me if he felt it would help him stay off the drink, and slowly I felt things began to improve for him.

I read parts of Paul's book when it came out but I found it very hard to get through, even though I knew how low he had been at times. There was something about seeing in black and white how bad things had been for him that was upsetting. He was very generous in the things he said about me, which was nice to read, but I like to think I would have done the same for any of my players. As a football manager, it sometimes felt like there was nothing more important in life than the performances on the pitch and the result on a matchday, but working with Paul reminded me that all players can have problems at times and those problems don't evaporate just because they are footballers. In fact, they can sometimes feel harder to handle.

Paul played on at the top after I left Villa. He played for Ireland in two World Cups, he was loved and respected by the Villa crowd, he was the PFA Player of the Season, and he was part of the Aston Villa team that beat Manchester United in the League Cup final in 1994. His life since retirement has not always been easy but it could certainly have been a lot worse, and so if one or two of the things I said to him have helped him along the way, I am very glad, because Paul was a first-class player and is a first-class person. He is rightly loved by the Villa crowd and they still call him 'God' to this day, although I keep meaning to have a word with them about that, because I thought there was only one God at Villa Park.

23

Close to the sack

I'm convinced to this day that I came very close to being given the sack by Deadly Doug in September 1989. Our start to the season had not been good, with only one win from the first seven league matches. The last of those seven was a 3-1 home defeat to Queens Park Rangers on a day when we played very poorly. We were sitting in seventeenth place in the table and things weren't looking too rosy. Next up were Derby County at Villa Park and on the morning of the match I got a call from our commercial manager, a man called Abdul Rashid, saying that the chairman wanted me to meet him in his office after the game. This was unusual because Abdul was not someone who would have got involved in football matters all that often. I wondered why it was him and not the club's secretary Steve Stride who was passing on the message.

When I saw Steve I said: 'He's going to sack me, I know it.'

Steve replied: 'No, he would have told me.'

'He wouldn't have. He knows we're close.'

Doug might very well deny it, and I have no proof other than my own instincts, but I am absolutely certain that had we not beaten Derby that afternoon, I'd have been sacked. So I am very grateful to the team, and to David Platt who scored the goal, for saving me.

My suspicions were confirmed when I went to Doug's office. 'You want to see me, Mr Chairman?' I said.

Doug spoke about something or nothing for twenty minutes, certainly nothing of enough consequence to merit setting up a meeting hours in advance. When Doug left, I said to Steve: 'See, he was going to sack me.'

That victory over Derby started a run of only two defeats in eighteen league matches and we had a real run at the league title. I'd like to be able to put my finger on precisely what changed but, like so much in football, it was just a case of patience being rewarded. We had worked hard for two seasons to create the sort of working environment I felt we needed. I had brought in Dennis Booth as a coach and he freshened things up and added something different. I had not intended to play three central defenders, but Paul McGrath, Derek Mountfield and Kent Nielsen, who I had signed from Denmark, were all so good I couldn't decide who to leave out. Again, playing three at the back was not new in football but there weren't many sides in the First Division playing that system. It enabled my full-backs to get forwards to support the attack and supply the crosses for my forwards. I had Ian Olney and Ian Ormondroyd who were both six-feet-plus. I don't want to sound too clever here but at the World Cup the following summer a lot was made of England's switch from a back four to a back five and how that contributed to them reaching the semi-finals, but I had played a similar system for almost the whole season. We also had David Platt and Gordon Cowans in the midfield and they worked so well together. Platty was terrific bursting through from deep and knowing that Gordon would sit and cover for him.

Unfortunately, we didn't have enough to push Liverpool all the way for the title. We hit the top of the table for the first time with a very good victory at Tottenham in February, only to lose the next game 3-0 at home to Wimbledon. That performance was very unlike us because we just didn't perform that day. I wondered if we had enough experience in the dressing room to keep the pressure on and get results even when we didn't play too well. Nigel Spink, Derek Mountfield and Gordon Cowans had won big trophies before, but for everybody else it was a new challenge. Although we did regain the position, Liverpool were the masters at winning the title and their run of form made it very difficult for us because they lost only one match between the start of December and the end of the season.

Finishing runners-up with Aston Villa felt very different to finishing runners-up with Watford because I had a feeling that, with a couple of additions, the side could push on and win the title in the next couple of years. However, as the season wound down I was already beginning to suspect that I might not be the man to take them any further.

Bobby Robson had already decided he would be standing down as England manager after the 1990 World Cup in Italy, and I had already been mentioned as a possible successor. I'd been involved with the FA since running the under-18 team and, shortly after I joined Villa, Bobby had asked me to take an England B team to play in Malta so I would be lying if I said the idea of managing England did not appeal to me.

One day Eddie Plumley, who was still chief executive at Watford, called me at Aston Villa to ask if my home phone number was still the same. It was a bit of a strange question so I asked him why he wanted to know.

'Graham Kelly at the FA has just been on to me, asking if I had your home number,' Eddie said. 'He didn't say this but I think he wants to talk to you about the England job.'

After a couple of meetings, the FA offered me the job and I did not hesitate. However, both the FA and I wanted to make sure nothing took attention away from Bobby and the England team who were going to Italy hoping to win the World Cup, so I had to keep it quiet even though it was an open secret in football circles.

The announcement was finally scheduled for 16 July 1990, two days after my daughter Karen's wedding. The announcement was delayed so that we could be certain nothing would overshadow my daughter's day. We certainly didn't want the press turning up at the church.

Can you imagine how proud I was, walking my daughter down the aisle on her wedding day, knowing that I would be unveiled as my country's football manager two days later?

24

A lonely job

When talking about the England manager's job I have to be very careful not to sound like I am making excuses, because that is the last thing I would want to do. A manager may not kick a ball, score a goal, or make a mistake on the pitch but I had been a manager long enough by 1990 to know that the buck would stop with me.

There's no point me trying to put a positive spin on things because everybody knows how it turned out. I can talk about the things that went right and the good results we got, but people will always remember that we failed to qualify for the 1994 World Cup. I cannot blame them for that because I feel exactly the same. As soon as anyone mentions the word England to me that is what I think about and I cannot get past it. Don't get me wrong, being England manager was a great, great honour. I was the seventh man to manage our national football team and I could not have been prouder to be asked to do the job. But not qualifying for the World Cup is something that I will take to the grave with me. That may sound like a dramatic thing to say but it is how I feel. Twenty or more years may have passed but it still hurts and, although I may have learned to live with it, I have not learned how to forget it.

As a result, it is not a period of my life I enjoy remembering. I find it very hard to think back to the summer of 1990 and recall the feelings of pride and excitement because I know in my mind what came next and that colours everything. We failed to qualify for the World Cup and I understand what that did for the country and I feel very responsible for it. I knew people were upset and disappointed, and I accepted the blame for that, but I will always maintain that I don't think anyone was more disappointed than me. I have carried that disappointment ever since because I know how badly I wanted to do well.

You might call me naïve for this but when I took the job I was not thinking about anything other than being successful, and that meant winning either the European Championships in 1992 or the World Cup in 1994. I had been a Football League manager for almost eighteen years and I had been successful more or less the whole time. I'd finished runner-up in the league with two different clubs. When I was at Watford I had been asked to take on the England under-18s and later, when I was at Villa, I took the B team to Malta, so I felt I had some international experience. I was almost forty-six years old, full of energy, at the peak of my career and ready for the challenge.

When I was given the job, it was not seen as a controversial appointment, although I always felt some people did hold two things against me. One was that I had not been a top player. I have always argued that playing and managing are two very different skills, and in recent years we have seen top managers such as Jose Mourinho, Arsène Wenger and others who have succeeded even though they did not play the game at the highest level. The second criticism was that, although my managerial career had been successful, I had not won a trophy or managed one of the very top clubs, and yet my track record stood up against anyone else who might have been in the running for the England job. When you look back at who had managed the league champions in the past decade or so, Bob Paisley and Joe Fagan of Liverpool had retired, as had Aston Villa's Ron Saunders. Kenny Dalglish of Liverpool and George Graham of Arsenal were Scottish, and at that time the idea of the Football Association appointing a non-Englishman to the role was unthinkable. That left Brian Clough of Nottingham Forest, who had been overlooked before, and Howard Kendall of Everton, who I gather was on the shortlist but was not offered the job. I don't want to do myself down here but I have heard people ask why I got the job in the first place, as if it was a complete surprise, but it is worth remembering that I had just finished second in the league with Aston Villa, having brought them out of the Second Division. I am not blowing my own trumpet but I was one of the best club managers in the country at that time.

I went to the 1990 World Cup in Italy to write a column for *The Times* and, although it had not been confirmed that I would be succeeding Bobby Robson, everyone knew that Bobby was going and that I was firmly in the frame. He had already lined up a job in the Netherlands with PSV Eindhoven. I attended some of Bobby's press conferences at the World Cup, sitting at the back of the room and observing the tension between him and the journalists. Bobby handled it very well but later on I wondered why I had not realised what could happen to an England manager when things were going against him. Bobby had been given a rough time over the years, particularly by the tabloids. After losing all three games at the European Championships in 1988, one headline read: IN THE NAME OF GOD, GO.

The 1990 World Cup showed how quickly things can change. Before the tournament and after the first two games, which were draws against the Republic of Ireland and the Netherlands, it seemed everyone was against Bobby. Then England beat Egypt 1-0 in the final group game, David Platt scored in the last minute of extra time to knock out Belgium, and then England had to come from behind to beat Cameroon, before losing to West Germany on penalties in the semi-final. It was not a smooth passage through the competition by any means. I am not being in any way critical because that is the nature of international tournament football – there are a lot of tight games and the impression of a team's performance is determined entirely by the result. However, the transformation in attitudes was remarkable. People were very upbeat because England had reached the semi-final, losing only on penalties, and the World Cup was deemed to be a success.

GRAHAM TAYLOR

In July 1990, two days after waving my daughter Karen and her husband Stuart off on their honeymoon, I drove down to the Football Association's headquarters at Lancaster Gate in London. This sounds a bit daft but my first job was to find out what the England manager actually did on a day-to-day basis. I knew it would not be the same as club management but I really wasn't prepared for how different it would be. I started keeping notes and it is interesting to look back at them because they are an accurate record of what I did and thought at the time. Our memories of events fade and change as the years go by and so my notebooks have been very valuable in helping me tell the story of my time as England manager. People may not agree with what I thought or did, but I am glad to have the notes I made because at least I cannot be accused of applying the benefit of hindsight to events.

One of the first things I did was arrange to speak to as many of the former England managers as I could. Between them Walter Winterbottom, Alf Ramsay, Ron Greenwood and Bobby had almost half a century of experience in the job, and yet I didn't feel any of them were really able to prepare me for what I was about to face because it became apparent that each person had done the job the way they felt was best and I would have to do the same.

At the start, there was a lot to sort out and get to grips with, so it felt a bit like a busy pre-season. I had important decisions to make, like appointing my assistant, coaching staff and scouts, checking out our training bases at Bisham Abbey in Berkshire and Lilleshall in Shropshire, and smaller things like getting measured for my England blazer. Most of the fixtures had been decided before I took the job – our qualifying campaign for the 1992 European Championships in Sweden would pit us against the Republic of Ireland, Poland and Turkey and, with only the group winners reaching the finals, I knew how important it would be to get off to a good start. A trip to Australia, New Zealand and Malaysia had been planned for the summer of 1991, but before all that would be my first game in charge:

a friendly international against Hungary at Wembley on 12 September 1990. The rest of my time was spent learning about the job and speaking to people who were involved either as players or staff.

When I read through my diary now, I see that a lot of time was spent talking with Jon Smith, the agent who represented the playing squad, about the bonus scheme and players' pool, which was the percentage the players got from the FA's commercial arrangements. That was something I had not really bargained for and, although I always got on well with Jon, it did show me that for the players there was more to playing for their country than pulling on the shirt purely for the honour. I cannot really be critical of them for that because the FA would make a good deal of money from sponsorship arrangements, especially if the team did well, but I suppose I still had romantic ideas about what it meant to represent England. Having said that, I was being paid well so it wasn't like I was doing the job solely for love; it's just that the discussions about money and contracts always seemed to take up more time than I thought they should.

I realised quite quickly that the FA was leaky because my decision to ask Lawrie McMenemy to be my assistant appeared in the papers before I'd had a chance to speak to him. I met with Don Howe, who had been Bobby's assistant, and asked him to stand aside because I felt we needed to break from the previous regime. I also felt that having myself, Lawrie and Don might be too overpowering for the players and that we needed to balance the staff by bringing in a younger man. I explained that I wanted to do much of the coaching myself and that there was no way a man of his experience would want to put out the cones and hand out the bibs. I could see that Don was a bit hurt but he was nevertheless very generous with his advice as we sat and chatted about his experiences and how he saw the England set-up. He warned me about the number of players who would pull out of the squad, particularly for friendly matches, and that if there was a First Division match on a Sunday it might mean some of the players would not arrive with us until late morning

on the Monday, meaning the first training session of the get-
together could be messy.

I would go down to Lancaster Gate for meetings with the
international committee or Graham Kelly, the chief executive
of the FA, but I soon realised there was no point being down
in London all week. I learned that Bobby Robson had worked
from home in Suffolk, using his secretary who had worked for
him at Ipswich Town to do his administrative work, so I decided
to convert my study at home in Little Aston into an office. I got
a fax machine installed and set up a television and video so I
could watch tapes of matches.

Working at home was such a change from what I was
used to. You might say I should have realised beforehand how
different it would be – and of course I did to a degree – but it
was not until I actually took the job that I began to understand
what it was really about.

An international side plays maybe eight or ten fixtures a
year, instead of the fifty or so I was used to at club level, and
there would often be a month between matches. I wouldn't see
my players for weeks at a time – and even as I say that I have
to correct myself because the players were not *my* players, they
belonged to their clubs. I can't say I was ever twiddling my
thumbs because I would always find something to do, but so
much of my time was spent on the telephone, leaving messages with people, waiting for them to call back. The day-to-day
activity of a football club, the bustle and the banter, was not
there and right from the start I missed it terribly. Working at
home was not for me and I am sure I drove Rita spare. I would
get up in the morning, have some breakfast, then take a cup of
coffee into my office and start work. I'd go for a run to burn off
some energy because I was used to being active, but it wasn't the
same as training a squad of players every day.

A lot of what I enjoyed about the job and many of the things
I felt I was good at were gone or at least dramatically reduced.
I was a football coach. I enjoyed working with players on the
training pitch, getting my ideas across. For two decades the

rhythm of my week had been the same, with everything building towards matchday. Now I had weeks to fill. I even missed Doug Ellis interfering in things. I suppose it was hard because I am a people person. I like to be in company, chatting, joking, sharing ideas and talking about the game, and so after a short while I found it very isolating. I will go as far as to say that I realised quite early on it was going to be a lonely job.

Knowing I couldn't sit around in my office all the time, I wrote to the managers of all the clubs in the First Division to ask if I could visit so I could introduce myself to all the players who were eligible to play for England and to meet those who were in my short-term plans. As well as meeting all the players, whenever I arrived at a club's training ground I would offer to take a session, partly to keep my hand in but mostly because I missed coaching so much.

The first club I visited was Southampton and when I offered to take a session their manager, Chris Nicholl, asked me what I wanted to do. I threw it back at him and asked what he wanted and the outcome was that I ended up with the first-team squad, the reserves and a few apprentices – about 35 players in all – trying to run a cohesive training session. I knew they'd never usually train in such a large group and that he was either testing me or having a bit of fun at my expense, but that was fine by me, I enjoyed the challenge. At Liverpool, we played an eight-a-side game and they put me in one of the teams. I didn't realise this at first but all the players on my team had been told to pass the ball to me every time they got it, so I'd get the ball and pass it to John Barnes or Peter Beardsley or whoever it was, and they'd give it straight back so I barely got a rest. It wasn't long before I was absolutely knackered and in the end I said: 'Hang on, fellas, what's going on here?' and they fell about laughing. Later that same day they were going through some corner and free-kick routines and Barnesy came over to me and said: 'We never usually do this. It's just because you're here.' When I went to Nottingham Forest, Brian Clough invited me into the office but quickly made his excuses because he had to go and babysit his grandchildren, so he left me with his staff, Archie Gemmill and Ronnie Fenton. At Oldham Athletic, I had a very good chat with Joe Royle, who was one of the brightest English managers at the time and someone I had in mind to work with the under-21s or B team. Everywhere I went, I asked people what they thought of the England players because they were the managers who either worked with them or came up against them. I was always interested in hearing other managers' opinions about players.

There was something that surprised me, and perhaps it shouldn't have done, but I got the feeling not every First Division manager had an interest in the England team doing well. At Manchester United, Alex Ferguson was very polite and friendly but he seemed reluctant to let me watch training or speak to his players, although we did have a good lunch and a very interesting discussion about football. I found the same with George Graham at Arsenal. I think it is too simple an answer to say their indifference towards the England team was because they were Scottish. I know when I was at Aston Villa I felt just as proud when Paul McGrath was selected for Ireland as I did when David Platt played for England but perhaps that was because I believed international football was the pinnacle of the game and their recognition reflected well on the club. Meeting Alex and George – and in fact it was an attitude I found at several of the top clubs – I realised that they saw international football as an inconvenience. I can understand why. After all, what was in it for them? They sent their best players off to spend almost a week with England, knowing there was a risk they might come back injured. I tried to be fair with the club managers but my job depended on picking the best players and sometimes that meant there was some friction between me and the clubs.

My tour round the clubs and my conversations with the England players had been revealing. I visited Glasgow Rangers and had a long talk with Terry Butcher, who had decided to retire from international football after the World Cup. He told me the players often got bored during international get-togethers because there was a lot of time to kill. The more players I spoke to, the more this problem came up. I knew there were a number of obstacles to overcome if I was to create the sort of team spirit and togetherness that I felt was so important at club level. For a start, we would have much less time together as a squad to build an understanding on the football pitch and relationships off it.

I always believed that a happy group of players had a much better chance of performing well than an unhappy group. I wanted to make sure the experience of joining the England squad was enjoyable, so I decided to ask Steve Harrison to join the coaching staff. I felt he was exactly the sort of person to keep people entertained and to boost morale. Steve was from Blackpool and had he not made a career in professional football, he'd have had a career on the stage because he was a natural comedian. He could have the players in stitches with his end-of-the-pier act and impressions. He had a great knack of loosening people up but what he was also very good at was making sure players knew when it was time to focus on what we were working on in training.

I wanted everyone in the squad to work to the same rules – and that meant all reporting at the same time. When there were league matches on a Sunday it could mean half a dozen players were unable to join us until the Monday morning, so I decided that everyone could report on Monday morning. Our base was usually the Burnham Beeches hotel, a short drive from the training centre at Bisham Abbey, which was convenient to get to Wembley for home matches. Many of the players arrived in their own cars, which meant that the London-based players would sometimes go home in the evening and commute in again the following morning for training. I didn't want this happening, so I requested that all players should travel by train to Burnham and then take a taxi. I also explained that there would be no visitors while we were together as a squad, and that meant wives, girlfriends, friends, hangers-on or agents. During our time together, I wanted everyone's priority to be the England football team.

I spoke to Chris Waddle, who was playing for Olympique Marseille in France, on the phone and he said he felt there was too much food available and that he could easily put on two or three pounds if he was just left to his own devices and allowed to eat what he wanted. He felt that meals should be set, rather than letting the players help themselves from a buffet. It was an interesting comment because I had always been very keen on making sure players stuck to their ideal weight, even during the summer. Further conversations with people suggested that there were problems with players ordering room service, particularly drinks, and racking up huge phone bills, although that was not necessarily a problem for me if the FA were happy to pay.

There was also an issue with the amount of access journalists had. Some players felt uncomfortable having journalists in the hotel. The set-up at Burnham Beeches was such that after a press conference the journalists would hang around in the lobby and the bar, writing their stories, which meant many of the players went to their rooms and stayed there. That inevitably made the players feel like they were trapped in their rooms rather than free to relax. I decided that we would ask the journalists to leave after press conferences. The FA invited the media to fly to away games on the same charter flight as the team and, while I was perfectly happy with this arrangement, when I realised that the journalists were all used to sitting at the back of the plane where they could see everyone and everything, I decided to move them all up to the front. They liked to see who was talking to who, or perhaps walk up the aisle and have a word with a player without me knowing, so I felt that if there was anyone who should sit at the back of the plane and be able to see what was going on, it should be me.

I'd always had a good relationship with most journalists and when I took the England job, I was determined to be as open as I could with them, while also being fair to everyone.

When I was appointed, I was offered £25,000 – a very good sum of money – to do an exclusive interview with the *Today* newspaper, but I turned that down and decided I would not give any newspaper preferential treatment over another. I also resolved not to give any journalists tips about who might be in or out of my squad. I thought this was the smartest, fairest approach because then no one could get upset that I had given their rival newspaper a story they didn't have. I organised lunches for the reporters and columnists who covered the England team so that we could get to know one another and they could gain some insight into how I intended to do things. As time went on, I realised that in trying to be fair to everyone, I had perhaps made a mistake because it meant I didn't have too many allies in the press who would stick up for me or put my point of view across from time to time. In trying to treat everyone the same, I had not played the game to my advantage. I didn't have the sort of relationships with individual journalists that I think an England manager needed. I wasn't in a position where I could pick up the phone and give a bit of background information to a journalist, knowing that my thoughts would end up reflected in a newspaper column. Maybe it wouldn't have made any difference but it was probably naïve on my part and it did mean that when the press turned against me, they all turned against me.

Once the season got underway, I watched as many games as I could – sometimes four or five a week if it was possible – but it once again reminded me what I was missing. Arriving at a ground on a matchday and having no part to play was not a new experience for me but I knew I was not going back to work with players the following morning and would have to wait weeks for my matchday.

It's very difficult now to look back and remember the feelings of excitement I had, but I must have felt it. I *know* I felt it. It's just I can't separate the disappointment of what came later from that sense of embarking on something new and unknown. In the late summer of 1990, I may have been outside my comfort zone and working very differently, but I was the manager of England – the best job in football – and all my time, focus and energy was going into thinking about how to create the best possible team from the players available. So I went to matches and took notes. I tried to see every possible England player in action, I made sure I met them, and I started to think about who I would name in my squad for the first game against Hungary.

25

Judged on results

England had just reached the semi-finals of the World Cup in Italy and so I didn't feel I needed to make big changes to the squad. Besides, it wasn't as if there were half a dozen better players who had been left at home and were waiting to force their way in. However, there were gaps I needed to fill. Peter Shilton and Terry Butcher had retired from international football, which meant a vacancy in goal and in defence. Bryan Robson, whose World Cup had been cut short by injury, was not out of my thoughts although he was not the same force in midfield that he had been at the peak of his career. When I had visited Manchester United, Alex Ferguson told me he was considering using Robson as a sweeper, which was an idea I was keen to keep an eye on.

With Robson likely to be in and out of the side depending on his fitness and form, and following Shilton and Butcher's retirements, the first big decision I had to make regarding the playing staff was who to name as my captain. Among the candidates were those who captained their clubs – which meant Mark Wright at Derby County, Stuart Pearce at Nottingham Forest and David Platt at Aston Villa – but I opted for Gary Lineker, who was probably the most experienced player at international level in that he had played in two World Cups and one European Championships. I had selected a forward as my captain at club level on a handful of occasions before, but it was quite unusual for me to do so as I preferred a defender or midfielder to lead the side because I felt they had more of the play out in front of them. But I went for Gary for a number of reasons. He was well respected and when he spoke people did listen to him. I can't say he was a leader of men like Bryan Robson or Stuart Pearce, who would roll up their sleeves and show the way for the rest, but he had a quiet authority about him. If I am honest, I knew I needed Gary's influence on my side rather than against me, and giving him the captaincy was one way to do that. I also knew that the likes of Wright, Pearce and Platt would do their bit anyway, so in one sense I was giving myself a captain-type figure in several areas of the pitch. Gary was also very comfortable with the media, he spoke well and he was happy to appear at the press conferences whenever he was asked. I was also impressed by his disciplinary record, in that he had never been booked or sent off. He didn't talk his way into trouble with referees and I felt that was an important example to set for the rest of the squad. And, of course, at his best he was a world-class goalscorer. His reading of attacking play was so natural and so instinctive. He was quick, yes, but the timing of his runs got him into so many scoring positions. He knew forward play inside-out, he took responsibility for shooting, he took responsibility for missing, which is just as important, and he followed shots in just in case there was a rebound to put away. So although I had reservations about giving a forward the captain's armband, Gary had a lot of other qualities that made him the clear choice for me.

For my first game against Hungary, I decided to continue with the formation that had worked well for England at the World Cup, with three central defenders, two full-backs who could push up to support the midfield and two up front. Whether you call it three-at-the-back or five-at-the-back, it was a system I had used at Aston Villa for the simple reason that it was the best way to use the players I had available. A lot is made of formations or systems but picking a team is about making the most of your resources, and with Mark Wright, Des Walker and Paul Parker I felt I had three players who complemented one another in defence. Parker was a good marker who could also get forward, Walker was very quick, although I sometimes felt he used his pace to get himself out of trouble rather than spotting danger before it occurred, and Wright saw himself as a ball-playing sweeper who could bring it out from the back and start off the attacks. I was never too sure about that because I felt he slowed things down for us too much and that by the time he got up the pitch the opposition had cut off his options and he ended up playing the ball sideways or backwards. But having those three at the back meant the two full-backs, Lee Dixon and Stuart Pearce, could get forward. The midfield partnership of David Platt and Paul Gascoigne was like chalk and cheese. It's a bit unfair to say that Platt did all the graft and Gascoigne all the craft but I felt that if they were both on song they could develop a very good understanding. I knew David very well because I had signed him for Aston Villa and I liked him very much but I was aware that he was still relatively new to the England squad, having forced his way in not long before the World Cup. I deliberately did not speak to him before the squad met up for the Hungary game because I didn't want to put him in an embarrassing position with the other players, who might suspect I would ask David about them.

I knew I had to make a choice between John Barnes and Chris Waddle. There had been a lot of debate about whether they could both play in the same side and, while I thought that they possibly could in the right circumstances, I also felt that by accommodating two players who wanted to embrace a so-called 'free role' I would be creating problems elsewhere, particularly when you consider we would also have to cover for Paul Gascoigne at times.

It is no secret that I did favour John. I felt he was one of the country's most gifted players and many of his performances for Liverpool, particularly during his first couple of years at Anfield, had been magnificent. I remember shortly after he left Watford I was chatting to Liverpool's coach Ronnie Moran, who couldn't believe what a good player they had bought. 'He's so fit,' Ronnie said, 'and he doesn't need to be taught about the defensive side of the game, he just automatically slips back into a good position when we are out of possession.' I explained to Ronnie that at Watford we did not have the luxury of allowing Barnes to stand on the halfway line and wait to be brought into the game. We were not such a good side that we could spare him from the defensive effort, so he had to drop back in and help out and he was very good at that. At Liverpool, who enjoyed so much possession, he had really stepped up a gear and for two seasons he was far and away the best player in the country, in my opinion, but there had always been this question mark over him and his performances at international level. It had become a cliché: why was John Barnes not the same player for England that he was for Liverpool? I hoped that, because of my relationship with him, I might be able to bring the best out of him when he played for England.

When I took over as England manager, John was at a crossroads. He was almost twenty-seven and at the peak of his career, certainly at club level. He was talking to Liverpool about extending his contract but I knew he wanted to test himself abroad, preferably in Italy. We talked about how to give him the freedom to play for England the way he did for Liverpool but I could sense that the criticism he got for his displays at international level affected him. When I went up to Liverpool to meet him, we spent so little time talking about the simple joy of trying to play the game in an attacking, enjoyable way that I made a note in my diary that read: 'Where has the boy in him gone to?'

Chris Waddle, meanwhile, was a big hit at Olympique Marseille, although on some occasions when I went to watch him I was shocked by how poor the opposition offered by teams in the French league could be. Both John and Chris gave me the impression that they looked down their noses at British-style football a bit and I have to admit that disappointed me. Both of them were very talented but, for whatever reason, neither had really made a place in the England team their own and I at least wanted to give one of them, ideally John, the chance to do that and show he could be one of the best players in the world.

It's as true now as then that if you asked players, managers and coaches – and journalists and supporters for that matter – to pick an England squad of, say, twenty-two players, eighteen or nineteen of them would be the same. Very rarely is a squad named where there's a national debate about who should and shouldn't be in it. When it comes to picking the starting eleven, it is often a very different matter. Everyone has an opinion on that, which is fair enough. It shows how important the England team is to the country that people debate the team selection so passionately. But, when all is said and done, only one man is in a position where his selection is put to the test. Everyone else's team remains unbeaten. All the discussions are put on hold for ninety minutes and, although it may not be the case that everyone agrees with the selection if the team wins, when they lose people are very vocal about what was wrong. The England manager is judged on results, it's as simple as that. Of course, people will have their opinions on the performance too but if England win there will not be too much criticism.

My time as England manager started well. We won our first two matches. The friendly against Hungary was tighter than it should have been but we came through 1-0, and the opening European Championship qualifier against Poland was a fairly comfortable 2-0 win. I was very pleased because we'd won two games without conceding a goal, while showing signs that there was plenty of room for improvement. Then came a trip to Dublin to face Jack Charlton's Republic of Ireland. This was a week during which I experienced for the first time just how intense the spotlight could be on the England manager. I realised then that if you fail to win, everyone in the country thinks they can pick a better team than you can.

26

A troubled genius

The first time I met Paul Gascoigne after I'd become England manager was at Tottenham Hotspur's training ground one afternoon. He arrived for the meeting with a two-litre bottle of Diet Coke and a huge slice of cake, which was unusual enough for me to make a note of it in my diary.

There is no disputing Paul's talent. He was arguably the most gifted English player of his generation and it is such a shame that it was not possible to build a side around him, for a number of reasons.

I want to be very careful what I say about Paul, because he has had a very difficult time since retiring from football and his struggle with alcoholism is well known. He is a sensitive, vulnerable person and I am convinced that the intrusive press coverage of his life has not helped him. I don't think he's ever had a strong enough group of people around him to actually look after him and I always feel very sad when I see a photograph of him in the newspapers, particularly when he is looking distressed, because I think back and ask myself whether there was more I could have done, as his England manager, to influence him. The problem was that I found it almost impossible to get through to Paul, as did many others.

As a footballer, Paul could take your breath away one moment and have you tearing your hair out the next. He had such ability to twist and turn with the ball, he had wonderful feet and he could see a pass before anyone else, and he was comfortable dribbling the ball even in congested areas of the pitch, but his greatest genius – that he could play off the cuff – was also his biggest weakness. Sometimes Paul didn't know what he was going to do, which made him such a handful for his opponents, but that was also not easy for his team-mates.

There was so much hype around Paul because of his play, but it is also important to remember that there were two sides to his game, as we had seen in the World Cup semi-final where he made a rash challenge that earned him a booking that would have ruled him out of the final, had England made it.

When he was at his best, Paul could win you a game. He was one of those special players who caused the crowd to come alive when he had the ball, but there was such a lack of discipline to his play and he could indulge himself to the point that he put his team-mates in difficulty. His enthusiasm meant he went chasing the ball all over the pitch. I tried to tell him that I wanted him to play in the opponent's half of the field and we would get the ball to him, but he would drop back and take it off the full-back or go wandering over to the flanks to get involved. There was an almost childlike innocence to his play in that regard but it meant the players who were in midfield with him had to be prepared to do a lot of work to cover for him. People might say that with a talent as obvious as Paul's the manager's job is to give him the space to use his ability, and I tried to do that, but too often his performances were well short of what he was capable of producing, not just for England but for his club too. Of course, we remember the flashes of brilliance, the moments that light up a game, but, for me, they were too infrequent. Paul had played well against Hungary, but my notes following the win over Poland said: 'Very disappointing display. Not with it and contributed very little to the team's performance – in fact, it could be argued I should have replaced him. His mind seemed all over the place and his appreciation of the state of the game and the requirements of his colleagues was poor. Very emotional, lacks concentration.' I do not reproduce those notes to embarrass Paul but to shed light on my thinking going into the game against the Republic of Ireland in Dublin.

During my time as England manager I was in charge for thirty-eight matches and Paul played in only eleven of them. Most of the times he was absent were because of injury, but the Ireland game was the first time I left him out of the side when he was available to play, and it caused quite a storm of controversy.

Everyone knew that playing against Jack Charlton's Ireland at Lansdowne Road on a mid-November afternoon would be a battle. We'd already lost John Barnes with a hamstring injury and when we were waiting to get on the flight at Luton airport our doctor, John Crane, told me that Chris Waddle had complained of an ankle injury, so rather than risk him I pulled him out of my line-up and put Peter Beardsley in alongside Gary Lineker.

People have often asked me why I left Paul out of the side. Well, people can choose to believe this or not, but I had been told by someone I trusted that the Ireland side were planning to wind him up and try to get him sent off. Now, I cannot prove that, and people might dispute it, but that is what I was told and it reinforced my thinking that this was not a match for a volatile Paul Gascoigne to play in. Instead I went for the steel of Steve McMahon, who would roll his sleeves up and fight but had the discipline not to go over the top or retaliate, and the calm of Gordon Cowans, which enabled me to put David Platt just behind the two forwards where I felt he could make those late runs from deep he was so good at to give us an additional goal threat. My job was to pick a side I felt could win the game, which I did, but the fact was that if we could not win the game, we simply had to avoid losing it because in a group of just four teams, with only the top side advancing to the finals, there was precious little room to slip up.

As I expected, it was a poor game played in very challenging conditions. There was swirling wind and rain and, as was often the case against the Irish, it was an ugly match which ended in a 1-1 draw. People could say with the benefit of hindsight, as indeed they did, that it was a bad decision to leave out a creative player in such circumstances, but I would stand by my decision on the basis that it is only ever the manager's team selection that gets put to the test. The journalists and supporters can name their preferred line-up safe in the knowledge that they cannot be beaten. That is not me trying to sound clever, by the way, it's just a fact. Yet what did surprise me was the reaction in the press. They couldn't see that I had picked a team to suit the situation and the circumstances. I realised that leaving out any of the best players – even if they were out of form or if I felt there was someone else more suitable for a particular game – would attract a great deal of criticism.

Because of a niggling groin injury Paul missed the return match against Ireland at Wembley the following March, which also ended 1-1, and the win in Turkey, which put us in a strong position to qualify from the group with two matches still to play. In fact, he didn't play for me again for almost twenty months because of a cruciate ligament injury he sustained in a reckless challenge on Gary Charles in Tottenham's FA Cup final against Nottingham Forest. By the time he was fit to play for me again, he had transferred to Lazio in Italy and had missed the European Championship finals in Sweden. One of my biggest disappointments was that Paul Gascoigne was not available for selection for so much of the time I was England manager. Perhaps rightly, I was criticised for not selecting Paul against Ireland, but he was unavailable for almost half of my competitive fixtures as manager.

27

A team of individuals

There has always been an attitude, particularly among the press, that England should win every game they play, and I have no problem with such high levels of expectation as long as it does not become a sense of arrogance or entitlement. The England team's biggest problem has always been that it is the nation that invented football and then gave the game to the world, but it is important to remember that England have only won the World Cup once and that was on home soil in 1966. In the 1970s, we failed to qualify for two consecutive World Cups – 1974 and 1978 – and in the late 1980s and 1990s it is fair to say that many countries we used to consider minnows in footballing terms caught up with us. I don't think the players ever assumed they would beat a side simply because they had the three lions on their chest, but I do think that journalists and supporters assumed we would be successful simply because we were England.

One of the biggest difficulties I faced as an international manager was getting a squad of fully fit, in-form players together. When I look back through my notebooks, where I have listed every squad I ever selected, it is interesting to see how many players' names I had to cross through because they were ruled out by injury. I seemed to spend half my time on the phone to club managers, checking on the fitness and availability of the players. In my thirty-eight matches in charge, I selected the same starting eleven for two consecutive matches on only one occasion – and that was for my first two games, against Hungary and Poland. However, it would not be right of me to say all the changes were forced upon me because of injuries, because it was only natural that I would want to have a look at different players according to the circumstances, particularly when it came to friendly matches.

I would name a squad for an international match and then dread the phone ringing with the news of players who had picked up an injury and would have to pull out. Once everyone had reported for duty I could at least be secure in the knowledge that I'd have a whole two days to prepare for the match before waving goodbye to them again for perhaps the best part of a month. I am not complaining, I knew the deal and it had been no different for my predecessor, but I always had a sense of frustration that we had so little time to work together. We may have had two days or so to train together but with a match to play it wasn't like we could do long, intensive sessions because the players would get mentally and physically tired, so I had to be clever about how I used my time, working with the starting line-up and trying to get my ideas across simply and effectively.

This will sound obvious, but an international team is made up of a collection of individuals who are all used to doing things differently. You might have two or three from the same club but, in the main, they are all used to a different style of play, a different way of training and a different routine. It was impossible to accommodate everyone, and even the simplest things like the pre-match meal and routine would have to be a compromise so that, in effect, you might have an entire team of players doing things in a way they were not used to. There was nothing much I could do about that other than set things out the way I felt was best and hope that the players could adapt. To be fair to the players, I never felt any resistance from them and no one ever complained, but I knew they were not preparing for England games the way they would have done for games with their clubs. People might say that as they were the best players in the country they should be able to adapt to anything, but as a manager I wanted them to feel comfortable.

Every player I selected for an England squad was a first-team player for their club and was not used to being on the bench, let alone left out of the matchday squad, and so I quite soon realised that if I left a player out he might not think too highly of me. If I did it a couple of times in a row, he might really not like it, and so I had to work hard to keep everyone involved otherwise they'd soon think it was a waste of time turning up. I had to think about it from a player's perspective – did they want to spend the best part of a week travelling to Hungary, Turkey or Czechoslovakia and not get on the pitch? So many of my conversations with players were encouraging them to feel part of the group even if they weren't in the team. In those days we could name five substitutes and when we played at Wembley the players who were not named in the matchday squad would sometimes go home instead of watching the match from the stand. You might think that would indicate they were unhappy with me, but I didn't mind them going because it meant they could be back in time to train with their club the following morning.

All this was new to me and it meant that building relationships with the players was not particularly easy. At club level, players had been my players. In many cases, they were people I had chosen to sign. We had worked together on a daily basis and everyone had got to know each other well and so a team spirit had evolved. It was so different when it came to the England team and, while I accept that the manager's job is to work with those constraints and make it work despite the lack of time together, it was not easy.

At the end of my first season in charge, we had a tour to Australia, New Zealand and Malaysia organised. The location and the schedule would not necessarily have been my choice, but it was planned before I took over and because two matches had been organised to celebrate the New Zealand Football Association's centenary there was no way we could pull out. But playing four times in twelve days, hopping from Sydney to Auckland then Wellington and finally Kuala Lumpur was not ideal. However, it would at least give me a chance to work with a squad of players for an extended period of time, even if it turned out that no one from Arsenal, Liverpool or Manchester United came with us. We agreed with those three clubs that their players would not be called up, which was frustrating but it would at least give me a chance to see who else was capable of stepping up.

The game against Australia in Sydney was a hard, bruising match, completely unsuitable for the end of a long season and meaningless in terms of learning anything about the players or preparing for a European Championships campaign. We won it 1-0 but it was a horrible game. The match two days later, in Auckland against New Zealand, was even worse but we managed to win that 1-0 as well. After that it was on to Wellington, where we played on a rugby pitch that was hard and bumpy and the weather was cold and windy. We were without Gary Lineker for this game because we had agreed that he could go to Japan to play in a match as he was just beginning negotiations to move to the Japanese league. Lineker came back in time for the match against Malaysia and he scored all four goals in a 4-2 win that at least meant we ended on a positive note, but my thoughts on the trip as a whole were not positive.

In hindsight, I didn't feel the trip should have been given full international status, but then again, if it had been a B-team tour even more of the established players would have pulled out. Whenever England play, there is pressure to get results and even though we won the games, we did not do so in an impressive or pleasing style and so the press coverage was understandably negative, which we could have done without. There were too many uncapped players in the squad and they were all nervous about whether and when they would get to make their debuts, so there was a level of tension around the camp that was unnecessary. And, of course, the Australia and New Zealand teams needed no incentive to raise their game against the English and so they played out of their skin, even if the quality of the games was extremely poor. Against New Zealand we tried to control the matches but we ended up playing little nothing passes rather than really getting at them and showing we were the better side.

Despite my worries, and the grumbles in the press, I had ended my first season as England manager undefeated and yet I was frustrated by so many things: the stop-start nature of the season, the lack of continuity in my squad selection, the rising tension in my relationships with club managers, and the overall lack of control I had over things that I felt were important. At club level, I had been the captain of the ship, plotting a course, changing direction if I felt we needed to. Being England manager felt more like steering an ocean liner and my job was to try to avoid the many icebergs in the way.

My unbeaten run as England manager lasted one day short of a calendar year. We played Germany in a friendly at Wembley on 11 September 1991 and lost 1-0. However, we clinched our place at the European Championships by doing just enough to beat Turkey at Wembley the following month and getting a draw in Poland in November thanks to a late Gary Lineker equaliser. The finals were to be held in Sweden and we were drawn in a group with France, Yugoslavia and the hosts. With a tournament on the horizon I began to feel positive about our chances, particularly when we beat the French 2-0 at Wembley in February and played very well in doing so. I gave Alan Shearer his debut in that match and he scored a good goal and looked impressive. I felt that in Alan we had a centre-forward who could lead from the front, someone I could gradually introduce into the team so that when Gary Lineker retired he would be ready to take on the responsibility.

In March and April, we had friendly matches against Czechoslovakia in Prague and against the CIS, which was the name the old Soviet Union team was playing under, in Moscow, and this is where my problems with the big clubs came to a head. I want to be clear that in later years I like to think I got on very well with Alex Ferguson and Graeme Souness but at that time I found them very difficult to work with. At times it was farcical. There was a period where I was phoning Liverpool's training ground and spending more time speaking to their groundsman than I was to Graeme. Once I phoned and I heard a Scottish voice in the background say: 'Tell him I'm not here.' You can imagine how frustrating it was but I had to accept that some managers would put their club's interests ahead of the England team's.

The Saturday evening before we were due to face Czechoslovakia, word reached me that all of Manchester United's players in my squad – Paul Parker, Gary Pallister and Neil Webb – had picked up knocks and would be unable to travel. The following day I got a call from Neil who said he was fit and didn't know why he'd been pulled from the squad, so I rang Alex and we had a very bad-tempered conversation for ten minutes or so. That's actually an understatement. I was on the receiving end of Alex's so-called hairdryer treatment, but think I gave as good as I got. I was extremely irritated that he had pulled his players from my squad when I had every right to call on them, and he was angry that I had spoken directly to one of his players.

In fairness to Alex, the England team was not his priority and why should it be? Manchester United had a very realistic chance of winning the league championship that season (although in the end they lost out to Leeds United) and they were entering a crucial period, so I could well understand him being unhappy that almost a third of his team was being asked to fly to eastern Europe and back.

I later learned that after they only managed a goalless draw with Wimbledon that Saturday afternoon, Alex had told all his international players they could forget about joining up with their national teams that week. I felt very sorry for Neil because he only started a couple more matches for Manchester United that season, having been a regular in the side up to that point, and I could not say with much confidence that the two things were unconnected.

We had arranged a B-team fixture in Czechoslovakia the night before the full international so that I could have a look at as many players as possible to see if there might be someone capable of forcing their way into my thoughts for the European Championships, but having so many players to deal with was a challenge. A group of four of them who were travelling to our hotel together reported late on the Sunday night. They called me on their way to say they had been held up in traffic, but when they arrived I was a bit suspicious about the condition one or two of them were in. One player in particular reeked of garlic and I had a very strong idea that he was trying to cover up the smell of alcohol.

While we were in Prague, a letter was left for me at the reception of our hotel. It was from an English businessman who had seen two players in England tracksuits in a nightclub at 1:30 a.m. behaving less than perfectly. On the way home, I also had to deal with three players who'd had too much to drink in the airport bar. Sometimes it felt like the job of England manager was in fact that of chief babysitter and at times I bored myself giving them the speech about how they were representing their country and that their conduct, particularly abroad, was of paramount importance. I was left with the feeling that some players treated an England get-together as an escape from their clubs. Some saw it as a chance to see what they could get away with and others followed.

28

A football decision

I've just chuckled to myself because I've read a line in my diary that tells me that on 8 May 1992, I went to the Duchess Theatre in London for *An Evening With Gary Lineker*. I must admit, I can't remember anything about the play but I should have taken it as a sign because there would be plenty of drama concerning Gary Lineker later in the summer.

Our final home friendly before the European Championships was against Brazil and I already had my squad for the tournament settled in my mind but I wanted to wait until after the match before naming it. At the risk of sounding like I'm making excuses, we had a number of injury problems. Paul Gascoigne was out. John Barnes had been injured on and off for months and was struggling with a calf problem. Stuart Pearce had not played a first-team game for Nottingham Forest since late March but was recovering his fitness just in time to join us. At right-back I had problems because Rob Jones, the young Liverpool player who had forced his way into the squad and done well, was suffering from chronic shin splints. Lee Dixon had injured his knee and so I had to call up the third-choice right-back, Gary Stevens of Glasgow Rangers.

The aftermath of the Brazil match brought some tension between Gary Lineker and me to the surface. He had announced that he would be retiring from international football after the European Championships and everyone knew he was off to Japan to play his club football for a team called Grampus Eight after the tournament. Having reached forty-eight international goals by scoring in the 2-2 draw against the CIS, he was one behind Bobby Charlton's England record.

Since we had qualified for the championships, I had used the friendly matches to look at other players, meaning Gary had not started every game, which was not something he was used to. I played him for the second half against France at Wembley and he scored and worked very well for the team, which was not necessarily a part of his game.

After about ten minutes of the Brazil match, we won a penalty and Gary placed the ball on the spot. He attempted a delicate little chip over the goalkeeper but he got his connection all wrong and the Brazilian only had to fall in the way to gather the ball. We drew the match 1-1 but afterwards I was asked by the journalists what I thought about Gary being stuck on forty-eight goals with the record in sight. I said it was something I wished would be out of the way as soon as possible because I felt it was on his mind. I also said the unsayable as far as Gary was concerned, suggesting that we wouldn't have been any worse off playing with ten men because his contribution to the rest of the play was almost non-existent. Gary was not happy at being criticised in the press, and asked to see me. I could understand him not being happy but we didn't fall out. I told him he was still my first-choice striker but I also said that I needed to see more from him in terms of his team play. As the captain and the most experienced voice in the dressing room, I expected him to lead by example on the pitch and that meant that if the goals were not going in, he had to be prepared to change the way he played so that he offered something to the team in terms of creating chances for other people.

We went to Helsinki to play Finland in our final warm-up match, then had a few days back in England before flying out to Malmo for the tournament. It made sense to play against Scandinavian opposition but, as often happens with games like this, the conditions were not perfect. The grass was far too long and I suspect that was a factor in why we picked up injuries. After about fifteen minutes John Barnes ruptured his Achilles

tendon, which meant we would lose him from the squad. Gary
Stevens came off at half-time with a foot injury and that left
me without a recognised right-back for the tournament. And
although I didn't know it until a few days later, Mark Wright
also injured his Achilles tendon, which was to cause us a lot
of disruption in the final week leading up to the tournament.
David Platt scored both goals in the 2-1 win but it felt like
a typically nervy pre-tournament game. Gary had not scored
and I was worried that the record was in danger of becoming
an obsession.

Until that point, we had been expecting to face Yugoslavia in
our opening game of the tournament. But civil war in Yugoslavia meant they were taken out of the competition just ten days
before it began and replaced by Denmark, who had finished
runners-up in their qualifying group to the Yugoslavs. I cannot
remember being overly concerned by that. Even though we had
done a lot of work on our three opponents, it was not like the
Danes were going to be a surprise to us. Besides, I had problems
with my own squad to address.

I had submitted our squad to Uefa a few days before the
deadline and so there was still time to replace John Barnes with
Andy Sinton, who had been on standby in case Barnes broke
down, and the Manchester City central defender Keith Curle,
who could play at right-back in place of Lee Dixon. What threw
me was that Mark Wright revealed a few days after the Finland
game that he had aggravated an old Achilles injury. I assume
he delayed telling me because he hoped it would clear up in
time. I put Tony Adams on standby to replace him just in case.
What followed was a chaotic and frustrating week. We arranged
for Wright to have an MRI scan at Stanmore hospital the day
before we were due to fly to Sweden. The scan showed Wright
had tendonitis, which our medical staff felt was unpredictable.
It might clear up in a week or it might cause him problems for
longer. There was also the possibility of making it worse if he
did play. I felt we would be better off without him because it

wasn't just the injury that was a problem; the disruption and uncertainty was affecting him too.

The Uefa deadline had now passed, so we had to ask permission to call up a replacement. Uefa told us Wright had to travel to Sweden to be assessed by their doctors before we'd be allowed to bring in Tony Adams. The rule was that we could replace an injured player as long as it was a 'new' injury. Wright flew via Copenhagen to join us in Malmo for Uefa's medical only to be told he then had to go to Stockholm. After all that, Uefa dismissed our request to replace him in the squad. The whole situation was a complete farce and it took up far too much of my time – and all of that time was wasted, seeing as the decision went against us and we had to play the tournament with nineteen in the squad instead of twenty. Losing a central defender would also affect my plans to play with three at the back, but they were the cards I was dealt and there was no option but to get on with it.

Preparation had not been ideal. The injuries just kept coming and I was relieved to finally be in a position where I at least knew who was available and who wasn't. I brought everyone together in a meeting room at our hotel to name the squad and, when Neil Webb realised he wasn't in the side, he got up and walked out and I had to send Lawrie McMenemy after him. I liked Neil as a player and I felt responsible for the fact he had barely played for Manchester United since I'd confronted Alex Ferguson after the Czechoslovakia game. In hindsight, I perhaps shouldn't have picked him for the European Championships because he was short of matches, but I had put him in that situation and so I felt I had to stand by him. I didn't expect him to be happy about not being in the side but I couldn't have him walking out of a team meeting either.

Our opening game with Denmark was goalless, but I felt we had more of the play and certainly more chances – six on-target efforts to their one – to have deserved a narrow victory. Denmark possibly finished the game slightly more strongly, and I felt that influenced the reaction of the journalists when I faced them afterwards. It was not a vintage performance by any means, but with only two points available for a win and one for a draw it was far from a disaster either. I'd opted to play a back four but I felt Curle struggled to cope with the occasion and so for the second match, against France, I went with three at the back – using Carlton Palmer as a sweeper with Martin Keown and Des Walker either side of him – five across midfield, and Gary Lineker and Alan Shearer up front. It was a tight, tactical game and the French paid us a lot of respect but I thought we were the better side. Although chances were few and far between, we cleared a French header off the line and Stuart Pearce hit the bar with a free-kick not long before the end, so a draw was probably about right.

We travelled to Stockholm to face the host nation in our last game, knowing we would probably need to win to go through to the semi-finals. I changed the team again, reverting to a back four, which meant playing David Batty out of position at right-back. I put Neil Webb and Carlton Palmer in the centre of midfield, which I hoped would allow our two wide players, Andy Sinton and Tony Daley, to get forwards to supply the service to Gary Lineker, who had David Platt just behind him to support and attack from deep. The experts said afterwards: 'Why did you change the side? Why did you drop Shearer, who had played well against France?' Well, my answer to that is simple and it's the same as it's always been: I selected the team I felt had the best chance of getting the win we needed.

We couldn't have had a better start, because Platt scored inside the first four minutes and we had other chances to go 2-0 ahead, and if we had done so I am confident we'd have won the match. But we were never in control of the game and the second half was extremely disappointing. We couldn't keep hold of the ball and when Sweden equalised I felt we were in danger of going behind.

Over the years, people have asked me about my decision to substitute Gary Lineker and I have been ridiculed for it, but I will always maintain that the decision was one I made in an attempt to try to win the game. In one sense I can say it was an easy decision because as I watched the game unfold in front of me, it was very clear that the ball was not sticking up front. That was not necessarily Gary's fault. As a team we were not giving him the sort of service that he could turn into goals. Gary was a goalscorer – one of the best this country has ever had – but when we were unable to create chances for him there was not a lot else he could offer the team. He was not one for closing people down or to go looking for the ball. As I say that, I can hear people reading it as a direct criticism of his game but it is not. I knew exactly what Gary was good at and what he was not good at, and in that particular game we needed something else. It's important to also bear in mind that this was not a one-off. Gary had not scored in his previous five internationals. Of course, the counterpoint to that argument is that many of the most naturally gifted strikers often do not look like scoring until all of a sudden they have the ball in the back of the net. That is a valid point but, as I said, we simply did not look like getting the ball into the areas where Gary could score because every time it went forwards it came straight back at us again.

Gary was an excellent goalscorer, but he was not playing well and a pattern had been established over a number of matches where his influence on the game seemed to be getting less and less. That's not a criticism of Gary either because even the best players go through difficult spells. I will not say Gary was not trying, because I am certain he was, but he was not performing. But we cannot have a situation where a player is thought of as untouchable and cannot be replaced in any circumstances. That does not help anyone.

People sometimes assume I must have sat on the bench agonising over whether to replace the England captain, weighing up the pros and cons, thinking about the potential backlash from the media, but that simply didn't enter into it. What the journalists would make of my decision did not come into my mind, even for a second, because all I was focusing on was making a change to our team that might help us score a goal and win the game. It's only in hindsight that people say: 'Well, you took off Gary Lineker, who had scored more goals for England than everyone apart from Bobby Charlton, and replaced him with Alan Smith. What were you thinking?'

At the time, it felt like the right thing to do. Alan was a target man, and a good one at that. He could hold the ball up when under pressure and was good at buying the time needed for his team-mates to support and give him a player to pass to. I was the manager and that was the decision I took in the situation I was confronted with. Everyone is entitled to say it was a mistake. Everyone is entitled to say I should have done something different. But the only person who had to take responsibility for that decision was me and, although it didn't work for us, I am big enough to stand up and take that responsibility. After all, that is what being the England football manager is all about. In hindsight, the safe decision would have been to leave Gary on the pitch and take off someone else. Perhaps that would have worked out better – we can never know – but when people criticise me for what I did, the one thing they cannot say is that I took the easy option.

A lot was said and written about my decision but I can say for sure that it was not personal. I wanted Gary to play well and score. I wanted him to break Bobby Charlton's record because that would have meant he'd scored a couple of goals for us. I wanted Gary to lead the team out all the way to the final, and my decision to replace him was all motivated by trying to win. The coverage afterwards did sting me because I had not substituted Gary out of spite as was suggested. I could handle being criticised for making a mistake but to suggest it was anything other than a footballing decision is wrong.

Sweden scored eight minutes from the end and we lost the game 2-1, so it may have been the wrong decision – and I can understand people saying that – but we all make mistakes. Where I had perhaps been naïve was in not realising that the spotlight would fall on my decision to take off the captain. Had I been worried about the reaction and left him on the pitch, I'd have been shirking my responsibility but no one would have known.

I didn't expect Gary to be happy with the decision but what did upset me was that he threw the England captain's armband to the ground as he came off. I know he has said himself that he regrets that because it turned out to be his final act as an international player. I have never spoken to Gary about my decision to substitute him, though, and when we bump into each other we are perfectly civil to one another. I couldn't blame him for holding it against me, and I suppose I have given him the opportunity to be very critical of me and it is to his credit that he has not done so publicly. I know Gary didn't want his international career to end like that, but I didn't want it to end like that either. I would have loved nothing more than for us to beat Sweden and for Gary to go on to score for England in the semi-final and the final and to end his international career with a medal around his neck and a trophy in his hands.

29

Crossing the line

I didn't expect positive newspaper headlines after going out of the tournament in the group stage. The *Sun*'s headline the next morning was the now-infamous SWEDES 2 TURNIPS 1. There was nothing offensive about that. It was a good tabloid headline, if you like that sort of thing. Of course, I wish they had never been given the opportunity to write it, but I knew that the tabloids could be very direct when England failed to perform and I was braced for some strong criticism after we'd been knocked out of the European Championships. What I wasn't prepared for was the profound effect that a newspaper's coverage could have on me and my family over such a long period of time.

By Friday morning I had arrived home from Sweden, still numb with disappointment, when Lawrie rang me to ask if I'd seen a copy of the *Sun*. I told him I hadn't. 'I think you'd better have a look,' he said.

When I saw a copy of the paper, I saw the picture of my face merged together with a turnip and the headline GO NOW. It wasn't flattering and I wasn't exactly pleased about it but, at first, I couldn't see there being too much harm in it. After all, as the old cliché goes, today's newspaper is tomorrow's chip paper. Little did I know that it was an image that would follow me around for a long while.

In the beginning it was not a problem, but a year later, when we lost a World Cup qualifier in Norway and then lost 2-0 to the United States in Boston, it came back to haunt me. Don't get me wrong, I didn't expect the newspapers to be sympathetic when we lost, particularly when we lost in the manner of those two defeats. I wasn't expecting them to write: 'Bad luck, Graham, never mind.' It wasn't even the severity of the criticism in the newspapers that concerned me, it was all the other things that went on that people don't know about.

There was an impact on my family that I felt was unacceptable. I could understand the press having a go at me because I was the England manager, but it was nothing to do with my family, yet they had to witness certain things that were not right. After one of those defeats, a television crew visited my parents' home in Scunthorpe. Instead of knocking at the front door, they went round the back and tried the door there, which they must have had a good idea was unlocked because people of my parents' generation were not used to locking their doors. They walked in, filming. My parents were in their seventies, and were absolutely stunned by the intrusion. They had seen the criticism their son was getting in the papers and it was hurting them too, but to have a camera crew invading their privacy like that was so far over the line as far as I was concerned. My agent and I had to act very quickly to make sure the television station did not broadcast the footage, and I called my parents to check they were OK. I understood that I was the story but my family had done nothing to deserve that sort of thing happening to them. People might wonder why I was angry about the coverage I got; well, it was incidents like that. The way the newspapers went for me was one thing but the consequence was that some people thought that anything was fair game.

While this was going on, I was thousands of miles away in America, knowing we had two games still to play and wondering what would happen back at home if we were to lose them. Some newspapers had called on me to resign, which I was never going to do, and so the focus remained on my family.

I was asleep in my hotel room one night when the phone rang. It was Rita. She sounded shocked but stoic. She told me she had come back from the supermarket to find a couple of journalists and photographers waiting in the road outside the house. She was looking after her elderly mother, who was in a wheelchair, and was unpacking the shopping from the boot when the journalists approached. Rita was making sure the photographers couldn't see what was in the shopping bags in case they got a shot of any fruit or vegetables. That might sound quite amusing now but it was how ridiculous things got.

One of them said: 'Can we do an interview with you, Mrs Taylor?'

Rita said: 'I'm sorry, I don't do interviews.'

The reporter shot back: 'Well, you'd better fucking start, love.'

Rita is made of strong stuff and she certainly didn't want me to be worrying while I was on the other side of the Atlantic, but I did worry because this was a level of intrusion that she should never have been subjected to. As much as I didn't like some of what was written about me, I accepted that I was a public figure and as manager of the country's football team I had a job that attracts criticism when things are not going well. But my family didn't ask to be followed, yet they were brought into it. I was concerned that the spotlight might switch to my daughters but as they were both married neither had my surname, which possibly helped because it made it more difficult for journalists to find out who they were.

Being depicted as a turnip was not fun but I could cope with that, but having my family harassed was completely out of order and I think one thing led to the other. I won't say for a moment that it was an intended consequence but I do believe that, once I had been turned into a turnip by the biggest-selling newspaper in the country, it gave the impression that my family and I were fair game – both for news reporters and for certain members of the public.

I understood enough about journalism to know that the people who made my face into a turnip were not the football reporters who covered matches up and down the country. It was down to someone in the office, a sub-editor, who would never have to come face to face with me. They had a computer that was capable of creating that image and I have no doubt they thought they were being funny and knew it would grab attention. But it also had an effect on some of the people who read that newspaper and I believe it appeared to give permission to some of the less intelligent people in our society to do and say what they wished.

Some of the journalists on the *Sun* apologised to me and distanced themselves from it. One said to me: 'Come on, Graham, it's just a joke.' But it stops being a joke when someone spits at you in a football ground, as happened to me when I went back into management with Wolverhampton Wanderers. It was at Sheffield United's Bramall Lane and I tried to grab hold of the fella so the stewards or police could deal with him but he slipped away and disappeared into the anonymity of the crowd.

It went on for years. While I was at Wolves, the opposition supporters would sing: 'Turnip, turnip, give us a wave.' OK, that's pretty harmless and fairly light-hearted but it was meant to ridicule me. I was grateful of a thick skin at times.

Another time, at Brentford when I was back at Watford, I was walking to the officials' entrance, past one of the pubs outside the ground when a man with two pints of beer lurched towards me. A steward managed to grab his arm so the liquid missed me, but if he'd got his way I'd have been standing there with beer dripping down my jacket. I tried to laugh it off and see the funny side but there's very little funny side when someone is trying to do that to you.

Funnily enough, it very rarely happened when Rita was with me, which tells you something about the type of people who would give me abuse in public, but for several years I was permanently on my guard when I was out in public and at football grounds. Ninety-nine per cent of people are thoroughly decent, friendly and respectful, but I was never allowed to forget and when people did approach me to say hello, shake my hand or ask for a photograph or autograph there was always a split-second where I hesitated and wondered what sort of situation I was going to get into.

I only reacted badly once and if the person is reading this, I will apologise to him again because I should never have done it, but I snapped because I'd had enough of it. I was walking down a street and a couple walked past me and, just as they were past, the man said: 'That's the idiot who cost us a place in the World Cup.' It wasn't even one of the nastier comments, but I snapped and before I knew it, I'd turned and grabbed him by the shirt. I said: 'Now say that to my face.' He suddenly panicked and his lady friend yelped and said: 'Don't hit him.' Of course I wasn't going to hit him, but she wasn't to know that. I came to my senses, let go of his shirt and said: 'Oh forget it,' and they scurried off. It was absolutely stupid of me to do it because anything could have happened. I had no idea who I was confronting – he could have got angry and hit me. Or he could have gone to the newspapers or the police and I wouldn't have had a leg to stand on. That was the worst I reacted and I felt terrible about doing so and told myself that I must not get myself into a silly situation even if someone did say something.

At some point, my agent and I decided we had to go and see the *Sun* and tell them that their constant turnip references were having an impact on my professional reputation. The final straw was when I accepted an invitation to be one of the best men at a Watford supporter's wedding. I didn't know the couple personally, although I knew they were avid Watford supporters. The groom's 'real' best man wrote a very nice letter to me, inviting me to be the 'other' best man. Every now and again, when the fancy took me, I would accept these kind of invitations simply because it was fun to do so. It was a private event but the *Sun* found out about it and made reference to the 'turnip' attending the wedding. I thought, can I not do anything without them calling me that? So Ian Wilson, my agent, and I went to the *Sun*'s offices and spoke to the editor, explaining the impact this was having on me and that if they were to continue calling me a turnip we would have to do something about it.

We got them to agree that they would stop calling me it, but the image lived on in the minds of some of the public.

In recent years the comments have become much, much less frequent, partly because of the passing of time and partly because I'm an older man and I'm no longer working in the game. The reception I get from people I meet is, by and large, very warm but there will still be the odd person – usually someone who was a teenager or young man when we failed to qualify for the World Cup – who will say something.

Some time ago, the sub-editor who was responsible for the headline was having a leaving do and I got a message asking if I would go along and make some kind of presentation to him and say a few words. I was polite enough but my response was along the lines of: 'Are you kidding me?'

I am not asking for sympathy and I am not trying to put people off journalists because many of them are decent people. I used to joke that they're a lovely bunch of bastards. I am sure when they drew up that page back in June 1992, feeling very pleased with themselves about how clever and funny they were, they had absolutely no intention of causing me the grief that they did. I am absolutely sincere about that. It demonstrated to me that some journalists – not all – do not have much idea about the strength and power of the words they write. They don't realise the consequence. I am certain they didn't know, because if they had known, they wouldn't have done it.

30

Still in our own hands

The European Championships had been so disappointing but I still believed in myself and in the squad's ability to qualify for the World Cup. The thought of not qualifying for the tournament in the United States did not cross my mind.

The summer of 1992 saw a significant change in English football, because the Premier League was created, although the implications of that would not be felt immediately. One of the reasons the Football Association had been keen to go along with the clubs in breaking away from the Football League was that they felt a Premier League could help the England team. The aim was to reduce the top flight to twenty clubs, which would mean fewer games and less stress on the players. There was also the introduction of four free weekends between key England internationals. It wasn't quite the international break we know now but I was looking forward to being able to bring my squad together for a few days at least four times during the season. I hoped this would help me because I'd have longer to work with the players on the training pitch and to build team spirit. I hadn't anticipated that it would actually create a whole different set of problems.

Of course, over the following two decades or so, the Premier League dramatically changed the face of football in this country. When I was the England manager, I could go to any top-flight fixture and be confident that each side would have at least seven or eight English players on show, sometimes more. There were Scottish, Irish and Welsh players and a few foreign players but they were in the minority. Those ratios have completely reversed now and sometimes it is pointless the England manager watching a game between two of our top six clubs because there might be only a couple of Englishmen on the pitch.

Back in 1992, one of the explanations for our shortcomings at international level was that our top players were not tested against the best in Europe often enough. There had been the five-year ban from European club competitions as a result of the crowd trouble at Heysel, which had arguably had an effect. Relatively few English players went abroad, although in 1992 I had Paul Gascoigne, David Platt and Des Walker playing in Italy for Lazio, Juventus and Sampdoria, which I hoped would expose them to a different type of game and help make them better players.

Going into the World Cup qualifying campaign, I brought in the former Liverpool defender Phil Neal (not to be confused with Phil Neale who played for me at Lincoln) as a coach. In terms of honours, Phil was one of the most successful English players of all time. He was experienced at the very top level and had won the league title eight times and the European Cup four times. I made Stuart Pearce my new captain because he had shown leadership qualities and I was impressed by how he talked whenever we had sat down to discuss the game. I felt there were some good players coming through and I had high hopes about Alan Shearer stepping up to be the sort of centre-forward who could score goals but also contribute meaningfully to team play. He was still young and inexperienced at the top level but, having transferred to Blackburn Rovers for £3.6million, which was then a record fee for an English player, I knew I was about to find out if he could cope with that kind of pressure.

We had seven World Cup qualification matches to play during the 1992-93 season and, although it was not an easy group, we should have been perfectly capable of finishing in the top two. A lot is made of the defeats in Norway and the Netherlands in the second half of the campaign, but dropping points against both sides at Wembley before that was just as damaging. I wonder what would have happened if we had managed to hold on to beat Norway at home in our opening game. It might have made all the difference. As it was, Kjetil Rekdal scored a stunning equaliser so we had to settle for a point.

I soon found out that the extra time we had as a squad because of the free weekends in the league campaign prior to midweek internationals was a curse as well as a blessing. The get-together before the Norway match felt particularly disjointed. We had some commercial engagements to fit in – including a photoshoot at Lilleshall. Paul Gascoigne disappeared off into Stafford to buy some trainers and we didn't see him again until the evening. A few players got knocks, which interrupted the flow of our training. Then a press conference overran because there was such a queue of journalists and film crews waiting to speak to David Platt about his having just joined Juventus that the whole squad was sat on the team bus for half an hour while he finished up, meaning we were late for training.

The following month, before the game against Turkey at Wembley, I allowed the players to have a drink or two one evening and it got out of hand. The result was a broken hotel-room door, one of the players had been sick in his room and had moved into another one, and there was a complaint from the staff that someone had urinated in the sauna. There was also an argument because the Arsenal lads were being wound up by one of the players from another club and Phil Neal had had to step in to calm everyone down. I found out who broke the door and made sure they paid the bill to have it repaired and when I spoke to the players I made it clear that, although I hoped it would all stay under wraps, they could have no complaints if the press found out and made a big deal of it. We were staying in a hotel and there were staff and members of the public who could have taken a very dim view of their behaviour and made an issue of it.

I was used to being able to lay down the law with players but it felt at times like my words fell on deaf ears. I wouldn't wish to tar everyone with the same brush because the majority of my squad gave me no problems at all, but there were a handful who were always a challenge and who would behave like kids and were incapable of taking responsibility for themselves.

Fortunately we beat Turkey 4-0 at Wembley and then beat San Marino 6-0 at Wembley, as we should have done, although the forty-minute wait for a third goal meant the crowd got restless and they started to boo John Barnes, which was not nice to witness. I could understand England supporters getting frustrated with their team because the expectation was that we would run up a big score against San Marino, but booing was not something I could get my head around, particularly when they were singling out an individual. We then went to Turkey and won 2-0, which was another good result, and at that stage I felt very confident that we were on course to reach the finals.

The home match against the Netherlands in March 1993 was pivotal. John Barnes scored with a magnificent free-kick in the first minute and David Platt added a second midway through the first half and we looked totally in control. The first half an hour was as good as anything we'd produced in my time as manager, although we gave the Dutch the encouragement they needed by allowing Dennis Bergkamp to pull a goal back.

Gascoigne was playing his fifth consecutive England match – the only time he was able to put together such a run of appearances for me – and although he had blown hot and cold in the first four games of the season, he was very impressive in this match. Unfortunately we lost him for the second half because the Dutch player Jan Wouters caught Paul's cheekbone with his elbow when they both jumped to try to win the ball in the air. Losing Paul didn't help us and, although I thought we did reasonably well in the second half, the equaliser was on the cards. It was very frustrating that we helped them on their way – Des Walker pulled down a Dutch player in the penalty area about five minutes from the end and another point slipped away.

All of a sudden, a strong position had been significantly weakened and we knew we might have to win one or two of our away games in order to qualify.

One of the great questions that we shall never know the answer to is how much Paul Gascoigne could have achieved if he had been able to stay clear of injury and focus on football without the many distractions in his private life. I make no apology for returning to the subject – and I hope that if Paul reads this he understands that I am not having a go at him or holding him responsible. I am simply explaining some of the things that went on that people were not fully aware of at the time.

From the outside it must have looked so simple. Paul Gascoigne was our most gifted player, so all I had to do was give him the number-eight shirt and let him get on with it. But as much as I believe Paul would have loved his life to be that simple, it rarely was, and I'm afraid I was not alone in failing to help him come to terms with some of the difficulties he faced, although I did try.

Paul Gascoigne had been all set to move to Lazio in Italy when the transfer was delayed because of the injury he did to himself with that challenge on Gary Charles in the 1991 FA Cup final. The move was delayed a year and so, after more than a year out of action, he moved to Rome to play in Serie A.

As I leaf through my diaries covering the second half of my time as England manager, I am struck by how many entries concern Paul. I made numerous trips to Italy, not just to see him play but also to keep tabs on him and try to reinforce the message about living as an athlete and looking after himself. Managing Paul was almost a full-time job and it required the patience of a saint at times. I could phone him four, five or six times without getting through. I'd leave messages on his answerphone or with his brother or his friends or whoever it was he was with. At one point he was worried that journalists might ring him, impersonating people he knew and so for a time we had a code-word system. I see from my notes that at one stage the code word was 'Kevin Brock' – the name of a Newcastle United midfielder. It was quite bizarre at times.

Paul was a person who needed to know people believed in him and so I tried to reassure and encourage him by telling him that if he was fit and playing well, he would be the first name on my teamsheet. The move to Lazio did not settle him. For a start, he'd been out injured for a year and so his fitness was a long way short of where it should have been. As a result, his place in the Lazio team was not guaranteed and so he was always on edge.

Against Turkey at Wembley, though, he was in sparkling form. Although he was not lightning quick, he had a little side-step move that enabled him to get past opponents. He was strong and powerful but not at the expense of his touch and he was an entertainer. If we could get him to a level where we could ensure at least a seven-out-of-ten performance from him every match, he would be a tremendous asset to the team and we could work round his shortfalls, such as his tendency to leave his position and go wandering. But what we got with Paul was nine out of ten one match and five out of ten the next. I could live with that uncertainty, even if you never knew which Paul Gascoigne you were going to get.

However, there were deeper problems than his fitness and his footballing performances. He was a troubled young man in a high-pressure situation, and with the longer international get-togethers the extent of his problems became clearer to me.

After the game against San Marino, I had a word with him about his drinking. Two days before the game, he spent £140 in the hotel bar on brandy. The money wasn't the problem; the fact it was three-quarters of a pint of brandy was, especially on top of a couple of pints of Guinness. Now, I later became aware that other players would put drinks on Paul's room so I couldn't find out who was having what, but the fact was Paul was drinking too much. It's no secret there was a drinking culture in the game and some very good players had a problem with alcohol. It was impossible and impractical to ban alcohol. Besides, there's nothing wrong with players having an occasional beer or glass of wine, but some didn't know when enough was enough. And some could handle it better than others.

The game against San Marino was won convincingly but the play completely passed Paul by and, to excuse his poor performance, his agent had told one of the papers that he had been suffering from flu, even though Paul had told him not to. I talked to Paul about it but a lot of the time he was fidgety and struggled to concentrate, and if you weren't talking to him about football he often wasn't interested. I was never convinced he was taking it in, or really understood the points I was making. I remember going to Rome to see him and he told me he'd turned over a new leaf and was in the habit of having pizza and no more than two beers at lunchtime.

I have to say, Paul never gave me any real problems in the sense that he was not badly behaved or rude. He was a soft, sensitive boy who wanted to be loved. I could see the hurt in his eyes when he knew he'd upset me, and sometimes he just made me smile and want to give him a big hug, which I often did. One time he arrived with us from Italy with a sunburnt chest, having spent all afternoon in the blazing sunshine, and I later found him in the hotel's sauna where he said he was trying to cool his skin.

His other problems were no laughing matter, though. We gradually became aware that he had an eating disorder, and he spoke to our psychologist about that. Sometimes he would miss the team's dinnertime and come down an hour later, I suspect so he could order from the hotel restaurant's menu and have a big bowl of ice cream or something. His drinking concerned me. He used to order mineral water but I cottoned onto the fact that he was colluding with the bar staff when he poured orange juice into his 'water'. Clearly he was drinking spirits. His sleep patterns were erratic. He'd stay up half the night and then struggle to get up on time in the morning. One day, before leaving the hotel for a game, everyone was on the coach waiting and there was no sign of Paul. He was fast asleep in bed with the curtains drawn. In hindsight, I should never have played him in that match.

I tried to give him a lead. I knew that losing my temper with him would be pointless and might do more harm than good. I wanted so badly for him to make the best of his talent and I believed that he had to change his lifestyle completely in order to do that, but he was simply not capable of it.

In one press conference, I made a comment regarding his 'refuelling habits' and that backfired on me. The thing is, the journalists all knew what Paul was like. They knew the problems he was having, but I was the bad guy for saying something in public. Paul was upset with me for that, and I can understand why he was, but I felt that I had spoken to him time and time again without making any headway and thought that putting it in the public domain might have a different effect.

A couple of months before what turned out to be my final game in charge, I tried a different approach. The whole squad was going to Wembley for a training session and a press conference and, rather than travel on the coach, I invited Paul to come with me in my car.

We had about an hour together and I just let him talk. He was calmer, less fidgety, perhaps because it was just the two of us in the car and there was nothing to attract his attention. He said he was losing confidence in himself, that money had not made him happy, and that he missed his wife, Sheryl, terribly when they were apart but that they argued when they were together. He did not want to stay in Italy but he was frightened of being seen as a failure. And he acknowledged that he needed to get to grips with his problems with food and drink. After he had finished talking, I mentioned my friendship with Elton and how it had taken time but that he had managed to find a relatively calm and ordinary life behind the superstar image. Finally, as the twin towers of Wembley came into sight, we talked briefly about football and he said: 'I just want to play.'

I suppose that is the thing I find so sad about Paul Gascoigne. He was a lad who just wanted to play football but for one reason or another he was never allowed to be just a footballer. He could win a game with a pass or a piece of skill, yet self-destruct ten minutes later by picking up a needless booking that would rule him out of the next match. Managing Paul was one of the biggest challenges of my career and I'm sad to say I never quite managed to get through to him.

31

The biggest disappointment

At the end of the league season we had two qualification matches – away in Poland and then in Norway – that were now of paramount importance, followed by a trip to the United States to play games against the hosts, Brazil and Germany in three different cities. It turned out to be, without a doubt, the worst period of my football management career.

It was already apparent to me that the hardest thing about the job was getting the best eleven players on the pitch at the same time. There were injuries, personal problems and lack of form, and it seemed that just as I got two or three of them fit, another two or three developed a problem. I am not making excuses here because it has been the same for just about every England manager there has ever been.

Tony Adams was playing on even though he knew he'd need an operation in the summer, which meant he was unavailable for the America trip. Adams had also fallen over drunk in a nightclub and had needed twenty-nine stitches in a wound. I liked Tony, even though I knew he was one of the people who had an alcohol problem that had got out of hand. Not long after I'd taken over as manager he'd been sent to prison for drink-driving and I'd written to him to tell him that his sentence need not rule him out of my thoughts. People might wonder why, when I suspected some players had a problem with drink and others were capable of overdoing it, I let them have even a sip when they were on international duty. It's a good question, but I think that not only would an alcohol ban have been totally unenforceable at that time, it would have made for a very unhappy mood in the camp. Anyway, despite the occasional off-field incident, Tony was someone I thought a lot of because he would never let me down on the pitch. He was committed and he helped those around him as well. I have been very pleased to read in recent years that he has managed to stop drinking.

Alan Shearer injured his knee ligaments midway through the season. John Barnes was struggling for fitness and was planning some sort of training camp with the former Olympic-champion runner Sebastian Coe at some point, although that didn't happen in the end. Paul Gascoigne's general fitness was always a concern but, after sustaining the fractured cheekbone against the Netherlands, he had to play against both Poland and Norway wearing a cumbersome protective face mask, which can't have helped him. To add to that, my captain, Stuart Pearce, was also injured.

The two World Cup games were also taking place before the end of the Italian league season and Lazio were hassling me to allow Paul Gascoigne to fly back to Rome in a private jet so he could play against Napoli between our matches. That was a total non-starter for me but it was indicative of the sort of pressures that were put on him, because he felt like he was being pulled this way and that and no matter what was decided he felt some-one would be unhappy with him. We knew Paul would not be coming to America with us because FIFA's rules at that time only required clubs to release players for seven international matches each season, and Lazio were not willing to let him join us for the tour, but we absolutely had to have his full attention for the Poland and Norway games.

We were very poor in Poland and staring defeat in the face so I was very grateful to Ian Wright for coming off the bench to score a late equaliser. Wright was one of a number of forward options I had available but, in Shearer's absence, none of them really took hold of that opportunity and made a place in the team their own. Given his goalscoring record for Arsenal, Ian possibly feels he didn't get a fair run in the team. I left him out of the final squad for the European Championships and I would say it took me a while to be convinced by him at international level. He was quick and lively but he did give the ball away too much for my liking and I felt that the best use of him was as a substitute because he could hurt tiring defences with his pace and directness. He had that quality that all good strikers have in that he could find a goal when his team was in desperate need of one. He came on against Poland with twenty minutes to go during a period of the game where we were fighting to get an equaliser but really struggling to keep the ball, and he popped up with a goal that came out of nothing by getting into the six-yard box unmarked.

Les Ferdinand did impress me with his power and on occasions he looked excellent. I gave Teddy Sheringham his debut against Poland and I liked his hold-up play and awareness, which certainly compensated for his lack of pace. The other option was Nigel Clough, who I liked tremendously as a person but who I couldn't quite find a place for in the team. He preferred to play a bit deeper than Sheringham and when he was on the pitch I found that everything had to go through him and it meant we were slower to get the ball into wide positions. Having said that, his passing was excellent and as a person I thought he was first-class. Not only that, but whenever I named him in the squad, a bouquet of flowers would arrive at home for Rita from Nigel's dad, Brian, although that had nothing to do with me selecting him.

At the back I had concerns too, because Des Walker had been playing at left-back for Sampdoria and that seemed to rob him of all his confidence, and when I picked him to play in the centre he didn't look anything like as comfortable as he had done.

People might read this and feel it confirms the accusation that I didn't know my best team. In answer to that, I would say that I rarely had the luxury of being able to pick my 'best' team; I was always forced into making compromises here and there, and often I made changes to ensure I felt the balance of the team was right.

Having got the point against Poland, I felt that if we could just do the same in Norway the pressure would lift a bit and we could go to America and spend a bit of time working on some of the things we needed to improve. However, the match in Oslo was a disaster. I was criticised for switching to three centre-backs, but people forget that it was a system we had employed on and off for three years. Some of the players were different, but to say I just drew the formation on the board and told them to get on with it is certainly not the case. I am sometimes criticised for playing Gary Pallister at left-back, sometimes for playing Lee Sharpe at left-back, but neither of them were an orthodox left-back. Pallister was on the left-hand side of the three central defenders, and so naturally went wide into left-back positions to cover when needed. Sharpe was, if anything, a left wing-back who pushed up and dropped back as appropriate. Anyone can criticise me for the team selection, because we lost the game 2-0 in a very disappointing manner, but I do question whether people know what they were looking at when they fire accusations like that at me.

The irony was that I knew Norway's coach Egil Olsen had been working with Charles Reep and so I knew what to expect from them. One of the reasons for selecting Pallister was that Norway had a centre-forward called Jan Åge Fjørtoft, who was six feet four inches tall and was a real handful in the air. We'd also lost Paul Ince in midfield because he had been booked in Poland, and so I had to rejig the team anyway.

But, as I've said, my arguments are all irrelevant because the result went against us and I cannot defend the level of performance. It was the poorest display of my time as England manager. No one played well but I do remember Teddy Sheringham saying to the press that he was particularly disappointed with his own level of performance. That stuck with me because so often the players do not take responsibility in that way. I don't blame them for that because the buck stopped with me, the manager. It certainly did on that occasion because the criticism of me intensified significantly afterwards.

After winning promotion and surviving a brush with relegation in his first two seasons, Graham's Aston Villa challenged for the title in 1989–90, finishing runners-up. One of his best signings was David Platt, seen here scoring in the 3-0 win over Manchester United on Boxing Day 1989. © Bob Thomas/Getty Images

With Aston Villa and Liverpool neck-and-neck in the spring of 1990, Doug Ellis (right) allowed Graham to sign Tony Cascarino from Millwall. Graham hoped Cascarino would score the goals to clinch the title but it didn't work out. From the Taylor family collection

Paul McGrath (below) was one of the best defenders Graham signed but his off-field problems needed sensitive handling.

© Neal Simpson/EMPICS Sport

Graham's first match in charge of England was a 1-0 win over Hungary in September 1990 (above). Gary Lineker, who Graham had made captain, scored the only goal.

© John Stillwell/PA Archive/PA Images

Paul Gascoigne was one of the most talented players in England but he was so often injured and unavailable during Graham's time as manager. © Fiona Hanson/PA Archive/PA Images

One of the most controversial moments of Graham's England reign, although at the time he did not realise there'd be such a furore over substituting Lineker as they chased the game against Sweden in the 1992 European Championships. As he came off the field, Lineker threw the armband to the ground. © Mark Leech/Getty Images

John Barnes was spotted playing amateur football in London and spent six years with Graham at Watford before moving to Liverpool, although he struggled to reproduce his brilliance at club level for England. Barnes played in the 2-0 friendly defeat against the United States in June 1993 as pressure mounted on Graham. There would be no return to the USA for the World Cup. © Phil O'Brien/EMPICS Sport

The turning point in the fateful World Cup qualifier against the Netherlands in October 1993. Ronald Koeman escaped with only a booking after fouling David Platt on the edge of the area, then scored a twice-taken free-kick at the other end. © Ross Kinnaird/EMPICS Sport

Graham speaks to the linesman during the closing stages of the Netherlands v England match. His words were picked up by a microphone for the documentary *An Impossible Job.* © Ross Kinnaird/EMPICS Sport

The press spotlight and intrusion were intolerable at times and being England manager often felt like a lonely job. Here Graham faces the media after beating San Marino in his final game before resigning. © John Stillwell/PA Archive/PA Images

All smiles with Jonathan Hayward, son of Wolves owner Jack Hayward, as Graham returns to club management in March 1994. After losing in the play-offs during his first full season, and following a bad start to the next campaign, the smiles had faded.
© Paul Marriott/EMPICS Sport

The dream team of Graham Taylor and Elton John returned to Watford in 1996 and, incredibly, history repeated itself with two successive promotions to take Watford to the Premier League.
© Alan Cozzi/Watford FC Archive

Luther Blissett and Kenny Jackett had been key players during Graham's first spell at Watford. Now they were working with him as equals and part of a coaching team that clinched a place in the 1999 First Division play-offs after a run of seven wins and a draw in the last eight league games. © Alan Cozzi/ Watford FC Archive

A 2-0 victory over Bolton Wanderers at Wembley confirmed promotion and restored Graham's reputation as one of the best club managers England has produced. © Alan Cozzi/Watford FC Archive

After retiring from management with Watford in 2001, Graham could not resist when Doug Ellis asked him to take the hot seat at Villa Park for a second time. He quickly realised it had been a mistake. © Mike Egerton/EMPICS Sport

Graham and Rita went to Buckingham Palace after he was awarded the OBE for services to football in the 2002 New Year's Honours. From the Taylor family collection

Retirement from management gave Graham more time to spend with his family. Here are Graham and Rita on the beach in Norfolk with their three grandchildren, Jake, Rhianna and Elsie. From the Taylor family collection

While writing this book Graham visited places that held significance for him, starting off in his home town, Scunthorpe, where his house in Axholme Road is still standing despite only being intended to last twenty-five years. © Simon Gill

In 2014 Watford named a stand at their Vicarage Road home the Graham Taylor Stand.
© Simon Gill

The Graham Taylor Stand is decorated with pictures that tell the story of his two spells as manager. Here Graham looks at a picture of him leading out the Watford team at Wembley for the 1984 FA Cup final. 'Don't I look young,' he said. © Simon Gill

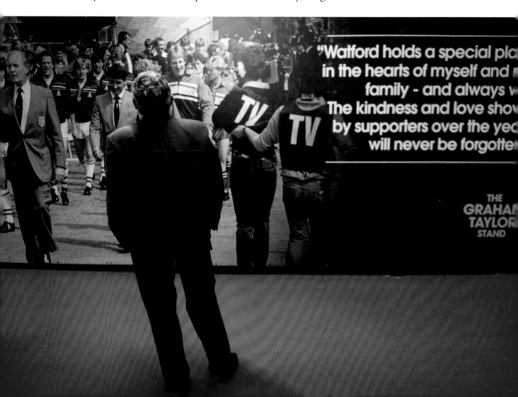

The trip to America was very poor. On the eve of our departure, Des Walker phoned me and said he felt it was best he didn't come. He wasn't injured, but he had not played well in Poland and had been at fault for one of Norway's goals, and his morale was on the floor. But I felt that he needed to be with the squad and work on his game rather than drop out of the trip.

A 2-0 defeat to the United States made an already bad situation worse. Losing to Norway had been a setback for our World Cup qualification hopes, although there was still time to correct that. Losing to the United States was a humiliating result, although we did OK to draw 1-1 against Brazil and we were not too bad against Germany, despite losing 2-1. The tour was possibly most notable for the fact that Paul Ince became the first black captain of England, not that the colour of his skin had any bearing on my decision. Paul was developing into a very good central-midfield player and was a natural leader. A year or so ago, a book came out that claimed I had said that the Football Association had wanted me to limit the number of black players I selected for England. I said at the time and I will repeat it now: there's absolutely no truth to that. And if anyone at the FA had told me who I should or shouldn't pick I would have told them team selection had nothing to do with them. People who know me should know that the colour of a player's skin would have no bearing on who I picked.

After a very good 3-0 win against Poland at Wembley, we had two games to go in the group and our fate was in our own hands but, once again, suspensions and injuries mounted up before the game against the Netherlands in Rotterdam. Paul Gascoigne was booked against Poland, so he was suspended. My captain Stuart Pearce was injured. Les Ferdinand, who had scored against Poland and looked very strong up front was also injured, although we did have Alan Shearer back again. Carlton Palmer is often singled out for criticism and, although he did not have anything like his best game against the Netherlands, he had done well enough for me over a period of two years, wherever on the field I had asked him to play. Carlton was not a pretty player and so he stood out for people, but he could be very effective and he helped those around him.

The number of injuries we sustained was quite remarkable and, when David Seaman walked into a window-cleaner's ladder at our hotel on the Saturday morning before the match and needed to have stitches, I thought that just about summed up my luck.

We played quite well against the Netherlands but it was a game that was all about the result and that went against us.

Throughout my career I tried to respect the decisions of the officials. One of my pet hates was players showing dissent towards referees and linesmen. Now, that does not mean I was an angel. I often expressed my opinion about officials on the touchline, but I did recognise that they were doing a difficult job. They had to make hundreds of decisions in the course of a match – in real time, without the benefit of a slow-motion replay. And we have to bear in mind that every free-kick that is not given is also a decision that has been made. The referee and his two linesmen have to keep an eye on everything that is going on around them and give decisions according to their interpretation of the laws of the game.

That is why I felt we had been robbed in that game against the Netherlands. In the film that came out afterwards, I used the word 'cheated', which is a very strong word and it is not one that I would have used in the cold light of day, but at the time I felt cheated because one key decision was not made in accordance with the laws of the game.

The match itself was open, attacking, exciting and full-blooded because it was just as important to the Netherlands and their hopes of qualifying for the World Cup as it was to us. It was a winner-takes-all game and it had a cup-tie feel about it. We were perhaps fortunate that they had a goal disallowed in the first half, but as the second half got underway I felt the match would tighten up and would be decided by perhaps one key moment.

In the end, a sequence of key moments were our undoing. The game was still goalless when everything changed for us. I can still see, in my mind's eye, David Platt running through on goal, about to fasten onto the ball over the top. He has Ronald Koeman with him, and Platt manages to get in front of the Dutch defender and chests the ball softly to give himself space to shoot. As Platt is about to break free, Koeman pulls his arm sharply and Platt goes down. The first contact was outside the penalty area so I can understand why the referee gave a free-kick. But what I am absolutely certain about is that Koeman denied Platt a clear goalscoring opportunity and for that he should have been sent off. With the World Cup approaching, FIFA had been making it very clear that professional fouls, as they called them, would be punished with a sending-off. There was absolutely no doubt about it, Koeman should have gone, but the referee only booked him.

Koeman knew he was lucky. You can see on the film he's smiling and shaking his head. I don't blame him for that. There was no way he was going to defend against Platt fairly in that situation and, although I can't applaud that sort of cynicism in the game, I also understand that players will always do whatever they can to prevent an opponent scoring. In that split-second, Koeman had three options – none of them good. He could let Platt go on and have a shot and, most likely, score. He could wait another second and give the referee no doubt it should be a penalty. Or he could tug his arm before Platt got into the box and hope for the best. So I don't have any ill-will towards Koeman, although I've not rushed to watch one of his sides since he's become a manager in the Premier League. No, the responsibility was with the referee to give the correct decision.

Our resulting free-kick, taken by Tony Dorigo, was blocked by a Dutch player who was very quick to break out of the wall, but the referee said nothing and play went on. Barely three minutes later, the Netherlands won a free-kick right on the edge of our box, and who stepped up to take it? Ronald Koeman. The first kick was blocked by Paul Ince, who broke out of the wall too quickly, and this time the referee ordered the kick to be retaken. Koeman then flicked the ball over the wall into the corner of the net to give the Dutch the lead.

I will maintain that Koeman should not even have been on the pitch. He should have been in the dressing room, having been sent off.

We lost the game 2-0, although we had good chances to equalise before they got their second, but I believe that short passage of play cost us the match. You might say that it's wrong of me to focus on one or two incidents in that match when we lost 2-0 anyway, but I believe the game swung away from us at that moment. No one can say we definitely would have won it had we been up against ten men for half an hour, but our chances would have been greatly increased.

That was the worst I have ever reacted on the touchline. It's long done and gone now but I am still upset about it. I can't help but wonder what might have happened. And, of course, my reaction was filmed and so it is one of the defining images people have of me. A documentary crew were filming us and, although I knew the camera would be on me, I simply could not restrain my feelings. If you've seen the film, *An Impossible Job*, you'll know that I lost my cool and that I said things to the fourth official and the linesman in the final minutes of the game that I should not have done. At one point, I tapped the linesman on the back and said: 'I was just saying to your colleague, the referee's got me the sack. Thank him ever so much for that, won't you?'

I won't say that the referee, who was a German called Karl-Josef Assenmacher, was deliberately favouring the home side, although that is what I felt at the time. But I will say that those decisions were extremely poor ones to make in a match of that importance. I think FIFA agreed with me because Assenmacher was due to referee another World Cup qualifier the following month but he was replaced and he never took charge of an international match again.

None of that helps me or the England team, and I am very well aware that no one else was to blame for us getting into the position we found ourselves in. If you want to say to me: 'Well, you should have beaten Poland and Norway away from home,' I cannot really argue any different.

The calls for me to resign were louder than ever but I had no intention of quitting while there was still a chance, no matter how slim. The final game was against San Marino in Bologna on 17 November 1993. We needed a miracle to qualify for the World Cup. We had to win by seven and hope the Netherlands lost in Poland. They won their match, which meant it was irrelevant what happened to us.

Straight from the kick-off, one of the San Marino players pounced onto a weak back-pass from Stuart Pearce and scored. San Marino had only scored one goal in their previous nine qualification matches and here we were, trailing them inside sixty seconds. We recovered to win the game 7-1 but at that moment, I looked up to the sky and I said: 'God, what have I done wrong? I am not a bad man.'

32

Punishing myself

I offered my letter of resignation to Bert Millichip of the Football Association six days after the San Marino match, knowing that it would be accepted. It was a very hard thing to admit to myself that perhaps I wasn't good enough, but the results tell the story and I could not hide from that.

I was not used to falling short. I'd had a long career in management during which so much more had gone right than wrong. But when it came to the top job, I had not delivered. It was a very painful time because I did not want to resign. I wanted to get it right and, although my confidence was knocked, I still believed in myself. Yet I knew that if you fail to qualify for the World Cup there is no way you should continue.

If there was one thing I was glad to see the back of, it was the newspaper coverage, some of which had been so hostile. Never mind being depicted as a turnip, I can tell you it is not a nice feeling to see a picture of your face with a target on it printed in a newspaper.

A couple of months after I resigned, with everything still so raw, *An Impossible Job* was broadcast on television and, although some people took from it what I had hoped they might, I was ridiculed and criticised once again by others. I've been asked many times over the years why I did the film and if I regret it. Contrary to what has been written, I did not agree to do it in order to restore my reputation after the European Championships, or in an attempt to make myself look good. I did it because I knew there was so much about the England manager's job that the public did not know – and could not possibly know – and I felt that if I opened the doors and let them see what it was all about they might have a greater understanding. Call me naïve if you want, but that was what I hoped.

I'd been approached several times by television production companies who wanted fly-on-the-wall access and I had always declined, but there was something about these people that impressed me. The director was a man called Ken McGill and there was something about his seriousness and that of his colleagues that impressed me. I was able to have grown-up conversations with them about what was and what was not acceptable. I was perfectly happy to let them have the access as long as they played fair when it came to editing the film. I knew there would be some members of my staff and some of the players who would not want to be in the film, and we got an agreement that those people would not be shown if they did not give their consent. The feeling I got was that they were not a bunch of people looking to sniff out controversy, but that they had a genuine desire to record what it was like inside the England football team. So we agreed they would join us each time we got together. They filmed me at home and at work and came with me to see David Platt when he was on a training camp in Spain with his club, Sampdoria. We allowed them access to the training sessions and the dressing room but we had final say and when I said the cameras had to go, they went.

As the qualifying campaign went on and a couple of results went against us, the film became less about the England team as a whole, which had been the original intention, and began to focus more on me, which was understandable. At some point, I think after the Norway game, the film company offered me the opportunity to pull out. They were obviously wondering which way things were going to go for the team and, having spent so much time and money on the project, presumably didn't want us to pull the plug at the end if things went badly and we failed to qualify. They wanted a commitment from me that if they went on we would not stand in the way of the film being released. I thought carefully about whether to go on and I decided to because my original intention had been to show what went on, whether it be good or bad. I also knew that several journalists were aware the film was being made and I felt that if I did pull the plug it might be perceived as me having doubts over whether we would qualify, which would throw up a negative headline.

When it was finished, I was given the opportunity to watch the film, and if I had wanted to I could have asked for things to be cut but, to the best of my knowledge, I let it go out as they intended. I was not unhappy about it – after all, everything on the film was accurate. I didn't feel I had been edited in such a way to make me look stupid. It was a faithful record of what had gone on so I didn't feel it was right for me to go through and change it to show me in a better light. And so, in that regard, I was perfectly happy with the film. It showed us in good moments and bad. It showed us under pressure. And it showed what happened on the training pitch, in the dressing room and on the bench.

In this respect, though, I had not fully appreciated that a lot of people – including journalists who work in the game – were not used to hearing the types of conversation we had on the bench and so were surprised by some of the discussions. It was unfortunate that people came to the conclusion that my coach, Phil Neal, was a 'yes man' because he wasn't. Often conversations on the bench are reinforcing our pre-match planning and preparation. We would plan for certain scenarios that might unfold in the match, and so when I said to Phil, as I did in the film: 'It's time for Wrighty, isn't it?' and he agreed, he wasn't blindly going along with what I said. Perhaps people had an impression that long, complex tactical discussions go on between a manager and his coaches on the bench, but that generally isn't the case. The work has been done, the game is unfolding in front of us and all we can do is react to what we are seeing on the pitch in a way that might positively affect our team.

The film also lumbered me with a few catchphrases – 'Do I not like that,' and 'Can we not knock it?' – but I didn't mind that. I sometimes have a particular way of speaking and I'm not going to apologise for that. But if I have one regret about the film, it is my language. In one of the newspaper reviews, somebody counted up the number of times I used the F-word in the programme, and I was embarrassed by that. I would say that in football circles my language is far, far from the worst but when you add them up in a programme that is an hour-and-a-bit long it leaves a certain impression.

A few days after it had been broadcast, my phone rang at home and it was a lady from Immingham, in Lincolnshire – my neck of the woods. She said to me in no uncertain terms that I should be ashamed of myself for swearing like that. She said her nine-year-old boy had stayed up to watch the programme and she called me a disgrace. I replied: 'What was your nine-year-old boy doing up watching that programme? It was on after the watershed. He should have been in bed.' The swearing must have caused a bit of a stir, though, because I remember receiving a letter from an ex-military man who told me to ignore people who were having a go at me for my language. He said that in the army nearly all of his commands had a swear word in it.

I am not a person who swears much in everyday life but it was different when I was at work. I am not saying it is right, or that it is particularly pleasant, but the language of the training ground and the touchline is not the same language I would use elsewhere.

Had I realised how it would be received by some people, I might have asked for some of the language to be cut out. Yes, emotions were running high during the games, but it left an impression of me as a person that I didn't feel was quite right.

After I resigned as England manager I felt very down. I am a firm believer that if you are down and you make no effort to pick yourself up, people will walk all over you, but if you show you are trying to get back on your feet people will come forwards and help. It was such a gloomy period for me that I went to see a doctor who said I was depressed. Rita and I went on holiday but I was anxious to get back into management as soon as possible because I felt I had to prove to myself that the England job had not made me a bad manager.

There was only one problem: the phone didn't ring. There was not a queue of clubs waiting to give me a job. If I had been prepared to wait a bit longer I might have had a chance when a vacancy came up at a Premier League club but I knew that the more time went on, the more I might be considered damaged goods. It might get to a stage where only a very brave chairman would give me that opportunity.

I was determined not to be ruined by the England experience. I read a column by a journalist that said I should not manage in England again and that hurt me a great deal. Bobby Robson had resumed his career with PSV Eindhoven in Holland, but there was absolutely no way I was going to leave the country just so I could get back into work, not least because Rita and I had just become grandparents and we didn't want to be away from our family.

For a brief time, it felt like failing to qualify for the World Cup might be the end of my career, and yet I was still only forty-nine. During that period, I did dwell on things too much. I could never say I regretted taking the England job, and if you had told me beforehand how things would eventually turn out it wouldn't have stopped me accepting it – partly because at that time I'd have refused to believe you. Now I look back on my life, I do wish the opportunity had come along later, when I was older and a bit wiser. I wonder what might have happened if I'd stayed at Aston Villa and taken them through the European competition we'd qualified for. Maybe an opportunity at one of the biggest clubs might have presented itself. But it's pointless wondering because what is done is done and, as I've said, there was no way I was going to turn down the chance to manage my country. I just wish I had been fifty-five rather than forty-five because I think I'd have been better equipped for it.

In March 1994, I was offered a chance to resurrect my career by Wolverhampton Wanderers and I was so pleased to be asked to do the job. A journalist called Dave Harrison helped me get that job by suggesting my name to Sir Jack and Jonathan Hayward, the father-and-son team who owned the club. Sir Jack was a lifelong supporter of the club and a very wealthy man. He did so much for Wolves, who had fallen from the top flight to the bottom division and were still making their way back up the ladder when he took over.

Wolves were not in the Premier League but they were a big club, and I felt a lot of warmth as soon as I met the people there. I won't pretend I had many alternatives but I was so grateful to them for giving me that chance.

When I took over, there were eleven games remaining and Wolves were midway in the First Division, which is now the Championship. There was an outside chance we might be able to force our way into the play-offs, but we fell three points short and finished eighth. At the time, I thought being back at a football club was the best thing for me. I threw myself into the day-to-day business of managing the team, taking training sessions, getting to know the players, speaking to my staff and getting to grips with how the club operated. But in hindsight, it was too soon. On one hand I desperately needed to get back to work, to feel the buzz of a matchday and the thrill of a victory. But on the other hand I was so worn out by the way my time with England had ended that I needed to recharge my batteries properly. I suppose I was working hard to block out the hurt and disappointment. It was only over the summer that I began to realise this was the case.

I could have gone on holiday when the 1994 World Cup was on. I could have taken Rita and myself off to a part of the world – perhaps the West Indies or Australia – where I had a decent chance to avoid the games and any news from the tournament, but I didn't. Instead, I stayed at home and watched nearly every match on the television. I didn't invite anybody round for company, I watched most of the games alone, and some days it was not easy but I needed to do it. It was almost like I was punishing myself and, although this sounds like a crazy thing to say, I felt it was part of the process of getting over it.

I feel almost silly admitting this, but after some of the games I would feel emotionally exhausted. I couldn't help thinking I should have been out there in the United States. I'd watch a game, wondering if this was the group England would have been in had we made it.

After the final whistle blew for each game, I would go out alone into our garden and take a football onto the back lawn and just kick it about gently for ten or fifteen minutes. I'd be there by myself, quietly rolling a ball around, feeling the cool evening air and looking up at the stars, just in a world of my own for a little while. It was like therapy for me, I suppose, a chance to get it all out of my system. I disliked watching that World Cup so much because I had spent years thinking that I would be a part of it with England, and I wished so badly that we were over there preparing for our next opponents.

It was such a relief when the tournament eventually came to an end because I felt like I could move on.

276

33

Which way from here?

I wasn't too sure how the players would react to me when I went back to work. I was still the same Graham but I did worry whether my authority had been undermined by the newspaper headlines. I knew that I had to repair my reputation as a football manager and so I felt I had no choice but to work exactly the same way as I always had.

Getting back in the game had been so important for me and once I'd got my mind right over the summer, I felt we were ready to challenge for promotion to the Premier League. That was certainly what Sir Jack Hayward expected me to do and he backed me when it came to signing new players to improve the team. In many ways, Sir Jack had rescued Wolves from oblivion. Molineux – which had been a fine stadium in the 1950s when the team was the best in the land – had fallen into a terrible state by the end of the 1980s, but Sir Jack spent a lot of money rebuilding it. By the summer of 1994, he was in a position to spend on the team and he enabled me to buy Tony Daley and Stephen Froggatt from Aston Villa. I had always liked Daley's pace, even if his legs were almost too quick for him sometimes, and Froggatt was someone I'd seen come through Villa's junior ranks and as part of the England under-21 squad during my time as manager. I changed the staff too, bringing in Bobby Downes and Steve Harrison so that I was surrounded by familiar people again, and as the season kicked off I felt very confident.

We began the season very well and lost only one of our opening ten league fixtures – that was at Vicarage Road against

Watford. Isn't it funny how life works out sometimes? We beat West Bromwich Albion early on too, and that would have gone a long way to winning over any Wolves supporters who'd had doubts about me.

Because the Premier League was being reduced to twenty teams, only the champions would go up automatically and so I was very happy that for most of the autumn we were top of the table and looking good. Despite a bad run in December, we were still well placed to challenge for the title but eventually a string of injuries caught up with us. Daley barely played, Froggatt got injured, and Geoff Thomas, who had been signed for the club by my predecessor Graham Turner, was also out for a long time. Towards the end of the season, we were still very difficult to beat but we drew far too many games – seven of our last nine were drawn – and we had to settle for the play-offs and a two-legged semi-final against Bolton Wanderers.

In the first leg at Molineux we played well enough to win more comfortably than 2-1. Bolton had forty-five-year-old Peter Shilton playing in goal because their regular keepers were unavailable, and he played out of his skin that night. We threw everything at him but just could not get an extra goal that might have given us a better chance of holding out at Burnden Park. The second leg was one of my most disappointing nights in football. It was 1-0 to Bolton at the end of ninety minutes, which meant we were tied on aggregate and so we went to extra time. Bolton scored again and that was the end of that. The fact that the scorer of Bolton's winner was John McGinlay, who earlier in the match had got away with punching our forward David Kelly during a goalmouth scramble, added further insult to the result.

Finishing fourth in the table was Wolves' highest finish for ten years and, although I believed progress had been made, the level of expectation around the club was so great that missing out in the play-offs was seen as a failure. The fact that the club had not long before been relegated from the top division to the bottom in successive seasons and therefore had no divine right to get into the Premier League was overlooked by some people.

The board were enthusiastic, though, and Sir Jack's passion for the club could not be doubted. Billy Wright, the legendary Wolves and England captain, was one of the directors. When I was at Watford and I was being criticised for playing so-called long-ball football, Billy had got in touch and I invited him down to meet the players. His view was that if we were being criticised, we were clearly putting noses out of joint because we were being more successful than people thought we should have been. At Wolves he was always very supportive. Rachael Heyhoe Flint, the former England women's cricket captain, was also on the board and I always enjoyed talking to her about either cricket or football. Sir Jack lived in the Caribbean and, as he was not around on a day-to-day basis, the running of the club was in the hands of his son, Jonathan. I got on fine with him but I felt he was impatient to push on.

I liked Wolves as a club but there was something about the place I could not put my finger on. I often wondered what conversations went on when I was not around. I didn't feel like I was as close to the heart of the decision-making as I had been at Lincoln, Watford or Aston Villa. I could cope with that because I never felt my efforts as manager had been undermined, and the club backed me financially as much as they could and trusted my judgement when it came to signing players. But I had a sense that I was disposable, which I suppose is a feeling all football managers have to come to terms with eventually. Everything was fine while we were doing well on the pitch, but when results went against us I felt I was out on a limb.

At that time, if you thought about Wolverhampton Wanderers, the first name that came to many people's minds was Steve Bull. I don't use the word lightly but he was a legend at Wolves because he had joined them when they were at pretty much their lowest ebb and he represented the survival and gradual regeneration of the club. I got on OK with Steve most of the time, and he was a reliable goalscorer for us, but I always wondered if he held it against me that I had eased him out of the England squad. He said he didn't, but I wasn't too sure. Steve had earned his place in Bobby Robson's World Cup squad in 1990, despite the fact he was a Second Division player, because he was prolific. He was a cross between a target man and a battering ram. He could certainly score goals in the Second Division, although I felt his game was lacking in too many areas for him to make the same impact at international level, especially as there were better players coming through, all of whom were playing in the top division.

After I arrived at Wolves, we had some fairly frank conversations and I don't think we always saw eye to eye. That was fine, because Steve was scoring goals, but I still needed him to fit in with the discipline I wanted at the club. In early November, he picked up an injury that would keep him out for a few games. I liked injured players to come to the ground on matchdays and watch the first team play at home. I didn't insist they travel away from home, although they could if they wanted. Sometimes I would relax this and say to the players they didn't have to come to a home game if they didn't want to, but if I said they were to attend then I expected them to be there. We had an Anglo-Italian Cup match at Molineux and I wanted the players to be there. Steve didn't show up and we had a few cross words after that. Perhaps it was turning into a bit of a battle of wills – he was trying to assert himself, knowing that he could do no wrong in the eyes of the supporters, and I was making sure that, as manager, my word was the final word.

In the summer of 1995, we had an offer of more than a million pounds for Steve from Coventry City, who were in the Premier League. It was a good offer for a striker who had only played a couple of games in the top division – and those only back when he was a youngster at West Bromwich Albion. He was so popular at Wolves, and whenever he was not in the side or if I substituted him there were always questions. As good as he was in the Second Division, he was still untested at the top level and I felt he could have improved as a player if he had gone up against the best defences every week.

It was probably a bit naïve of me, but when the offer came in I was happy to accept it. I knew it would cause a stir but I didn't think that the idea of selling Steve was so far out of the question for so many of the supporters. With the benefit of hindsight, I can see that I put myself in a vulnerable position by accepting Coventry's offer. It was even trickier when Steve said he didn't want to go. But I felt it was the best move for both him and the club – Steve would have had a new challenge and I could have made the changes I felt necessary to give us the best chance of achieving promotion. I could understand the supporters not being happy, but a manager has to be allowed to do things if he feels it will improve the team. Bull stayed and, although I didn't appreciate it at the time, it was a turning point for me at Wolves because, when the season started poorly, I was quickly under pressure.

My concerns about how the team would respond to having lost in the play-offs were well founded because we began the season in a very sluggish fashion. It's all very well telling players to put the past behind them and look forwards, but the disappointment of losing a play-off match like that can linger on. They are all people and sometimes it is hard to get over something like that. If I am honest with myself, I was struggling to get over it too. We won only four of our first sixteen matches and were sitting eighteenth in the table in mid-November, and I knew I was going to have to make further changes to the team if we were to get it going again.

It was one of the most difficult periods of my management career because I felt the players were happy enough for me to bear the brunt of the blame. I've said many times that as a manager I was perfectly happy that the final responsibility rested with me, but on the other hand, once the players have crossed the white line, their performance is down to them alone. I tried several techniques to try to turn things round. I could only give the players both barrels when they really deserved it because otherwise I would lose them, but it didn't feel like I was getting through to them.

Although I could feel the mood around the club had changed, I still felt it was too early in the season to rule out climbing the table and forcing our way into the promotion battle. Sir Jack and Jonathan Hayward felt otherwise.

A couple of days after we'd drawn 0-0 with Charlton Athletic, I was asked to meet Sir Jack, who was over from the Caribbean. I was driving on the M6 towards Wolverhampton when I heard on the radio that the board were considering my future. I had thought we were going to have a serious talk about the team's results but, as soon as I heard that on the radio, I realised I would be leaving the club. I got to our meeting, we talked for a while and Jonathan Hayward asked me to resign.

When I joined the club, I had been given a three-year contract. There was nothing in that contract that said I had to get promoted to the Premier League within a certain timeframe, although of course I knew there was an expectation. We had finished fourth in my first full season and, while my second season had not started well, I was still only halfway through that contract. Had it been down to me, I would have carried on because I felt that even if we didn't get promotion in that year, we were building towards being able to take Wolves into the Premier League. There was a lot of work that had been done behind the scenes, particularly in trying to secure a permanent training ground for the club, because they didn't have one at that time. I understand that supporters judge their manager on what happens between 3 p.m. and 4:45 p.m. on a Saturday afternoon, but I had hoped the board of directors might have noted the other work that had been done.

While I say I would have continued as manager, I was not going to do so without the support of my board and the chairman. When I signed my contract, Wolves had requested a clause that would entitle them to a certain amount of compensation if another club came in for me and I left. I had no problem with that clause, but what I did ask for was a similar clause that meant I would be compensated if they sacked me. Wolves didn't want it to appear in the press that they had sacked me – they wanted me to resign – but we're splitting hairs here because what is the difference between being sacked and being asked to resign? We talked about the details and it was all fairly amicable because they honoured that payment.

I am sure many people must think that because I'd been in football for so long, and had been the England manager, money must not have been an issue for me. I had been well paid but the sums of money in football then were very different to how they are now, and although we were comfortable we still had a mortgage. The severance pay from Wolves enabled me to pay off our mortgage, although that didn't do anything to lessen the disappointment. Leaving the England job had been the hardest thing I'd had to cope with, but in many ways leaving Wolves left me in an even worse position. I had gone back into club management with a club that was outside the Premier League and had not managed to achieve what we set out to achieve. I was very worried about what the next step might be, and whether leaving Wolves might signal the end of my club management career.

The news of me leaving Wolves had yet to be officially confirmed, and that afternoon I had an appointment at a local school to present some prizes. I didn't want to let them down, so I went to the prize-giving as agreed. The teacher introduced me as the manager of Wolverhampton Wanderers and I said: 'I have to correct you there…'

At home that evening, the phone went. It was Geoff Smith, who had been vice-chairman and a director at Watford throughout my first spell there. I knew what he was going to say and I cut him off mid-sentence: 'The answer is no, Geoff.' The time just was not right to hop from one job to another. Unlike after resigning as England manager, when I felt the best way forwards was to get straight back to work, this time I needed to give myself a break. I felt tired and bruised that it had not worked out at Wolves. England had been very disappointing for me because I had fallen short of what I expected of myself, but that was international football, where I was testing myself at a different level. But to lose my job at a club that was playing in a division I knew I could be successful in knocked me sideways. To try and pick myself up, Rita and I went to South Africa to watch England play a Test match and have a holiday. It was one of the very few times I was able to take a proper break during the football season and it did me the power of good.

I do believe I would have got it right if Wolves had given me a bit more time, but every manager who loses their job thinks that. I don't like to rub it in, and I certainly don't say this to sound clever, but it's worth pointing out that I did in fact make it to the Premier League before them.

34

Never go back?

For the first time in a very long time I was able to do all the things I told myself I'd only be able to do when I retired. I went to the theatre, spent time with my family and went walking in the Yorkshire Dales. I could watch football matches just for the sake of watching a game.

All football managers try to convince themselves they are happy to have the free time that being out of work allows, but the truth is that being out of the game does leave a big hole to fill. I loved my work, I missed it and I was too young to spend my time pottering in the garden and walking the dogs full-time. The ups and downs were what drove me and it is very hard to replace the excitement of being a manager, working with players and not knowing what Saturday's result will be.

I wanted to return to football but I wasn't all that certain football wanted me. After I left the England job I knew it would be a brave Premier League chairman who would give me a chance. Now I'd left Wolves, I accepted that I was carrying even more baggage. Anyone looking to hire me now needed to be very bold indeed.

There had been offers from abroad – someone acting on behalf of the Iranian national team got in touch, but that wasn't for me – but I wanted to get back into club management in England. As the weeks turned into months, I wasn't too sure where or when an offer might come. Then one day the phone rang and it was Elton. We spoke quite regularly in those days so that wasn't unusual, but the tone of his voice was different this time.

'It's time to come back, Graham,' he said. 'You need to be somewhere you're still loved.'

Elton had sold the club a number of years earlier to a businessman called Jack Petchey, but he was still honorary life president and had a lot of influence at the club. He explained that he had been thinking of getting more involved again, although not in quite the same way as he had been before. He was working on putting together a consortium who could buy out Petchey, and he felt that having me at the club might make it a little bit easier to attract people.

It was well after Christmas and Watford were struggling, some way adrift at the bottom of the First Division. Relegation back to the lower divisions was looking a distinct possibility. Because of the position the club was in, and because I was out of work, it was perhaps no surprise that people started to speculate that I might go back, although I was very reluctant to speak about it because I always felt it was disrespectful to comment on being linked to a club that already had a manager.

When Watford then dismissed Glenn Roeder, I agreed to take the position of general manager, although I would also manage the team until the end of the season with the aim of keeping them in the division. They say you should never go back, and in general that is probably pretty good advice, even if I ignored it more than once in my career. It was not a difficult decision to go back – not least because it was a part of the country where people happened to think I wasn't a bad fella – but I was also taking a risk because, if things didn't go right, the people of Watford might no longer think so fondly of me.

We had a press conference at Vicarage Road and – with Elton and I back together again – naturally we were asked if we could repeat what we had achieved the first time round. I had to say right from the start that it was foolish to expect a repeat. For a start, I was no longer the thirty-two-year-old with all those unfulfilled ambitions and aims. I was an older man, and a lot more experienced in many ways, but things had also changed in the English league. Although the Premier League was only a few years old at that stage, the biggest and richest clubs had begun to pull away from the rest and a gap had opened up between the top two divisions. There was much less chance a club like Watford could finish second in the top tier. I felt that anywhere above mid-table in the First Division would be a bonus.

I asked two of my former players – Kenny Jackett and Luther Blissett – to join me so that we had a three-man management team. Partly this was because we were planning for me to move 'upstairs' at the end of the season, whether we stayed up or went down. Kenny was already on the staff and was coaching the youth team. I felt Luther also had a lot to offer, not least in coaching the forwards. I knew there was an unhappy atmosphere among the supporters and that bringing two very popular people onto my staff would give us a lift immediately. We certainly needed that because the team was so far away from safety.

There were only a few days to prepare for our first game, at home to Ipswich Town. We led 2-0 but lost 3-2 and, although we became more difficult to beat in the following weeks, we couldn't win enough games to pull ourselves away from the foot of the table. By Easter we were in real trouble and had no option but to go for it without holding anything back. At times we played with four or even five forwards on the pitch and looked to get men and the ball forwards as much as possible. I knew we would concede goals but it was our best chance of winning matches. There was a sense of desperation about it perhaps, but when I look at the results now, I can see it worked. We beat Port Vale 5-2, Reading 4-2 and Grimsby 6-3 in consecutive home games to give ourselves a chance. A very good 2-1 win over Norwich City at Carrow Road meant we at least had a slim chance of survival going into the final game of the season, against Leicester City, who were themselves trying to clinch the last spot in the play-offs. We were unfortunate, in a way, that so much hinged on that final game, but it has to be acknowledged that, even if we had beaten Leicester, we still would have needed two other results to go our way. We lost 1-0 and the results of both the other games went against us anyway, so it certainly wasn't our day and we slipped into the Second Division.

There was some pressure on me to continue as the manager but that was never on the cards because there was so much work to be done behind the scenes to get the club back on track. I don't want to be accused of making out that everything we had done in my first spell at Watford was perfect and everything that had happened since had been bad, but it was clear that the club had lost so much in the nine years I had been away. It was a rudderless ship, a pale imitation of the club it had been, and the happy, purposeful, committed group of people had gone. That's not to say they were bad people – in fact many of the people behind the scenes were to be a part of the recovery – but the environment was totally lacking drive and enthusiasm. A lot of the community work we had done had been scaled back and I found that when I went into local schools and asked 'Who supports Watford?' and 'Who supports Manchester United?' a lot more hands went up the second time. We also needed to find a regular training ground of our own and there was a lot of work to do to bring together the group of people capable of buying out Jack Petchey.

Fairly soon after I arrived, I wrote a five-year plan that had prepared for the worst: relegation to the Second Division. I thought it might take two seasons to return to the First Division and another three before we were ready to push on to the Premier League. People looked at me a bit strangely when I talked about the Premier League as we were staring relegation to the third tier in the face, but it was a question of changing people's attitudes and mindsets. Before you can achieve something, you have to believe it can be done; before you set off on a journey, you have to know where you're heading. I had to try to convince people that we were going to start looking upwards, rather than accepting the inevitable and slipping downwards, even if we had to take a step backwards first before we righted ourselves and moved forwards. I felt we had to start thinking more positively. Of course, no one likes losing but I've always believed that it is the manner of a defeat that is important. If you can look in the mirror and say you gave it your best shot then there is at least some pride to be taken from the performance even if the result has not been good. I've always been a person who has looked for the positive rather than dwell on the negatives, so it was not hard to put a smile on people's faces by giving them a simple 'well done' or a pat on the back for doing something well, rather than poking holes in everything and looking for faults. Because, dear me, there were plenty of those and I knew it would take a while to sort things out, but there was no way we would improve anything by focusing on all the things that were wrong.

As I stepped upstairs, Kenny Jackett took over as first-team manager, and I realise now what a hard job that must have been for him. Kenny is an excellent football manager, and he has proved it by winning promotion with Swansea, Millwall and Wolves, but he was still a young man of thirty-four when he took charge at Watford and the expectation was that we would win promotion at the first attempt. He was presented with a very difficult set of circumstances. There was almost no money to spend on players – in fact, the only people we were able to bring in were Alec Chamberlain, as a back-up goalkeeper for about £40,000, and two free transfers. We lost a few players too, including the captain, Andy Hessenthaler. He was a player who had impressed me a good deal during my few months back at the club, but he lived way round the M25 near the Dartford tunnel. We had players commuting in from all over and you'll know my thoughts on that, so we asked them to move closer or we'd try to help them move on. Gillingham came in for Hessenthaler and, as we were not in a position to match their offer, we let him go.

As well as having a young playing squad and not a lot of money, Kenny also had me looking over his shoulder. I tried to take a back seat and give him the space to be the manager because I believed he could do the job. I knew the supporters would expect me to get involved if things were not going right, but I had to send the message straight away that I was not going to do that. My role was completely different during that season and it would have been very unfair of me to meddle in team matters. I tried to be to Kenny what Bertie Mee had been to me all those years earlier. I was there as a sounding board whenever Kenny wanted some advice but I gave him the room to manage as he saw fit.

The team did quite well and was always in the hunt for a play-off position, but when injuries hit there was not enough depth to the squad and we fell away to finish thirteenth. Kenny was relying on youngsters, loan signings and free transfers and there just was not enough quality. I tried to persuade Jack Petchey to give us a bit more money to spend because it might have been a case that bringing in just one or two extra players would have been enough to give us a shot at the play-offs. But Petchey was determined to sell the club and, understandably, did not want to put in any more money, especially as he might not get it back when he finally did find a buyer.

During his time as the club's owner, Petchey's popularity had declined. I have to say I never had a problem with him because I always felt he was straight with me. He told me that he ran the club like a business, that he was not going to pump in money that he would never see again, but if the club generated some money then we could spend it. In that sense, he never promised something he was not prepared to deliver and so, although the supporters don't like to hear that sort of pragmatic attitude, I couldn't complain because he was only ever direct with me about that.

It took the best part of a year to bring together the collection of businessmen who had the money and inclination to join Elton and take over the club from Petchey. It was a tense time because I felt we had to know who we were getting into bed with, so to speak. It wasn't like the previous time where Elton's fellow directors were lifelong supporters of the club. I wanted to find out what everyone's motives were, and that was not necessarily an easy task.

The whole deal was almost derailed because when it came to completing the sale it emerged that a considerable amount of money Elton had lent the club when he had owned it in the 1980s had been left on the books as debts to the owner. During the sale from Elton to Petchey, those debts had not been written off and so, when it came to selling, Petchey was able to say that he was owed the money. Legally speaking he was, but Elton was understandably miffed at the thought of paying back money he had lent the club in the first place. In the end it was agreed that the money would be left as outstanding debts and would be paid back over time, which was not ideal because it would hang over us for a good couple of years.

On 26 April 1997, before our home game against Bury, I was able to walk onto the pitch at Vicarage Road and announce to the supporters that Elton was coming home. He would become the club's chairman once again, leading a board of businessmen who all had different interests and ideas. I've had to look at a list to remind myself of the names, but there was Rumi Verjee, Brian Anderson, David Meller, Terry Rosenberg and Haig Oundjian, who was the cousin of Nigel Wray, the owner of Saracens Rugby Club. The only member of the previous board to remain was Charles Lissack.

The other big change was that we were going to share Vicarage Road with Saracens. It was a good arrangement because it enabled us to improve the stadium and it brought in some money. I was concerned about the impact it would have on the playing surface, but one of the first things we did was install a new pitch with artificial fibres woven into it so that it would be more durable.

By the end of the season, after a year spent in the office, I was ready to return to being a football manager again. I had not really enjoyed working behind the scenes, away from the players and the training ground. I wanted to take control again and make decisions that had a direct impact on the pitch. Kenny and Luther once again became my coaches, and I brought back Tom Walley to work as a coach but also to take over the running of the club's youth development system. Kenny could have been very upset about that. He could have said: 'Hang on, I'm the manager here,' and decided to leave or he could have been difficult about it, but he wasn't at all. I wasn't taking over from Kenny because he'd done a bad job but because the circumstances at the club had changed. This time I was the manager, but I delegated more than I had previously, not least because I had promised Rita I would not get married to the club again. Kenny and Luther had learned a lot from being manager and first-team coach and they were better for the experience, even if it had been a frustrating one.

I made a few signings that I thought would give us a chance to get out of the division. It felt very like 1977 all over again to me because I had the freedom to build a team using the players I inherited and by bringing in some players who would help us overpower teams. I signed Jason Lee, a striker who had lost his way at Nottingham Forest, partly because he had been mocked for having an unusual hairstyle on television by the comedians David Baddiel and Frank Skinner. They sang: 'He's got a pineapple on his head,' because Jason had worn his hair up. Of course, opposition supporters quickly embraced the song and for a while it was very difficult for him. I was asking him to drop down a division, which was a risk for him, but I knew he had to start scoring goals again. I said to him: 'You're a pineapple, I'm a turnip, so I'm sure we'll get on fine,' and he seemed to relax a bit. I could see I would need to work on his confidence, but I told him I was going to play to his strengths and that if he worked hard and got into goalscoring positions things would work out for him. I was so pleased when he scored the only goal of the game on his debut for us against Burnley on the opening day of the season. He did very well for us that season but I had to sell him early the following season because he was unable to move down into the area. All year he had said he was looking for a place to live, but there was always a problem or a change of mind, and in the end we sold him to Chesterfield so he didn't have to uproot his family.

Gerry Armstrong, who had scored our first-ever goal in the First Division back in 1982, had recommended a lad called Peter Kennedy, who was on the verge of giving up professional football and returning to Northern Ireland after spending a season at Notts County. Peter had such a good left foot, I was sure we could make use of him. I signed a midfield player called Micah Hyde who had been captain of Cambridge United when he was only twenty-one. Then, on the eve of the season, I managed to get Ronny Rosenthal. It was one of the directors, Brian Anderson, who told me that Ronny might be available from Tottenham Hotspur. There was no transfer fee but Ronny's wages were a considerable outlay for us, and in order to get him ahead of some other clubs we had to be prepared to offer him a three-year contract, which was a big gamble considering he was almost thirty-four. But I thought it was a risk worth taking because he was still so quick and would frighten defenders to death.

I felt the mix of new players was just right – there was a couple who had a point to prove, one who was ready to step up a level and one who was nearing the end of his career but who might just be too good for opposition defenders to handle.

I told the players that promotion was the target but that it wouldn't just happen for them. I was confident that if we gave our best effort in every game we would be good enough to go up. We started very well and were never out of the top two all season.

The game against Burnley on the opening day of the season was hyped up because it was my first game back in the dugout and Chris Waddle was taking his first game as player-manager. He made some comments in the press about our style of play, calling us a long-ball side, and said that we'd see who was highest in the table at the end of the season. I said that Chris ought to concentrate on either his playing or his managing because it can be very difficult to do both, which was naughty of me really because I shouldn't have got involved in that sort of talk. When they beat us 2-0 at Turf Moor later in the season Chris made the point that they'd beaten us 2-1 on aggregate. I explained that wasn't really how the league worked, which became even clearer when they only stayed up on the last day.

In early September, Elton finally did come home. We played Wycombe Wanderers at Vicarage Road the day after he had sung 'Candle in the Wind' at Princess Diana's funeral, and he came to the match. The warmth in the ground that day really did make it feel like the old days, especially as we won and stayed top of the table. The following month we hammered Luton Town 4-0 at Kenilworth Road, which was especially nice because Watford hadn't beaten them in the league for about a decade.

Even more satisfying was that the team had hit the ground running and were showing that they were good enough to go up. It was not always pretty and there were plenty of occasions when we had to grind out a result but we were able to do that more often than not. There was the predictable wobble in the new year, of course, when a couple of defeats and a few draws saw us lose the top spot to Bristol City, but I never felt promotion was going to slip away from us. After Ronny Rosenthal got injured we lost a bit of our attacking strength and – apart from that victory at Luton, and perhaps one or two other games – we were not a side that won games comfortably, but we did win them, and that spoke volumes about the character in the team.

The problem for us, perhaps, was that promotion had looked on the cards right from the first month of the season. If you win six of your first seven league games, as we did, everyone's expectations are raised. The second half of the campaign was less of a thrilling ride and the stumble we had in the spring was not necessarily down to the players. I picked up a virus and felt ill for a few weeks. Then our kit man, the lovely Roy Clare, passed away and that hit me and the staff very hard because we went back such a long way, to my first spell at Watford.

It's funny how things turn out because, as the season wore on, it became increasingly clear that the battle for the top two places would be between us and Bristol City, who were managed by my good friend John Ward. In the end, a 1-1 draw with them at Ashton Gate on Easter Monday meant both sides confirmed promotion and then we had three games to sort out who would win the silverware.

At the start of the season, promotion had been the goal and I was delighted that the players had managed to achieve that because it meant so much to the club to get back to the First Division without too much fuss. But I remember telling them more than once that for the sake of their own careers they had to go on and win the title. When you think about it, there are very few opportunities to actually win a medal in professional football and any opportunity to do so should be taken. When they are young men they perhaps don't understand the significance of it. Maybe they are confident enough to think that other chances will come along, but there are many, many former professional footballers who do not have something tangible in their possession to go alongside their memories.

We knew we more than likely had to win our last two games to win the championship. Our game in hand over Bristol City was a midweek match at home to Bournemouth. If we won it, we'd go into the final match at Fulham tied on points with Bristol City. I could tell the players were uptight but I struck upon a gimmick that I thought might divert energy away from our worries and loosen everybody up on the night.

Someone had pointed out that Steve Palmer had worn every shirt number from one to fourteen, apart from number one and number nine. This was in the days before squad numbers, of course, and, as far as we could tell, no one had ever worn the full set in a season. A silly idea occurred to me. What if we could arrange it so that Steve could wear the numbers one and nine in the final two matches and see if we could set some sort of record? This is where it started to get complicated. Goodness knows why we couldn't print an outfield shirt with a number one on it and give Alec Chamberlain an outfield player's number, but we couldn't. Perhaps there was a rule that said the goalkeeper had to wear number one, I don't know.

I refused to give up on this idea so I decided to name Steve Palmer as number one on the official teamsheet, with Chamberlain number four. We agreed with Bournemouth and the match officials that Steve would take up a position in goal and that the ball would be kicked out of play straight from the kick-off to give Steve and Alec a chance to swap shirts before resuming the game. It was a daft idea, really, and planning it took up far too much time than was sensible, but in a funny way it changed the mood around the place. Instead of fretting about whether they could beat Bournemouth, the players were laughing and joking about whether their manager had finally lost the plot. We won the game 2-1 and gave ourselves a chance to win the title at Fulham on the final day. Steve Palmer wore the number-nine shirt to complete the set and provide the answer to one of football's more obscure pub-quiz questions.

Looking back at some photographs of the last game of the season at Craven Cottage, I wonder why we played in our grey and blue striped away shirt. What a shame we weren't in yellow and red. I'm pretty sure that can't have been my decision. Whatever colours we were playing in, it was a wonderful day because we won 2-1 and heard that Bristol City had lost at Preston.

It was a very good feeling to reach the end of a season having achieved what we set out to achieve. I had a very good group of players who were committed to giving their best and had shown themselves to be quick learners. I felt we had the basis of a squad that could survive in the First Division without too much trouble and, with the right additions, might push on in a year or two and keep us on track to complete my five-year plan.

Everything should have been perfect but there was tension in the boardroom that had become more of a problem as the season wore on. Rumi Verjee, who had started the season as vice-chairman, had resigned. I could not say for certain what caused the tensions, but there were too many directors. When the new board members all arrived there had been a lot of goodwill towards them from the supporters, largely because they were not Jack Petchey and because they were part of a consortium that included Elton. Some of them had a habit of walking around the ground in front of the supporters and lapping up the applause. I had no particular issue with that, but I did notice they didn't tend to do it when results were not going so well.

Although I was the general manager, I think some of them were surprised by how much influence I wielded. I suppose I was a nosy so-and-so – and I did ask awkward questions considering I was an employee and not a director – but, as I saw it, my role was to improve several aspects of the club, not just the playing side. At that stage, it was not a major issue but I did get the feeling that there were too many competing influences and that not everyone in the boardroom was rowing in the same direction or putting as much effort into it.

It was a situation that diverted my attention and energy away from the football too often, and not necessarily always in a constructive way, but it was the reality I had to deal with. Football, even at Second Division and First Division level, had become so expensive that a club like Watford needed more than just one or two people putting in their money. Of course, many of the people who had come on board were businessmen, and very successful ones at that, and successful business people were not in the habit of losing money. At that time football clubs needed a constant stream of finance and I do not blame anyone for wondering what sort of return they might see on their investment.

My five-year plan had been to consolidate our position in the First Division for a couple of seasons before mounting a challenge for promotion to the Premier League, but of course the players once again paid no attention to what their manager was telling them. Honestly, it sometimes felt like I was talking to myself.

Before the season kicked off, I was getting a bit of criticism from the supporters for not spending a lot of money on new players. We brought in Nick Wright and Allan Smart, two forward players from Carlisle United, who had been relegated from the Second Division the previous season, for a combined fee of about £175,000. I also broke the habit of a lifetime and signed a player on the strength of a highlights video supplied by his agent. The player in question was Michel Ngonge, a Belgian-born Democratic Republic of the Congo international striker who had been playing for Samsunspor in Turkey. I didn't watch him play live, which was very unusual for me, but I thought it was worth a risk. I liked Michel a lot because he was so positive and upbeat and he made a good contribution, but my suspicions about highlights videos were confirmed because what they don't show is the bad bits of a player's game. He was an unpredictable player because he was just as likely to blast the ball yards wide or over the bar as he was to put it in the back of the net. I also brought in Tony Daley, who I'd had at Aston Villa and Wolves and had selected for England. Even though I knew his injury problems would limit his time on the pitch, I felt he could still have an impact.

I understood that the supporters were not exactly thrilled by the new arrivals, but I felt I had a decent enough track record of bringing in players who added something to the team that they could trust me. I received a letter from one supporter complaining that we were not showing enough ambition, so I gave him a call and just asked him to wait and see how we did before judging the new players.

We won our first three league games, lost our next three, then won the three after that, and I thought: 'Right, it's going to be one of those seasons, is it?' And it was, because we were very good at times and very poor at others. By early November we were happily sitting in the top three or four places, approaching the halfway mark in the season, when I began to think about whether we might have a serious shot at promotion. Then something happened that made me re-evaluate everything.

One night I woke up coughing. My throat was closing up, I was struggling to breathe and there was blood on the pillow. Rita rang for an ambulance and as I lay in the back, listening to the siren and trying to read the faces of the paramedics, I thought back to something Heneage Dove had said to me right at the start of my managerial career at Lincoln City in 1972. He'd watched me tackle the job at a breakneck pace and had called me into his office for a chat.

'Graham,' he said, 'I have two things I want to say to you. Firstly, there are only twenty-four hours in a day, and if you can't get everything done in twenty-four hours you are either not up to the job or you are disorganised. Secondly, if your health goes, you are no use to anybody, so look after yourself.'

As I headed to the hospital, I thought: 'You were right, Heneage, my friend.'

It turned out I had an abscess in my throat that was blocking my windpipe. The doctors said I was very lucky because if I'd not woken up, or if I'd left it much longer before getting treatment, I could have been in very serious trouble.

I spent a week in hospital, then took it easy while I got back to full health, and the team stayed in the hunt for a play-off position until a poor run of results in the spring. We lost three in a row and then drew 0-0 against Oxford United and Bury, who would both end up getting relegated. It felt like we had run out of steam just at the point of the season where we needed to push on and make one of those play-off places our own.

It was around this time I turned to a sports psychologist called Ciaran Cosgrave. I had worked with sports psychologists before and had found they could have a very positive effect on a group of players, but the impact Ciaran had contributed to a remarkable run of form that spanned two months and would take us all the way to Wembley and beyond. I won't say it was all down to Ciaran because that would be to undermine the work of the players and staff, but there is no doubt that having a different voice around the place had an incredible effect.

For a couple of weeks or so, I had been telling the players that they needed to liven up and improve not only the results but their performances if they were to cling on to a play-off place. The season was in danger of petering out for us, which was perhaps understandable given we'd had eighteen very intense months and were no doubt exceeding expectations by being anywhere near the top six. I told them that there is always a team that ends the season strongly and carries a run of form into the play-offs and ends up winning the whole thing. I genuinely believed that could be us, but I knew we needed a catalyst, a spark to get us going again because the games were running out.

The moment we needed came in a home game against Tranmere Rovers. The atmosphere was very flat as we trailed 1-0 after my old Wolves striker David Kelly scored. Peter Kennedy equalised for us but still we couldn't get going. In the end, it took a series of controversial moments to bring us to life. Richard Johnson, a tough-tackling midfielder who never went in for a challenge with anything less than full commitment, broke clear in midfield and overran the ball a little bit. He then went into a block tackle with a Tranmere player, and the referee blew for a foul before showing Richard a yellow card, which was his second of the match. As he came off the pitch, Richard turned to have a go at the linesman and I had to pull him away because on that occasion if anyone was going to have a go at the linesman it was going to be me.

Very near the end, we were given a penalty and I had some sympathy with the Tranmere players because I couldn't very well tell you what it was for. The penalty was saved but Ngonge scored from the rebound and, while half the team celebrated, the other half seemed to get involved in a scrap with the Tranmere players. Allan Smart became our second player to be shown a red card, and we had to hold on through injury time with nine men. While I would never condone my players getting involved in pushing and shoving with opposition players or shouting at the officials, on that occasion I was pleased to see a bit of fight in them – though I reminded them they had to channel their energies more positively.

It felt like something had changed after that game. There was a belief among the players that they could achieve something. I never got too involved with what Ciaran did because I felt it was important that the conversations he had with the players both individually and collectively remained confidential. I know Ciaran spoke to them about things that they may not have been too happy to share with their manager – their fears, doubts and insecurities, in particular – but I also knew that the mental side of the game was so important when the pressure was on at the end of a season, and Ciaran became an important part of the staff.

Every decision I made, or was forced to make, worked out. Tommy Mooney had been frustrated not to be a regular part of the team and had been on the verge of leaving the club weeks before. Tommy was one of those players who would give everything, regardless of the position he was asked to play, and in some ways players like that end up being victims of their own versatility. He was a forward really but when I returned as team manager I asked him to play on the left-hand side of three centre-backs alongside Robert Page and Keith Millen. He was very good at that in the Second Division because he could come out of defence with the ball, link up with the midfielders and even pop up in the opposition's penalty area. He was good enough defensively to cope with Second Division attackers too. When we got into the First Division, I was not so sure. I signed Dean Yates to play at the back and, although Dean got injured, Tommy lost his place in the side and couldn't get it back – largely because of the form of Robert Page and Steve Palmer, who had formed a very good partnership. I know Tommy was frustrated and was prepared to go away if it meant he could play more regularly. However, Allan Smart's sending-off meant I could put Tommy back into the team to play at Birmingham City in the game that followed our win over Tranmere.

I also put Tony Daley in the side for the first time in a month, knowing that as an Aston Villa man he would get booed all match long by the Blues supporters. Tony scored one and set up the other one for Mooney and we won the game 2-1.

After that, we just seemed to keep going. There was no great secret; it was just one of those periods that everyone in football strives for but which come along very rarely. We looked no further ahead than the next game, and the players had such belief that they could win no matter who the opposition were. We kept a relatively settled side, we stuck to what we were good at, and Tommy Mooney kept scoring as Bolton, Crewe, Crystal Palace and Port Vale were all beaten to make it six wins out of six. A draw at Barnsley and finally a victory over Grimsby on the last day of the season made certain of a play-off place that had looked very unlikely only six weeks earlier.

Once we had qualified for the play-offs, I felt very confident we would reach Wembley and win promotion. It's easy to say that with the benefit of hindsight, but there was such a positive feeling around the place. Every time we spoke about the play-offs, we talked about winning at Wembley. We were taking it one game at a time, of course, but one of the things Ciaran was very good at was making sure no one was frightened of thinking or speaking about winning the final. There was such a sense of purpose and togetherness in the squad for those few weeks, and even the players who were not part of the first team accepted that they might not play a full role but knew they nevertheless might have an important part to play, either by coming on as a substitute or just by being positive in training.

Before the league season had even finished, I decided we should finish each training session with a penalty shoot-out. It wasn't that I had some sixth sense that we would need to win a penalty competition to progress, but it was all part of making sure we were prepared for every possibility. I think it helped the players focus too. As we ran through the shoot-outs, I tried to make the experience as realistic as possible by dividing the players into two teams and making them stand in the centre circle before the walk forwards to the penalty area to take their kick. The players bought into the idea and instead of laughing and joking they created an atmosphere of tension. Of course, it wasn't possible to replicate the real conditions of a penalty shoot-out with promotion hinging on the outcome, but it was a useful exercise.

The first leg of the semi-final against Birmingham City at Vicarage Road was tight and tense but we won the game 1-0, which at least gave us something to defend at St Andrew's.

Having planned for almost every possible situation, it was very frustrating that we got stuck in heavy traffic on the way from our hotel and arrived at the ground for the second leg with less than an hour to go until kick-off. It was far from ideal but I had no choice but to give the team talk on the bus as we inched towards St Andrew's. As the game began, the players were unsettled, and in the first two minutes Birmingham hoisted the ball into our penalty area, there was a scramble and Dele Adebola bundled it over the line. We'd barely even started and our advantage from the first leg was wiped out already. It meant we were in for a long, nerve-wracking evening. We rode our luck at times but the team weathered the storm and defended brilliantly at times during the next 118 minutes and took the match to a penalty shoot-out. Whether our practice shoot-outs in training were the difference or not I couldn't say, but it certainly can't have hurt because we won 7-6.

A play-off final is unlike any other match in English football. A Wembley cup final is a special occasion and, although no one wants to lose, there is a sense of pride gained simply from being part of that occasion. A play-off final is all about the result as a nine-month-long season and forty-eight matches all come down to one last game.

To my mind there were two ways we could approach it: we could either try to pretend it was a match just like any other and prepare for it in the same way as usual, or we could treat it like a cup final. It was obvious to me that we had to think of it as a special occasion. I believed we had to take into account the fact that we'd be playing at Wembley in front of almost 80,000 people. We had to prepare for the occasion before we could prepare for the match. So we went the whole hog and ordered new suits for the players. We visited the stadium before the match and had a look round the dressing room. Ciaran spent time with the players, visualising what the day would be like, imagining walking out of the tunnel in front of a capacity crowd. We worked hard to make sure the players knew what they were in for and would be ready for it.

Our opponents, Bolton Wanderers, arrived for the game in their tracksuits. It seemed they were taking the opposite approach. I am not saying we were right and they were wrong, but we did what was right for us, and it worked.

The two players I'd signed from Carlisle United scored the goals. Just before half-time, we won a corner, which was not fully cleared by the Bolton defence. In my mind's eye I can still see Nick Wright's overhead kick as it dropped into the net. Everyone can look at that goal and say it was a one-in-a-million strike, and on the one hand they are right. The timing of his jump, the way he connected with the ball, and the trajectory of the ball were all absolutely perfect. Could he do it again if the ball fell to him? Possibly not. But on the other hand, Nick was in the position he was supposed to be in, on the corner of the penalty area, waiting and anticipating a clearance. He wasn't there by chance, he was doing what he was asked to do. When the ball came towards him he improvised brilliantly. Allan Smart's goal came right at the end when everyone associated with Watford was willing the referee to blow the final whistle.

I will never forget the celebrations afterwards. Almost all of the Bolton supporters had left, leaving one end of Wembley empty, and as I stood on the halfway line I could see 38,000 Watford supporters in red and yellow celebrating. I stood for a little while and made a conscious effort to commit the scene to memory because to know I had played a part in creating those moments – memories that would live with them for a long, long time – was very special indeed.

35

Time to go

It's easy to say now, with the benefit of hindsight, that we weren't ready for the Premier League, but at the time I believed it would be difficult but not impossible to stay up. I had perhaps underestimated how much the gap between the top two divisions had grown.

There were several things that worked against us. The players had been magnificent for two seasons, but many of them had been in the third tier just fifteen months or so earlier. No one had expected them to win successive promotions, but now they had to prepare to face the best teams in the country. We were very short of experience when it came to playing in the top flight. Although I wanted to give the players who had achieved promotion a chance to show whether they could make the grade at the top, the fact was I had very little choice in the matter. People may think that as soon as you are promoted someone from the Premier League pops round with a cheque for tens of millions of pounds, but we knew we would have to wait several months before the first instalment was due. We also still had to make our final payment to the previous owner, Jack Petchey. Although the board of directors were wealthy men by most standards, the fact was that none of them was willing or able to shoulder the full financial burden of trying to compete with the likes of Manchester United, Arsenal and Chelsea. The sort of money we were talking about at the time is almost small change compared to the sums that are in the game now but, as the new century approached, the game was already moving beyond the reach of mere millionaires and was on its way to becoming a billionaire's playground.

We simply weren't in a position to spend a fortune on new players. To give you some idea of the financial constraints we were under, when our wing-back Darren Bazeley decided to join Wolves, I had to replace him with a free transfer from Nottingham Forest, Des Lyttle. I understood and accepted the situation – and to be fair to the board, as soon as we were in a position to buy players, I was allowed to spend some money. We brought in a lad called Nordin Wooter from Ajax for almost a million pounds – which was a club-record fee at the time – and then spent well over a million on an Icelandic centre-forward called Heidar Helguson. One worked out, the other didn't, but those were the odds when spending that sort of money. It was a lot for a club like Watford, but in the grand scheme of things we were searching for bargains or taking a calculated risk.

The summer was far from ideal. Having won the play-off final at Wembley on 31 May, our season had ended a lot later than everyone else's and we were back for pre-season training after only four or five weeks. We had trips to Iceland, the Isle of Man and Dublin booked, and I realised too late that the matches we had scheduled were not going to give us the best possible preparation for the Premier League. I probably should have cancelled the trip to the Isle of Man because we played three very poor games, one against an Isle of Man team, on poor-quality pitches, but we had made the commitment months earlier and I didn't want to disappoint people by pulling out at short notice. It wasn't just a matter of being too polite, it was too late to organise alternative games against better calibre opposition anyway.

Never let it be said that the computer which generates the fixtures doesn't have a sense of humour. Our first game in the Premier League was against Wimbledon, who had just appointed Egil Olsen as their manager. He had been in charge of the Norway team that had beaten my England team in the World Cup qualifying match in Oslo to reach the tournament in the United States ahead of us and so it gave the press an angle to explore ahead of our opening match.

We lost that game against Wimbledon 3-2, and looking at our results that season does not bring back too many good memories. There was a very good victory against Liverpool at Anfield and a home win over Chelsea, but they were two of only six league wins all season. From mid-September to mid-October we faced all of the previous season's top five and, although we beat Chelsea, we lost all the rest against West Ham, Arsenal, Leeds and Manchester United. There was nothing too surprising or disgraceful about that, but the problem was that when the fixtures began to look a bit kinder to us we failed to pick up any wins. We went eleven games without a win – and drew only two of those – which made it quite a gloomy Christmas in the Taylor household.

It was not easy to accept that we were not good enough, but the league table rarely lies. We knew from the turn of the year that we were likely to be relegated, and in the end we finished bottom some way adrift. Midway through the season there had been discussions about whether to strengthen the team, but I felt that any money we spent would be put to better use trying to build a side capable of bouncing back to the Premier League at the first attempt. I wasn't throwing in the towel or admitting defeat but we had to be realistic. I didn't feel we could attract the right players to keep us up and so I decided to wait until the summer.

I thought we needed to be pragmatic and accept that it might take two or three goes at the Premier League before we managed to stay up and establish ourselves. Bigger clubs than Watford had gone up and down, and I always tried to explain to supporters that I believed that our natural level was to be among the top thirty clubs in the country. That meant either being in the Premier League or in the thick of the battle for promotion to it.

By and large, the board of directors supported me in that view and yet, as time went on, I started to have my doubts about the direction the club was going in. It would be unfair of me to say the board didn't support me because I never felt they had unrealistic expectations about what could be achieved, but I didn't have the feeling everyone was as committed as they should have been, or that there was the level of agreement between the directors that we needed. They all had other business interests and I wondered how high up the list of priorities Watford Football Club was for some of them. I was realistic and I knew that football had changed and that business people got involved with football clubs that they didn't necessarily support. One of our directors was a Chelsea supporter and he would attend our games with his teenage son. Sometimes I'd watch the first half of our home games from the directors' box and I'd always sit on the end of the row so I could duck down to the touchline quickly if I wanted to. Midway through the half, our director used to send his son down to the lounge to check the TV to see how Chelsea were getting on. The lad would come back and say: 'We're 1-0 up,' and the director would clench his fist. Perhaps I shouldn't have let it irritate me, but it did because I'd think: 'Hang on, you're supposed to be watching Watford here.'

It was different to what I'd been used to during my previous ten years at Watford. Most of the directors were based in London and they used to like to hold the board meetings in the city, which made it difficult for me to attend, especially if they wanted to meet on a Thursday. I would be trying to prepare the team for a Premier League match, so I couldn't take half a day out to go into London for a meeting.

Football was beginning to change in a lot of respects and I had to accept that the manager's role was changing. Owners and chairmen were becoming a lot more involved in football matters. During the summer, as we were preparing to mount a challenge for promotion back to the Premier League, I had decided to try to sign two players from Tottenham Hotspur – a goalkeeper called Espen Baardsen and the midfielder Allan Nielsen. I knew Tottenham's secretary, John Alexander, because he had previously been at Watford, so I called him to talk about the possibility of making a bid. The transfer fees for the two players added up to a lot of money for us, so I was trying to negotiate the total downwards. John said the chairman, Alan Sugar, wanted a word.

Sugar came on the phone and said: 'What the fack are you trying to pull here? Do you think I'm some kind of mug who's going to let players go on the cheap?'

I gave as good as I got but couldn't help noticing that the trend at some clubs was for managers to have less and less of a role in the buying and selling of players.

We started the season back in Division One so well, winning twelve and drawing three of our first fifteen games. After a third of the season, ourselves and Fulham were well clear of the rest and we'd put ourselves in such a strong position to win promotion that it's very difficult to understand what went wrong after that. Towards the end of that run, we faced Manchester United at home in a League Cup tie and were well beaten. The score was only 3-0 but I wondered if, for some of them, it brought back bad memories of what the Premier League had been all about. Perhaps that is unfair of me because as their manager I was unable to arrest the slide.

By the spring, I was beginning to feel that it was time for me to retire. When I had rejoined Watford, I'd promised Rita I would not get married to the club again, but that was a promise I had not entirely kept. However, I was not enjoying things as much as I had been. In March 2001 I announced that I would retire at the end of the season. I hoped we might have a final push for promotion or at least the play-offs, but my decision seemed to have the opposite effect on the players.

Well before the end of the season Watford announced that Gianluca Vialli was going to replace me and, as all hopes of promotion disappeared, there was to be no fairy-tale ending to my managerial career. Everything has to finish at some time, and the reception I received from the supporters at the end of my final home game against Tranmere Rovers was very touching.

The cliché says that you should never go back, but my second spell at Watford had been far more good than bad. I was confident that the club was in a much better condition than it had been when Luther, Kenny and I first went back. I could understand the directors and Elton being excited at having persuaded Vialli – who had been a wonderful player and had managed Chelsea – to take over from me, even if I did suspect they were a little more starstruck than they should have been. Before I left, it became apparent that the new manager had a clear idea who he did and didn't want to keep, and that he didn't fancy having to tell the players he was rejecting that they should move on. I felt the least I could do was to sit down face to face with the players the club no longer wanted and be straight with them, even if it really wasn't my responsibility to do so.

As far as I was concerned, that really was it for me as a football manager. Some people said I had retired too early but, having reached the milestone of 1,000 league matches as a manager, I felt I had done enough. I did not have the drive or energy I'd had when I was a younger man, and I was not prepared to compromise the way I worked to lessen the workload or make life easier for myself.

A few months later, when Doug Ellis rang me to ask if I would consider becoming a director of Aston Villa, I told him that the idea appealed to me on one condition: that I would not be asked to take over as manager, even in a caretaker capacity. He agreed to that, and for a few months I enjoyed getting to grips with a very different role at a football club I knew and liked.

I stressed to John Gregory, our manager, that I had no intention of taking his job and I hope he never felt I was trying to move in on his territory. But at the start of 2002 it became clear that John had been talking to Derby County about going there and, when John finally resigned, Doug asked me to step in as manager. It's easy to say now that I should have said no, but at the time I felt the break I'd had from management had refreshed me. It was also an opportunity to manage a Premier League club. If there was one thing that caused me to hesitate, it was the possible reaction of Watford supporters. I can quite understand some of them feeling let down because they had thought I was retiring. I hadn't intended to manage again but I felt I couldn't turn down the opportunity when it was offered to me.

I was manager of Aston Villa for almost fifteen months, and it gradually dawned on me that I had been right to retire the first time. Football had changed and I was not prepared to compromise what I thought was right. The amount of money in the game was now so great that very ordinary players could easily become millionaires. That wasn't the fault of the players because we would all accept that money if it were offered to us, but it did change the relationship between the manager and his players. The Aston Villa team was one that had been in decline and, although Doug was a very wealthy man, he did not have the sort of money to keep pace with the likes of Manchester United.

My first signing was Peter Crouch from Portsmouth, who was a player I had admired since the first time I'd seen him. He had played for Queens Park Rangers against Watford at Vicarage Road and the Watford supporters gave him a bit of stick that afternoon. Peter is very tall and because of that he stood out and attracted attention. He was like a lot of very tall players in that his ability to control and play the ball was underestimated, but at the end of the game I deliberately waited for him to come off the pitch, offered him my hand and said: 'Don't let anyone tell you that you can't play.'

I liked Peter a lot but it frustrated me that he didn't move into the area and often commuted from the south coast. I would shake my head whenever he pulled into the car park at our Bodymoor Heath training ground and I watched him unfold his six-feet-seven-inch frame out of his car. Peter wasn't the only one who travelled a long distance in to training. Others lived in hotels or flats near Birmingham and travelled home when they had a couple of days off, and I had to accept that the players didn't want to uproot their families every time they were transferred and they were wealthy enough not to bother. They could afford to carry on paying the mortgage on their family home and rent a flat near the club. It was understandable, particularly for the ones who had children in private schools, but it was not what I wanted. The problem was, managers no longer held the power they once had. I couldn't put my foot down and tell a player where I thought he should live.

I signed a two-year contract with Aston Villa but my first full season was a slog. We finished a couple of places above the relegation zone and, as the months went on, the scale of the job that needed to be done at the club began to dawn on me. We lost a home game towards the end of the season and there was an angry atmosphere in the ground. I can still see the face of a supporter who came down the steps of the stand behind the dugout, his face all scrunched up. 'You're yesterday's man, Taylor,' he said.

For weeks I couldn't get his face out of my mind and the words stuck with me, possibly because there was an element of truth to them. On 14 May 2003, three days after the Premier League season had ended, I woke up and – instead of getting out of bed promptly as I usually would have – I stayed lying there. It was my daughter Joanne's birthday, which is another reason the date sticks in my mind. I was mulling over what the day might have in store for me at work and I came to the realisation that I just didn't want to do it any more. For the first time, it felt like a chore to think about getting up and going to work. It was an impulsive decision but I hastily hand-wrote a letter of resignation, drove my company car to Villa Park, and put the envelope and the car keys on the desk in reception and waited for Rita to come and pick me up. It was as easy as that to bring to a close more than forty years in professional football because it finally felt like it was time to stop without looking back.

36

I've enjoyed (almost) every minute

I was very happy to be able to continue working in the game as a summariser or co-commentator for BBC Radio 5 Live. I remember someone jokingly asked whether I was being paid by the word but I actually enjoyed the challenge of keeping my comments short in radio commentary. One of the easiest jobs in football is passing comment on others and pointing out people's mistakes, and I knew that the game always seems so much simpler to those of us sitting in the stands than for the players on the pitch and the managers on the touchline. After all, even the best players make mistakes. It's always so obvious to us what a team should do when it's not actually our responsibility. If a mistake leads to a goal, we can usually all see it. I was always more interested in the general pattern of play being employed by the teams and I tried to offer a bit of insight into why a side was having success in a particular area of the pitch.

My commentary work took me all over the world watching England and, although I tried to be impartial during the matches, I cannot pretend I was not hoping England would win. Unfortunately, apart from the 1996 European Championships in England, we have not lived up to expectations, which could be said to be unrealistic ones anyway .

Although I had retired from football management, I liked to stay busy and my diary was always full alongside my commentary work. Rita will probably say I took on too much but I found I was happier when I had a busy schedule. I enjoyed public speaking and working for the charities I had become involved with. I would accept any opportunity to put on a tracksuit and spend a bit of time on a training pitch and so when I was asked to manage a team of celebrities for a charity game and television programme on Sky, I jumped at the chance. It was a bit like all those years ago when I had been just starting out as a manager with Lincoln City and I went to coach amateur sides. There was the same sense of enjoyment at seeing players improve in small but significant ways.

One invitation I turned down, though, was to go on *Strictly Come Dancing*. It's a programme I have always enjoyed, and more than once Rita and I have been to sit in the audience. What I like about it is that the professional dancers have to take into account the ability of their partner. I can only imagine the amount of patience and work it takes to teach the amateur dancers their routines. There is so much about it that is similar to coaching a footballer – explaining the moves, practising so that they can work together as a pair, and then hoping for a good performance on a Saturday.

I was quite envious of John Barnes because he did go on the programme. I always knew he had a wonderful left foot. Well, a few weeks on *Strictly* proved he had two wonderful left feet. I am only joking, because John did quite well on the show and he had the courage to go on it and test himself. I would love to have been brave enough to accept the invitation but I don't think my two daughters would have forgiven me for embarrassing them every Saturday evening. I cannot dance, but I'd have liked to see whether I could have learned, although perhaps not with millions of people watching every step on television.

In 2009, I was asked to become a non-executive director of Watford Football Club and I accepted, not realising that I would end up getting a lot more involved than I had bargained for.

The club was not in good shape. The majority shareholder was Lord Michael Ashcroft and the chairman and vice-chairman were two brothers, Jimmy and Vince Russo, who owned a salad-growing company. The Russos' company had lent the club almost £5million and towards the end of the year, they resigned from the board suddenly and announced that they wanted their money back more or less immediately. Had they gone ahead and insisted on calling in those debts, the club would have gone into administration and would have suffered a points deduction that would have put us in grave danger of being relegated from the Championship. I had agreed to become the interim chairman because I was so concerned about what might happen to the club. Jimmy Russo had said in an interview that he had not become a bad man overnight, and when I was interviewed by Sky television, I said that his threat to put the club into administration did make him a bad man. It was not, perhaps, my wisest comment but I felt the club was in the middle of a tug of war between Lord Ashcroft and the Russo brothers and that if we all weren't careful it would suffer badly. Jimmy Russo was not happy with my choice of words, to say the least, and I can understand that because it wasn't me who had lent millions of pounds to the keep the club going. I shouldn't have said what I said but at the time I was the interim chairman and my responsibility and loyalty was not with either side but with the club and its supporters. I suppose I should have been a bit calmer about it because my word carried some weight with the supporters. I genuinely didn't mean any disrespect to Jimmy Russo and I apologised but I did feel that, by demanding the club repaid millions of pounds he knew it didn't have, he was risking the club's future.

I felt we had assembled a good board of directors and we had an excellent chief executive called Julian Winter, but in the end it became apparent that the club had jumped from the frying pan into the fire when a man named Laurence Bassini bought the club. I just couldn't work him out. I didn't know enough about him – in fact I'm not sure anyone did – and any attempts to ask him about his background quickly became confused. I couldn't get to the bottom of what was motivating him. It was a very difficult period and more than once I felt I wanted to resign but I felt it would have been irresponsible because the supporters would have interpreted it as a vote of no confidence in Bassini. At one point, we had arranged a fans forum, where supporters could come along and ask us all questions about the club. Bassini had been due to attend but at very short notice he called to say he was unwell and wouldn't be coming. The supporters were not happy and nor was I, but I had to accept his excuse because I had no evidence to counter his claim that he was ill.

With all the uncertainty and disruption, our manager Sean Dyche worked miracles. He had barely any money to spend on players, but he managed to create a team that could get results and we finished eleventh in the table. It has been absolutely no surprise to me to see Sean do so well at Burnley because it was obvious he had a lot of the skills required to be a top manager. If he was foreign, I think his name would be near the top of the list whenever the top clubs have a managerial vacancy. I really hope that his background as a no-nonsense centre-half who played the majority of his own career in the lower divisions does not count against him as he goes on because he is a very bright football manager.

The only way Watford could break the cycle of struggling financially was to attract wealthy owners, and in 2012 the Pozzo family – Giampaolo, who had owned the Italian club Udinese for many years, and his son, Gino – emerged as the favourites to take over. As chairman I did as much as I could to ensure the potential buyers were the sort of people who would at least be able to offer the club some financial stability. I hoped for the best and when the takeover went through, I resigned as chairman, although I remained as an honorary life president.

It took Watford three seasons, and twice as many managers, to get into the Premier League. They almost did it at the first attempt, but lost to Crystal Palace in the play-off final in May 2013. That night, my phone buzzed. It was a message from Laurence Bassini gloating about Watford's defeat. I know I was not the only person connected with the club who received such a message that night.

People ask me what I make of the way Gino Pozzo and his people have worked at Watford and I must admit that it is a very difficult question to answer because, as a football manager, I would have hated it. I certainly couldn't have been a 'head coach'. I would have wanted total control over which players we signed and sold. I have always believed that stability is required if you want to be successful – at least where the manager is concerned. The season Watford were promoted they had four head coaches. They got promoted and replaced Slavisa Jokanovic with Quique Sanchez Flores. Sanchez Flores kept them in the Premier League, and they replaced him with Walter Mazzarri. It shouldn't work, and yet it has done and so who am I to question the approach? When I think back to my managerial days, I would change the team over a period of time, replacing players, ensuring things kept evolving so we didn't stand still. Watford's way these days is to take that same approach and apply it to the managerial and coaching staff too. I certainly couldn't have worked that way, but any manager going into Watford cannot claim they did not know how the club operates so they can have no complaints. As with anything in life, there is no right or wrong way, and if the club remains in the Premier League then who can say it is the wrong way?

On 29 November 2014 I strode onto the pitch at Vicarage Road, flanked by a guard of honour formed by some of my old players, many of whom still call me 'gaffer' even though I reassure them it's OK to call me Graham these days.

Everyone in the stadium seemed to be on their feet, applauding. A huge yellow banner was being passed from hand to hand by the supporters in the Rookery End behind one of the goals and as it unfurled I saw that it featured the faces of some of Watford's best-loved players… and me. I was in the middle, in a black blazer with the club crest on the breast pocket. I must admit, it was a very good likeness. Luther Blissett and John Barnes were on there too, as were Nigel Gibbs, Tommy Mooney and other players from my two spells as manager of Watford.

Not all the faces featured were players of mine but most of them were. The words at the bottom said 'We're Still Standing', which is an adaptation of one of Elton John's song titles and a reflection that the club has endured difficult times as well as great days.

I was presented with a silver salver and, as I turned to look for Rita in the stand behind me, the supporters began singing: 'One Graham Taylor, there's only one Graham Taylor.' I waved to Rita and then my eyes settled on the smart yellow lettering on the front wall of the upper tier of the stand. It read: 'The Graham Taylor Stand'. I don't mind admitting that I could feel the tears beginning to come.

When I got the call to say that Watford wanted to name a stand after me, I had a tremendous sense of pride, as you would expect, but to be in the stadium and feel the warmth and love of the supporters is overwhelming. I smile to myself because this is the sort of thing that usually happens only after someone has passed away, and so I am very happy to be around to witness it and to say thank you to the football club and the people who gave me and my family so much.

I must admit, I was slightly surprised that the club had taken the decision to name that particular stand after me because it already had a name, the Sir Stanley Rous Stand, but I certainly wasn't complaining because I recognised that the club had no obligation to make such a gesture towards me. In this day and age, when a stand at a football ground is given a name it is often a company paying for the privilege. Later in the day I did joke to Rita: 'I hope we're not going to get a bill for this.'

Rita and I took our seats in the stand to watch the match which, unfortunately, Watford lost 1-0 to Cardiff City. It really wasn't a game that had very much about it at all and I felt a little awkward when people came up to me and said: 'You wouldn't have put up with a performance like that, would you, Graham?' or: 'You'd have sorted them out at half-time.'

When people say things like that, I smile and nod and say something like: 'Let's hope the second half is a bit better, shall we?' because I know that my Watford teams were capable of turning in poor performances every now and then. It's just that people tend not to remember the dull days, and I suppose that is one of the lessons of a life spent in football: supporters forget the bad days quite easily if you give them enough good ones to remember. The goalless draws and limp defeats fade away and, after a while, almost don't matter at all because if you are successful people will always have the memory of the good feelings they had when they were inside the ground watching their team. The excitement and buzz of following a club that is doing well – of winning matches, achieving promotion and knocking the big clubs out of the cups – live on long after the players and manager have left.

I have never changed my opinion that football is a game for the people. During my career, I tried not to lose sight of the fact that we were striving to be successful for the supporters as well as for ourselves. Yes, we could all carry on playing the game without them, but there wouldn't be anything like the sense of enjoyment and satisfaction when things go well. So to be recognised and appreciated by those supporters means a great deal to me.

Whenever I visit Vicarage Road to watch a match, people are so kind, although I notice it is usually older people who come up to me asking for a photograph or autograph. It pulls me up short to realise that someone would have to be in their mid-thirties to remember the tail-end of my first spell as Watford manager. Sometimes the supporters have their children with them and occasionally they will say: 'This is Graham Taylor, our greatest-ever manager,' which is very nice to hear, although I smile to myself when I look down at a blank little face and realise it means nothing to an eight-year-old who idolises Troy Deeney.

That is fine, by the way, but it is very nice that there are so many reminders around the ground of what we achieved during my two spells at the club. Those memories can never be forgotten, but I do genuinely hope that one day a future generation goes on to outdo what we achieved.

While I was writing this book, I watched the documentary, *An Impossible Job*. I didn't particularly want to, for obvious reasons, although it remains a very skilled piece of film-making and it does show what it was like to be the England manager at that time, so I have no complaints about it.

It was not an enjoyable watch but there were moments in it that I had long forgotten. At the end of the film, you can hear the team talk I gave to the England players before the World Cup qualifier against the Netherlands – the one that cost us our place in the tournament. I have given thousands of team talks during my career but this one summed up much of what I believe.

'In life there are so many opportunities, and they are always round about you. There are too many people in life that never see them. Then there are those people who see the opportunities but don't grasp them. Then there are other people, who are generally life's winners ... they see the opportunities, they go looking for them, and they take them. And that's what you are facing now on the football field. Now go out there and take it, it's there for you.'

Now, we didn't win that match, but I stand by every word of that team talk. In life you win some and you lose some; the secret is not to get too carried away by one or too dragged down by the other but to keep giving your best. No one can ask any more of you than that.

Acknowledgements

We would like to take the opportunity to express our heartfelt thanks for the support and kindness shown to our family since Graham's sudden passing in January 2017.

The public tributes to Graham, which flowed from people from all walks of life, were incredibly moving and helped us all enormously in those early weeks of grief.

We are also grateful for the ongoing support and generosity shown to us by Watford Football Club and the community. Watford will always hold a special place in our hearts.

Some of our grief was very much in the public eye. Like all families who have lost a loved one we have had our up and down days. We would also therefore like to say a big thank-you to our loved ones and friends who continue to be there for us.

Best wishes and thanks,

Rita, Joanne, Karen, Stuart, Rhianna, Elsie and Jake.

The publisher would like to thank Charlotte Atyeo, Ian Wilson, Simon Ricketts, Paul Parry, Simon Gill, Alan Cozzi, Steve Leard, Ian Ridley, Edward Pickering, John Ward, David Luxton, Richard Walker and everyone at Watford FC, Grimsby Town, Lincoln City, Aston Villa and Wolverhampton Wanderers.

Index

INDEX

INDEX